Remember Sto.

Ralph Ingleton

Past President ASLC.

FROM BURLEIGH
TO BOSCHINK

FROM BURLEIGH TO BOSCHINK

A COMMUNITY CALLED STONY LAKE

Christie Bentham
Katharine Hooke

NATURAL HERITAGE BOOKS

TORONTO

Published by Natural Heritage/Natural History Inc.
P.O. Box 95, Station O, Toronto, Ontario M4A 2M8

Edited by Jane Gibson
Design by Blanche Hamill, Norton Hamill Design
Printed and bound in Canada by Hignell Printing Limited

Front cover photograph, top, by Alan Wotherspoon.
Front cover photograph, bottom: *Gull*, *Skidley* and *Spree*.
Designed before 1900, they are still sailing in the new millenium.
Courtesy Martha Hunt Collection.
Back cover photograph, top: William Thompson steaming to
winter quarters in late fall before freeze-up in motor vessel *Niaid*
with his cold crew huddling in the bow, 1920s.
Courtesy Michael Fowler Collection.

Canadian Cataloguing in Publication Data

Bentham, Christie, 1930–
From Burleigh to Boschink: a community called Stony Lake

Includes bibliographical references and index.
ISBN 1-896219-63-2

1. Stony Lake Region (Peterborough, Ont.)—History.
I. Hooke, Katharine, 1932– II. Title.

FC3095.S76B46 2000   971.3'67   C00-931591-8
F1059.S76B46 2000

THE CANADA COUNCIL | LE CONSEIL DES ARTS
FOR THE ARTS | DU CANADA
SINCE 1957 | DEPUIS 1957

Natural Heritage/Natural History Inc. acknowledges the support
received for its publishing program from the Canada Council Block
Grant Program and the assistance of the Association for the Export of
Canadian Books, Ottawa. Natural Heritage also acknowledges the support of
the Ontario Council for the Arts for its publishing program.

Dedicated to the memory of two Davids

CONTENTS

FROM BURLEIGH
TO BOSCHINK

INTRODUCTION

EARLY IN the planning of this commemorative book the steering committee naturally cast about for an appropriate title. They wanted it be catchy, definitive and concise—a bit like writing a ten-word telegram in the old days. Christie Bentham captured the boundaries with Burleigh and Boschink and Marg Gouinlock identified the one word that underlies this written history that ultimately came together: *community*. Again and again it turns up throughout various accounts. It obviously refers to settlements, places where people put down roots to live and work. However, the word *community* in its many senses since the 1500s also means "life in association with others," "commonness," "a sense of common identity and characteristics." It is a word that in its history has never been used unfavourably. It is more tangible and immediate than the word *society*. Without experiencing community, however we define it, we may suffer "isolation...impoverishment of spirit." Thus, this relatively small geographical area of Stony Lake represents a community in an overall sense to those who have lived and visited here. How that experience has evolved is as varied as the people.

Throughout this book the reader will recognize common threads, but whatever has drawn and continues to draw people to Stony Lake cannot be explained in words alone. For some, the community is the natural setting; for others, extended summer families and familiar friends; like Wes Willoughby, some may say, "There's a lot that doesn't change here," and that may be what's important to them. We have tried to let the story tell itself through many voices and pictures. Our hope is that 100 years from now Stony Lake will still be a community.

Over the centuries, many people have written published accounts about the lake and its landscape. In succeeding chapters, the reader will be able to peek into cottage logs and diaries, letters and recorded recollections, interspersed with newspaper tidbits and other local writings that give perspective to the narratives. Regarding time periods, the major focus is on the first half of the 20th century, with enough looking back and ahead to provide perspective and some historical significance.

Our first practical question concerned the boundaries of the lake communities. These are not as clearly defined as those of townships or municipalities. We made some rather arbitrary decisions for the purposes of this book. For instance, cottagers at either end of Stony

Lake may well be members of our central Association. The one area of the lake that is somewhat self-contained is Upper Stoney (yes, the name of their Association has always included the *e*) which begins just east of Boschink Narrows and is represented by the Upper Stoney Lake Association (USLA). However, this account does include the Narrows, some of whose residents are also members of the USLA. We extend west through the Burleigh Channel to the Falls. About 20 years ago some of those cottagers formed the Juniper Point Association, partly for social reasons and partly because of development concerns. Kawartha Park has had a small but active association since 1915 (a larger evolve-ment of the Clear Lake Association of 1911). In the early years of the 20th century there were few cottages and virtually no development on the shores of Clear Lake. Those shores are now extensively developed and residents have formed a ratepayers' association. In summary, this book encompasses the life and times of campers, cottagers, and settlers from Burleigh to Boschink, as the title states, and southwest to Kawartha Park with some references to Clear Lake.

The next question is thornier and definitely emotional. Ask yourself, is there ever a greater controversy when writing about a geographical area, a town or, as in this case, a lake, than how to spell it? Arguments are mounted for

Rapids at Burleigh Falls, high water in spring, looking north. D&S postcard series #916. *Courtesy Katharine Hooke Collection.*

each possibility and proponents tenaciously defend their stand. The authors of this book represent both sides, but reached the consensus indicated in the title. The original Letters Patent of 1907 refers to the *Stony Lake Cottagers' Association, Limited*, a spelling which remained in effect until the formation of the *Association of Stoney Lake Cottagers Inc.*, March 24, 1950. However, within a year the "e" periodically disappeared in correspondence and other Association records, presumably at the whim of the writer. When the Yacht Club was incorporated, it omitted the "e". The question of the "correct" spelling will likely continue until the end of time, but it does appear that in spite of the official spelling, many members of the organization lean on the side of no "e". The following printed account (unfortunately no source or date is given) indicates the force of the debate.

"Some years ago, the Ston(e)y Lake Cottagers' Association attempted to determine the official spelling of Ston(e)y Lake. Edwin C. Guillet, then the provincial archivist and author of *The Valley of the Trent*, argued that the spelling should be with an "e". He went on at length citing numerous historical references for support. Guillet's cousin, Jack Guillet, also present, reported that all of these cited authors were wrong: the Stony in the Bible had no "e".[1] With this, all present [at an Association meeting] were made suddenly aware of the weight of their decision.

The Biblical argument did not win converts to the Stony Lake without an "e" counterattack. In a sampling of ten items bearing the name Ston(e)y Lake (not including the Bible), the score was tied at five with and five without. In the forefront of spelling Ston(e)y without an "e" was Leslie M. Frost, former Premier of Ontario. Support for this spelling comes from the *Peterborough Examiner* and a host of Trent Canal publications.

Edwin Guillet's argument for Ston(e)y with

an "e" gets support from *Peterborough Land of Shining Waters*, and the *Peterborough Historical Atlas*. At one time, proponents of this spelling toyed with the idea of resurrecting the flagship *Stoney Lake* of the Stoney Lake Navigation company as a symbol of their cause."[2] We are fortunate that early explorers, surveyors, visitors and settlers recorded their observations and sketched what they saw and measured. Join us now on a quick journey of over 200 years.

When we look back to Samuel de Champlain's late summer expedition in 1615, we have to stretch our imagination to picture the lake more than six feet lower than it is today. The plant growth was luxuriant. An excerpt from Champlain's journal comments on "...the vines and walnut-trees [that] grow there in great quantity. Grapes here come to maturity, but there remains always a very pungent acidity which one feels in the throat after eating many of them...The cleared portion of these regions is quite pleasant. Hunting deer and bear is quite common here...There are also many cranes as white as swans, and other kinds of birds, resembling those in France. It is certain that all this country is very fine and of pleasing character."[3] As Trevor Denton notes, "...it would have been a marvellous sight to see the 110 Huron canoes moving through the sparkling lakes...and rounding Hurricane Point."[4]

Moving on to 1835, we have Susanna Moodie's well-known account in *Roughing it in the Bush*. The Moodies and Traills had become close friends with Francis Young and family at Young's Mill (as it was known then). Susanna knew well the tranquil Lake Katchawanooka from her gathering of berries and fruit, but she had little experience of Clear and Stony lakes because to travel on them presented quite an expedition. Her descriptions are vivid and detailed."...Clear Lake, which gets its name from the unrivalled brightness of

Catharine Parr Traill (in flowered dress at left) with daughter, Katharine Agnes (Kate), grandaughter, Ethel Traill, and niece, Katie Traill, at 'Minnewawa,' Kate's cottage in the mid-1890s. *Atwood Family Collection, courtesy Katharine Hooke.*

its waters, spread out its azure mirror before us. The Indians regard this sheet of water with peculiar reverence. It abounds in the finest sorts of fish, the salmon-trout, the delicious white fish, maskinonge, and black and white bass. There are no islands in this lake, nor rice beds, nor stick nor stone to break its tranquil beauty, and, at the time we visited it, there was but one clearing upon its shore....The whole majesty of Stony Lake broke upon us at once, another Lake of the Thousand Isles in miniature, and in the heart of the wilderness! Imagine a large sheet of water, some fifteen miles in breadth and twenty-five in length, taken up by islands of every size and shape, from the lofty naked rock of red granite to the rounded hill

covered with oak-trees to its summit, while others were level with the waters, and of a rich emerald green, only fringed with a growth of aquatic shrubs and flowers."[5]

In 1838, Catharine Parr Traill published an essay entitled "The Mill of the Rapids" in *Chambers Edinburgh Journal* in which she describes Stony Lake: "At the head of Clear Lake are two islands, which form the entrance into Stony Lake. One, which I think I heard called Big island, was a majestic elevation of pines. The soft blue haze that rested on these islands had a charming effect, mellowing and softening the dark shade of the evergreens that crowned them with hearse-like gloom. This same Stony lake do I most ardently long to see. I am told that it contains a thousand wild and romantic scenes, and, in miniature, resembles the lake of the thousand islands in the St. Lawrence. In many parts the rocky islands are more picturesque, some of them shooting up in bare pointed craggy pinnacles abruptly from the depth of the water, while others are fancifully grouped, and clothed with flowers and trees."[6]

The following year an English traveller, James Logan, visited the Traills and recorded his impressions of Stony Lake: "The scenery of this lake is very beautiful, and its numerous wooded islands, its romantic banks, and dense forests, inhabited by woodpeckers, and other gaudy birds, wolves and squirrels merit a more extended stay."[7]

However, various surveyors during the first half of the 19th century were more specific and often less enthusiastic: "...swamps with islands of hard land, rock hills, swampy pond marshes, bad water on this ridge near Boschink, maple, beech, ironwood and elm, fit for settlement."[8] In spite of many reservations by the surveyors, particularly on the north shore, they were impressed by the variety of trees, clear streams and a potential for development, once roads were built. On July 14, 1865, the *Peterborough Review* was cautiously optimistic about the possible improvement of the 20 miles of carriage road beyond Burleigh Falls. "...Mr. T. Eastland from Peterborough carries a weekly mail delivery which no doubt will be a little less difficult thanks to a one hundred dollar donation from County Council to blast and break the continuous deposit of boulders."

By the time Susanna Moodie (age 69) and Catharine Parr Traill (age 70) returned to Stony Lake on June 22, 1872, after an absence of nearly 40 years, they still enjoyed the beauty even though extensive lumbering was denuding the shoreline. They boarded the *Chippewa* in Lakefield on a hot, sunny day to visit Mt. Julian. Susanna later wrote to a friend about the expedition: "The sail was quite enjoyable, and the wild rocky islands of Stony Lake still in the wilderness, very beautiful. 1200 of these islands have been surveyed, without counting numbers of bare granite rocks that rear their red heads above the water uncovered with grass or lichens, that look like the bare bones of some former world. We reached our destination about 3 o'clock and dined on board. A capital picnic dinner, the gentlemen having provided us with quite a feast of good things. After dinner, we all went ashore to look for flowers in the woods, but the sun was so hot and the path so steep, and the mosquitoes and blackflies so savage to have a picnic at our expense, that we were glad to return to the boat. I scared up a great snake, which scared me, though Mr. Clementi said, that he was a beauty. To me he looked as ugly as sin and I was glad to give him a wide berth. This Stony Lake is a very grand place, and will one day be as popular as the English Lakes to the sightseers."[9] Not only sightseers, as we well know, find pleasure in Stony Lake. The following chapters offer fascinating perspectives from all manner of people who call Stony Lake home.

One

THE LAND AND THE LAKE

WE LIKE to think of Stony Lake as a constant in our lives, yet the natural environment changes continually. Many of the oak trees have gone, victims of the gypsy moth, forest tent caterpillars and lack of moisture in the thin layer of soil. On the positive side, descendants of the white pines which were heavily logged in the last century have flourished. Invasive species such as Eurasian watermilfoil, purple loosestrife and zebra mussels have appeared, while the indigenous Canada geese, ospreys and cormorants are much more numerous.

It is difficult to imagine Stony Lake without its abundant life on land, in the water and in the air. However, in the past the landscape was often barren. At least one and a half billion years ago a vast range of mountains as high as the Rockies formed along the edge of a much older land mass, creating what we now call the Canadian Shield. Over time these mountains were worn down to their largely granite roots, thus forming the gently rolling landscape of the area north of Stony Lake. This is the land that frustrated early 19th century settlers enticed by free settlement grants. Small pockets of arable land are interspersed with marshes, shallow creeks, and the never-ending rocks.[1]

About 440 million years ago, a vast inland tropical sea covered the area; glacial till settling to the bottom of this sea created the layered limestone, some of which now exists along part of the south shore of Stony Lake. The warm, shallow water of the ancient sea was good habitat for numerous life forms, resulting in many fossils now found in this limestone. During repeated Ice Ages the powerful grinding action of the glaciers, with beds of ice as deep as three kilometres, along with the torrents of water from the melting glaciers, completed the formation of our lake and the surrounding land. The most recent meltdown occurred a mere 12,000 years ago.

After the ice finally left, diverse forms of life spread slowly northward from areas not disturbed by the Ice Age, with seeds, plants, insects, birds and animals, later followed by the first human inhabitants. White and red pines with hardwoods below were common in the rocky areas, while swamps contained tamarack, cedar, alder, elm and black ash. Surveyors made note of the species and speculated on possible uses of the land and trees.[2]

The intensive lumbering of white pine led to the most obvious devastation as noted by early tourists and cottagers. The logs were squared in the forest so that as many as possible could be loaded into the limited space in ships. The best of this timber was prized as

Log jam at Burleigh Falls, about 1900. If necessary, the "key" log would be removed or dynamite used. *Courtesy Michael Fowler Collection.*

Wooden log shute from a feeder lake into the waterway, about 1920. *George Douglas Collection, courtesy Katharine Hooke.*

Boom of logs off the east side of Big Island, looking east, 1907. Note the low water level. *George Douglas Collection, courtesy Katharine Hooke.*

masts for sailing ships built in Great Britain. Later, as sawmills were erected in the area, round logs were hauled and floated to the mills and sawn lumber was produced for both local consumption and the American market. Wooden log slides were built to carry logs and avoid the rapids. By this time, species other than white pine were saleable, so clear-cutting was practised. Debris left behind on the forest floor fed frequent forest fires. Neither the means nor the inclination to put them out existed; in fact, settlers welcomed fires as an aid to clearing land for farming. John Collins, of the Collins' family island, recalls a family story about an ancestor and friends paddling during a forest fire in the 1860s, and seeing large numbers of swimming animals fleeing the blaze. In conversation with Christie Bentham in the summer of 1999, he observed: "When I replanted a tree in 1996 I dug into the fire layer only a couple of inches below the fallen leaves and a very thin layer of humus. There was a black charcoal layer about a quarter of an inch thick and beneath that the fire-broken granite crumbled into a one-inch layer of sharp particles slightly bigger than grains of sand. Evidence after 130 years!" A government Forest Distribution map records that 20,000 acres in Burleigh Township burned in 1913.[3]

As mentioned earlier, most of the land cleared on the north shore was unsuitable for farming and almost all of it was abandoned. Although much of the topsoil from the cleared and burned areas was lost through erosion, now there is from partial recovery to good mixed forest, particularly near the shoreline. Thanks to the efforts of concerned cottagers and environmental guidance like Project Lifeline,[4] many property owners are carefully nurturing the habitat. In recent years, dozens of volunteers for Project Lifeline, sponsored by the Association of Stoney Lake Cottagers, completed a detailed inventory of the natural

and altered shoreline features of large areas of the lake. This information is now available for use by both the Association and the local regulatory bodies as a tool to influence future development of the shoreline. However, as a result of the recent funding reductions, governments at all levels have less capability to enforce regulations. Therefore, a group called the Stony—Upper Stoney Lake Stewardship Council has been formed to continue data collection and to encourage careful consideration of the impact of human use of the lake on the health and survival of other species. One of the initial projects of this group is to encourage individual property owners to restore altered shoreline to a more natural state.[5]

This joint venture began under the initiative of Kathleen Mackenzie and Roslyn Moore, with technical advice from the Trent-Severn Waterway. Janet Owens and Paul Kyselka from the Upper Stoney Lake Association have been enthusiastic liaisons from that area. Thanks to Phred Collins' computer expertise and wide knowledge of the lake habitat and species, the Association now has an extensive data base which is a valuable resource for other lake communities who may wish to undertake a similar project.

Catharine Parr Traill notes, in *Studies of Plant Life in Canada*, a flowering shrub that helps protect the shoreline. Sweet Gale "...forms a close hedge-like thicket near the margins of lakes and ponds; those lovely inland waters, where, undisturbed for ages, it has flourished and sent forth its sweetness on the desert air."[6] Many current gardeners with a strong naturalist's perspective are rejuvenating their property as will become evident through their stories.

We know that the fish population species have changed and if the early cottagers' accounts are reasonably accurate (they are fish stories), the numbers of fish have declined. One can read about the late fall herring run at least into the 1920s along the Douro/Dummer boundary. Settlers netted and salted them down in barrels. One account notes that forest fires in 1926 and '27 raised the lake temperature so significantly that the herring came to the surface and died. Tom Cole of Otter Island, summer home of various Coles since 1883, wrote an extensive family recollection in which he clearly remembers when and what fish were available: "Perch were important as well as black and green bass and 'lunge;' indeed, occasionally a perch of 12" to 15" would be taken and provide a good meal. The first rock bass taken in our camp was in 1924. No one knew what it was and the general surmise was a cross between a bass and a sunfish. Even though they grew bigger than sunfish they were about as unpopular of source of food because of the bone structure. That delight of epicures, the pike-perch, called in Ontario pickerel, in the U.S. walleye and in Quebec doré (how much nicer!), was first stocked in Stony in 1931 near Ship Island I was told—and the first in our camp was 1934 or 1935. Since then, also, the blue gill and the crappie appeared along with carp...suckers were always there and what we called catfish which were correctly named as well as eels. Upper Stony managed to produce immense white fish and occasional lake trout."

Terry Hall from Syndicate Island likewise remembers landlocked white fish and salmon being caught. Many people refer to the existence of lake trout in these waters (on earlier maps the lake is called Salmon Trout). An article on fishing in a 1984 April edition of *Out of Doors* states that "...stocking of lake trout in 1922, '24, '25 and '26 has been documented."[7] Don Elliott has determined that 18 species of fish, including walleye, have been introduced to the lake.

Mackenzie Bay, with very low water, looking north in 1909. Note the usual water level on the far rock. *George Douglas Collection, courtesy Katharine Hooke.*

Youngsters found many sources of live bait during the Depression. According to Tom Cole, his family found abundant sources "...of bait, perch, shiners, leopard frogs, green frogs, crawfish, white grubs and grasshoppers which were a source of both spending money and entertainment. Occasionally we would find hellgrammites and sculpin (darters we called them), but we never took to leeches." The fish they caught were a welcome addition to the family meal.

The landscape continues to change. Marilyn Ott observes: "Many huge pines have succumbed to strong winds. Small pines are being eaten by hungry beavers and the cedars get a regular pruning by the deer, even on the islands. Mink and groundhogs are becoming a nuisance, while snakes and frogs are fewer in number. We are thankful that the loons still lull us to sleep." Maintaining a proper balance of nature involves choices and knowledge. In 1954, the Cottagers Association endorsed the then-accepted practice of DDT spraying for tent caterpillars.[8] We are constantly learning.

For at least the next century, most changes will likely be the result of human activity. Many of the lifestyle modifications we make to reduce acid rain, global warming and damage to the ozone layer will be offset by continual increases in population, and the further spread of our high impact lifestyle. Each individual needs to take steps to soften this potentially negative impact.

At Stony Lake, acid rain damage will likely be confined only to trees and other plants on land, because of the neutralizing effect of the limestone. The risks to humans arising from ozone depletion can be minimized by sun block and protective clothing, but global warming could be a more serious problem. Even a modest increase in average temperature occurring as a result of more frequent periods of hot dry weather will cause increased moisture evaporation from plants,

the soil and the lake. Drought resistant species such as white pine, eastern red cedar and juniper will survive, but many deciduous trees and shrubs will suffer. Other plants now at the northern limit of their range may become more abundant, if they are adapted to survive drought.[9]

The Trent-Severn Waterway maintains a reasonably consistent water level in the system, but dry summers and little winter snow make water management increasingly difficult. As Don Elliott has determined: "Stony's surface area of 28 square kilometres is about average for the 15 largest Kawartha Lakes. The point of greatest water depth at 33 metres is north of Crowe's Landing. Stony's mean depth is just under 6 metres, exceeded only by Cameron Lake. This helps explain our relative freedom from surface water weeds. Although they are a nuisance in some areas of our lake, estimates made a few years ago showed that under 1% of the surface of Stony Lake is covered with plants. Compare that with figures ranging from 10% to 85% for six other Kawartha Lakes."

What flora and fauna have the cottagers observed? Tom Cole notes: "There has been quite a variety of fauna on Otter Island at different times. In addition to the usual squirrels of all shades and flying squirrels, various bats, chipmunks, mice, moles, shrews, voles, rabbits, hares, skunks, groundhogs, racoons, porcupines, weasels, mink, beaver and otter in summer, there are sometimes deer and wolves in winter. Not so many years ago, (1980), a herd of 30 deer was said to have wintered on the island. The bird life has been very entertaining and since [we were] small children we kept annual lists of sightings on (and, to include water-fowl and hawks, from) the island."

In 1913, young Freya Hahn recorded in her diary while at 'Woodonga': "I saw a redstart this morning. Heard loons and saw herons, hawks and blackbirds and chipmunks and, of course, the eternal pewee. Blueberries are ripe and we are going picking to-day. There is a beautiful little plant very much like squirrel-corn only quite a deep pink. A chipmunk was eating bread about three feet from the dining-room steps last night. Saw cedar waxwings at Perry's Creek on the 11th. Found a pitcher plant the same day and have transplanted it to the marsh. On the 14th I transplanted a rattlesnake fern watered it yesterday and it is quite stiff and fresh now."[10]

Don Elliott sees favourable changes at Stony Lake - on land and water. Certainly our landscape is no longer barren. In so many ways people are trying to make wise choices. Many will agree with his conclusion: "I am optimistic about the future of Stony Lake. With understanding and effort, the natural setting of the lake can continue to recover from the effects of logging, burning, disruptive recreation and other human actions. Gradually, the plant life surrounding the lake will more and more resemble its pre-1800 appearance."

Two

FIRST NATIONS—FIRST HERE

STONY LAKE and area are rich in ancient history, much of which has survived or is still being studied. As Helen Guillet summarizes: "Archeologists tell us that about 2500 years ago the Point Peninsula People travelled through the Kawarthas, and pottery from that time has been found here. Visitors from northern Europe explored and traded. The map of the valley of the Trent River by Samuel de Champlain, who was guided by Hurons, dates from 1616. Anishnawbe, Ojibway, and Algonkian tribes also hunted, fished and told their stories with words and rock pictures, or petroglyphs."

Since the mid 1950s, much information has become available on the Petroglyphs on the north shore, as well as the archaic period Serpent Mounds on Rice Lake. Not as well known is the Iroquoian village site five miles southeast of the Petroglyphs, in Dummer township, ultimately established in 1973 as an undeveloped provincial park on the Lyle Quackenbush farm. Nearly 13,000 varied artifacts have been identified in this area protected by the Ministry of Natural Resources. The date of this site is estimated at between 1450 and 1550 AD. In 1967, the leader of a Trent University dig "...speculated that the village may have been a seasonally-occupied manufacturing centre...for making tools to be used in trading with southern tribes."[1] Other Iroquois remains have been found near Gilchrist Bay (the Drain site) and at Mt. Julian (McCauley-Wilson site). It is possible that others exist on Jack's and Eel's creeks and also between the mouths of the two creeks.

The story of the well-known rock carvings, the Petroglyphs or Teaching Rocks, illustrates on-going problems with increased tourist traffic, even when it is on foot, to a fragile environment. A summary of figures and comments gives the picture. Local hunters mentioned the rock carvings in 1923, but it was in the summer of 1954 that three geologists made their observations known publicly. The Royal Ontario Museum and later Trent University did thorough anthropological studies. In the 1950s, both Edwin Guillet and Nick Nickels speculated in newspaper accounts that few people would be interested in tramping through the rough terrain to view the carvings. How surprised they would have been to learn that, in 1994, 30,000 visitors toured the site, now protected under cover from undue human stress and nature's acid rain. The Anishnawbe people call these rocks "Ke-no-mah-gay-wah-kon" (rocks that teach) because of the knowledge and spiritual guidance the carvings portray. Through oral accounts passed down from the elders of the tribes,

Native Peoples revere this significant artifact.[2]

Controversy continues about the age and origin of the carvings, although the major belief is that they were carved by hammerstones (found in 1967) by Algonkian-speaking Ojibway, somewhere between 500 and 1000 years ago. Current, controversial theory about the Petroglyphs' origins concerns possible contact by Celtic or Iberian peoples in the late Stone Age (7000–3000 BC).[3] There is no doubt of their spirit and nature and importance to the local Native bands. However, their supervision by the Ministry of Natural Resources and their tourist appeal raise questions.

Stony Lake and surrounding waters have been sacred to the Aboriginal people who valued the fish, animals and plants that flourished abundantly. Beginning about 1000 BC, the Ojibway people gradually worked their way south from the Lake Superior woodlands over a period of about 1500 years, slowly encroaching into Iroquois territory. However, from circa 1700, the Kawartha area was the territory of the Mississauga Ojibway. The various bands of this large tribe eventually were forced to settle into designated reserves, three of which are known locally as Curve Lake near Buckhorn, and Alderville and Hiawatha on Rice Lake. The origin of the term "Mississauga" is not certain, but one possible interpretation is "many river mouths."[4]

Water was most important to the Natives for travel and sustenance. Charles Weld, in "A Vacation Tour in the United States and Canada," wrote about a canoe trip he took with a local settler up to Boschink Narrows, a favourite site for Native encampments. He describes "...a wild whoop from my companion [which] was answered by an Indian who burst through the bush and motioned us to a little creek, where we disembarked. Following our swarthy guide, we came suddenly on a small clearing, in the centre of which was the lodge. A more picturesque spot could not well be conceived. The ground, mantled by a variety of wild flowers, sloped gently towards the Lake. Lofty trees shut out the oppressive sun, and a tiny brook gurgled sweetly as it leaped into daylight from the gloom of the forest. The lodge was constructed of birch-bark, open at the top for the egress of smoke. Around were various hunting and fishing implements. Portly fish, with strips of bear-flesh and venison hanging on poles in process of curing, attested how efficiently these had been used.

"Pushing aside the buffalo-skin serving as a door, we entered the lodge, from which, however, I was nearly driven by the dense and acrid smoke. The family consisted of the Indian's wife, mother-in-law, and two girls, who were squatted round the fire superintending a savoury mess of boiled ducks, fish and squirrels."[5]

Charles Weld was likely aware of these forced changes in the lives of the Natives. Here he glimpses some of the original traditions: "But though the Ojibways residing in Upper Canada pass a considerable portion of the year in the outskirts of towns, their hunting spirit breaks forth in the autumn, when, casting off the trammels of civilization, at all times galling and perplexing, they seek the wilderness, erect their lodges by the side of a lake or stream, and spend their days hunting and fishing; while their squaws make Indian ornaments, or sew the seams of birch-bark canoes, for which they have a constant demand from settlers. The Indian whom I visited had several of these graceful boats in hand, for each of which he was to receive six dollars.

"The Ojibways inhabiting this portion of Canada number about 1200. They are, however, like other tribes, decreasing. In an address which they presented to Lord Metcalfe in 1843, they touchingly remark:—'Great Father; We are feebly attempting to

Paddling through rice beds, 1904. *Courtesy Connie Wahl, from the log of the* 'Shanty.'

walk in the footsteps of your people: we see them increase while we wither and perish like the autumn leaf; but we, also, will cease to be hunters, and seek in the bosom of the earth that food for our wives and children for which we vainly toil in our rapidly disappearing forests.' "[6]

Weld's account was written when the Department of Indian Affairs was pressuring the indigenous people to give up much of their traditional way of life. In 1818, the representatives of the Crown and the chiefs of the Ojibwa nation "...signed an agreement surrendering native lands, in effect the present counties of Peterborough and Victoria and some surrounding townships. In return for giving up this land, they received an annual grant of $3,500 amounting at that time to $9 or $10 for each Indian man, woman and child."[7]

Eleven years later, in 1829, the reserve at Mud Lake (now Curve Lake) was formally established. Reserves in Upper Canada were developed, following similar measures in the United States of placing Aboriginal people on reservations, separated from white settlements. Both the Indian Department of Upper Canada and the strong missionary movement by the Methodist church to "civilize" the Indian population were the major influences in attempting to assimilate the indigenous population. Thus, the Native Peoples lost much of their original nomadic hunting and fishing way of life as they were pressured into agriculture and the white man's way of life.

From various accounts it appears that local Natives and early settlers like the Traills, Moodies, Choates and Youngs admired and helped one another. In *Yesteryear at Young's Point*, Aileen Young recalls that her great-grandfather, Patrick, was named "Nathaway" by nearby Indians. This high tribute, "Pale-faced Indian," honoured Patrick's friendship with these Native friends. There was mutual respect, understanding and learning.[8]

Locally, the Curve Lake Reserve is well known to Stony Lakers, now as the home of one of the finest native craft centres in Canada. In earlier times, cottagers recall Native women paddling from cottage to cottage with quill baskets and beadwork. Kady Denton recalls one woman in particular paddling with a continuous stroke, sitting on the bottom of her canoe—a lovely sight as she glided quietly among the islands. Rick Beaver, grandson of the former chief of the Alderville Reserve, notes that the Natives fashioned baskets, mats, and chair splints from reeds, black ash, woven rushes and cattails.[9] His great-grand uncle made cedar racks on which he burned designs with a coat hanger. He made the rounds of Stony Lake with his wares bartering on the principle of "the need of the seller and the desire of the buyer." Natives paddling from Burleigh Falls filled large laundry baskets with smaller quill and bead work pieces. They landed at Mt. Julian at least once a summer.

The woman whom Kady recalls could well

have been the grandmother of Curve Lake's recent chief, Gary Williams. Gary's father Wellington runs an annual September regatta at Curve Lake and has competed with and against area canoeists Les Crowe, Clarence McIlmoyle and Reg Blomfield and the famed Redpath brothers.[10] Wellington is a marathon canoeist who has paddled from Parry Sound to Trenton, stopping at various reserves. In the 1930s, Jack Matthews, now a long-time Stony Lake cottager, remembers as a young boy on Chemong Lake being taught to paddle by the then Chief, Dan Whetung.

The current Métis settlement at Burleigh Falls developed out of early camping expeditions of some members of the Curve Lake band who travelled up to the falls to fish, trap and hunt. Because of the early lumbering operations, followed by local building and ultimately a steady influx of tourists, Burleigh Falls became an area where many men could make a living. Traditionally, Natives gathered wild rice and picked cranberries from the many marshes along the north shore of Lovesick Lake. Before the rivers were dammed, wild rice grew in abundance in both Lovesick and Stony lakes as Mrs. Traill noted in a letter to her sister Agnes: "The squaws told me they got the sweet grass, or wampum, on an island in Stony Lake…. It is very long and rather harsh, but smells delightfully."[11]

Those early Native travellers to Burleigh Falls are the ancestors of the current Métis and non-status residents. A 1978 *History of the Burleigh Falls Métis Settlement* notes that "…the skills of making a livelihood from the local surroundings were passed down from generation to generation in good faith that there would always be a future for native people in the area."[12] Island 31 as seen on the Trent Canal charts for the area was their unofficial camping ground. It is well situated between Lovesick and Stony lakes, with a creek on one side and the canal lock on the other. However, gradually this land was taken over because of expanding dam and lock work

Katie Beaver, who lived with her family near White Lake, delivering various baskets on Stony Lake circa 1925. *Taken from Jean Cole's; "Origins of the History of Dummer Township." Used with permission of Jean Cole.*

Indian River, undisturbed wetland, 1909. *George Douglas Collection, courtesy Katharine Hooke.*

at Burleigh. When fishing parties in canoes hired guides in the '30s and '40s, up to 24 Native guides worked out of Burleigh Falls. The recurring family names were Taylor, Jacobs, Johnson and Irons. A guide had to cook an ample shore dinner of boiled potatoes, fried or broiled fish, or a chowder, and always a pot of tea. Like the settlers in the area, many of the Natives worked on the road crews in the 1930s when the Department of Northern Development improved Highway 36 (known locally as the Oregon Trail) to Buckhorn and the Burleigh Road to Apsley.[13]

Various recent programs at Burleigh include the Winter Warmth Project, the Burleigh Falls Canoe Factory and the opening of a community centre. Of special interest to members of St. Peter's-on-the Rock is the Lovesick Lake Native Women's Association, which since the early '80s, has undertaken many educational and recreational programs, especially with their young people. St. Peter's includes this Association in its outreach contributions. The women host a remarkable annual wild meat dinner and have published a comprehensive cookbook; part of their purpose is to "encourage others to make use of the natural resources in their area."[14]

One Native builder of note was Moses Marsden. He had an unerring ability to hew each corner notch of squared logs by sight, using a variety of building tools that he had made over the years. After he made a log cabin for U.S. Secretary of State John Foster Dulles on Duck Island in the Thousand Islands, his fame quickly spread beyond his home in Lakefield and his years as Chief of the Alderville band. In a 1958 *Globe and Mail* article he stated "...there is no special best time in which to build. Logs do not need to be cured and can be brought directly from the standing stump, peeled and set in place."[15] As a Native builder, Moses had skills and experience which many white men lacked.

Because of the Native Peoples' care of the waters and shorelines of the Kawartha Lakes, we are the beneficiaries. Always they would recognize healing qualities when they set up camp after the long winters. We have much to learn from those who were so attuned to their natural surroundings.

Three

THE EVOLVING COTTAGERS' ASSOCIATION

THE CURRENT Association of Stoney Lake Cottagers Inc., and its predecessor, represent nearly 100 years of official organization. However, a loosely knit group of avid cottagers in 1895 and 1896 was the catalyst for community activities on the northeast corner of Juniper Island. It is accepted that this is the second oldest cottagers' association in the province. There is much to be proud of. In the words of former president Ralph Ingleton: "We must celebrate our history and we must record what we can before memories, oral accounts and written documents are lost."[1]

Why would a group of cottagers be concerned enough about surroundings and daily activities that they would band together for the good of others? What were their interests? Why devote time, energy and money into this venture? All of the answers will probably never be known, but there is no question about the gratitude of succeeding generations. Cottagers have argued with one another about specific issues, heatedly and forcefully, but the principles of the Association seem more strongly upheld than ever as the 21st century begins.

The 1880s and '90s were delightful years for many tourists with an eye to summer living on a Kawartha lake. This was especially so on Stony Lake because of considerable adver-

tising of comfortable resorts and adequate train and steamer service. Canoeing was well-established following two American Canoe Association [ACA] regattas at Juniper Island. Newspapers extolled the virtues of healthy living on clean waters.

It was fortuitous that Judge G. Morrice Roger and Elihu Burritt (E.B.) Edwards were both members of the ACA executive and that they had purchased Juniper Island as a site for the first regatta, as well as for their own property. Thomas William (T.W.) Robinson of the Metropolitan Store in Peterborough, with an eye to a possible lucrative summer business, provided basic campers' supplies at the 1897 regatta from a small cabin with a shuttered opening. The potential must have been pleasing, because the following notice appeared in the July 19, 1892 *Peterborough Examiner*: "A new store and post office—Mr. T.W. Robinson, of the Metropolitian grocery has completed his handsome, two-storey structure on Juniper Is., Stoney Lake. The premises, which are well-adapted for their purposes, are used as a grocery store, where Mr. Robinson keeps on hand all that is required for summer tourists. This is a great convenience for the campers in that locality and one which will no doubt be appreciated. The daily mail route to the island established by the government to be open …July and August, is also another boon that will be appreciated."

The papers continued in 1893 to urge the cottagers to form some sort of group. The suggestion was "…to try and have the islands incorporated as a separate municipality and thus have control of the taxes and care of the islands and their properties in their hands."[2] On July 28, 1896, the *Examiner* noted that "…a letter was received by Mr. Edwards granting the request of the cottagers to be allowed to hold religious services on Sundays on a portion of Juniper Island…An appropriate minister will take regular morning services but the evenings are to be left free. Next Sunday's services will be on the old preaching ground." This is the land on which the pavilion was built late that fall.

These cottagers were referred to in the local newspapers as the Islanders and were obviously becoming organized. They met on July 27, 1896 to plan a regatta including an illuminated boat parade. They also formed a committee to provide religious services for all

denominations at Juniper, Headlands and Otter Island for three services: at 8:00 a.m. (Holy Communion); 11:00 a.m. (Morning prayer) and 7:00 p.m. (Evening prayer).

The 1896 regatta was a grand success although the sailing races were cancelled due to lack of wind. Miss Edith Stortly was proclaimed "lady champion of Stony Lake by clever rowing and paddling." Unfortunately no records have come to light of this early association, if indeed it kept any, but the Peterborough papers reported in detail who was staying where and what events were taking place. Over the next ten years this group, which included T.W. Robinson, continued to lease the land, but were working towards ownership by a duly constituted organization.

By summer 1907, plans were underway to form a limited company involving shares. Thus, in November 1907, the Province of Ontario granted a charter to the "Stony Lake Cottagers Association, Limited with a share capital of $40,000 divided into eight thousand shares of five dollars each. The directors are:

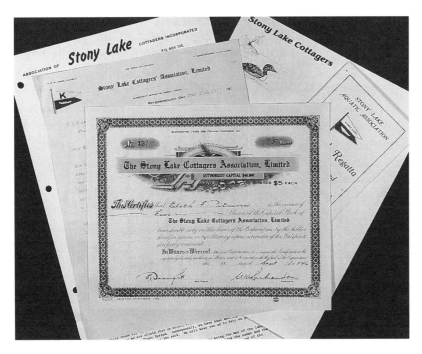

Association letterhead that has been used through the years. *Records of the Stony Lake Cottagers Association, Ltd. and the Association of Stoney Lake Cottagers, Inc.*

The first Juniper Island Store on the occasion of the second American Canoe Association Meet at Juniper, 1887. Left to right: Edie Clegg (sitting), Perry Hamilton, Laurs Goldie, Bill Hamilton, Edie Hamilton, Annie Brundrette and Tom Barrie (with ham). Tom Barrie, a fur trader and furrier, and Bill Hamilton, a grocer in the tradition of Fortnam and Mason or Michie of Toronto, were great friends, both of them from Peterborough. *Amys Family Collection, courtesy Jane McMyn.*

Early T.W. Robinson store at Juniper Island, 1900. The storekeepers lived upstairs. *Atwood Family Collection, courtesy Katharine Hooke.*

Samuel Henderson, Manufacturer; James Acton, Publisher; Henry Sutherland, Manager of Life Insurance Company; Robert Neill, Merchant; William Irwin, Lumberman; and any others who have or will henceforth become subscribers…to this corporation for the purpose and object to:

(a) acquire, own, improve and lease real estate
(b) acquire, build, own, lease crafts …conveyance of passengers or freight to the inland waters of the Kawartha Lakes
(c) trade in all articles of commerce…useful to members of the Association or visitors
(d) acquire, erect, own summer hotels or boarding houses
(e) sell or otherwise dispose of all real estate or other property acquired by the Association and to make regulations or bylaws to govern the affairs of the Association"

The land was conveyed by E. Burritt Edwards, G. Morrice Roger and J. Williams Bennett, whom we can assume, were satisfied that the directors of the Association were committed to the principles of public use of the store and pavilion. These two areas had become a drawing card for cottagers and visitors with a variety of community activities. Of the three original title holders of the whole of Juniper Island, only Judge George Morrice Roger remained in the picture. As the unmarried uncle of J.M.R. (Jack) Fairbairn, who inherited the remaining 44 acres of Juniper Island (the non-Association part), Roger initiated an extraordinary legacy, both through the Association and through his relatives.

The bylaws were drawn up in 1908, one of which stipulated a director must purchase a minimum of 200 paid-up shares. The annual fee of one dollar entitled the member and family "to all the ordinary privileges in connection with the pavilion and other property to be acquired. Guests of a director do not have to pay to be entertained on the property." The first treasurer's statement, reproduced below, gives an interesting picture of this fledging organization.

STONY LAKE COTTAGERS' ASSOCIATION, (Limited)

Treasurers Statement for period from November 18th, 1907 to December 31st, 1908.

To Loan from S. Henderson	$1,300.00
By cost of Property	$2500.00
– Draft on S. Henderson	1,200.00
– Search of title	2.70
– Payments on Stock	1,930.00
– Discount	12.90
– Regatta Subscriptions	47.15
– Cost of Charter	100.00
– Sale of Buttons and Badges	97.35
– Draft	1,200.00
– Fees from Cottagers	54.00
– Paid on loan	250.00
– Concert	33.70
– Interest on loan	72.10
– Sabbath Collections	129.15
– Furniture from T. Eaton Co.	109.39
– Rent of Store	200.00
– Lumber and other materials	87.91
– Balance from old Association	134.57
– Wages of employees	158.50
Expenses of regatta	128.64
Printing &c.	37.50
Stony Lake Navigation Co.	15.00
Steamer to Chemong	35.00
T.W. Robinson, light &c.	39.83
Postage & Minute Book	3.75
By Balance	372.70
	$5,125.92
	$5,125.92

In the early years, the Association published a 68 page yearbook, through the auspices of the James Acton Publishing Company, with approximately 34 advertisements of local businesses and those of Toronto businessmen who had cottages on the lake. The head office of the Association was at Confederation Life in Toronto where director Henry Sutherland was president. The committees represented the objectives of the Association: transportation, regatta, entertainment, dances and bonfires, and Sunday services (held at Juniper). The transportation directors were so keen to increase public service to the lake that, in February 1907, they had appeared before Peterborough city council urging the local City Radial Railway Company to build a line to McCracken's Landing. In December 1908, the Association sold to Public Works (Trent Canal Authority) the strip of shoreline fronting the pavilion and store on which they built cement wharves and installed lights.

Each building on the Association property has had a distinct character and variety of uses over the 20th century. Of them all, the pavilion has been home to many groups. In the early years Sunday morning services were held at the pavilion at which "loitering or talking outside…or in other ways interfering with the decorum of the hour and place will not be tolerated." Evening services consisted of camp fires at different cottages, "largely singing with a short scripture lesson." Preachers were advised to limit their address to 15 minutes. A popular method of transportation encouraged by the Association was the use of launches which could "promote attendance at services, regattas, etc., by offering to tow boats and canoes from a distance."[3] Summer religious services were immensely popular, especially at Otter Island on Sunday evenings.

The Association's history is well recorded in minute books, financial statements and correspondence which are fairly complete. Thanks to Don Walter's efforts in the early 1980s, all this material has been filed chronologically.

Occasionally, other files appear, coming to light when someone clears out a storeroom at the cottage or moves to an apartment. These documents represent a precious archive that needs to be properly housed, perhaps at the Trent University archives as an important adjunct to the Choate papers and the Douglas/Guillet correspondence. Some highlights gleaned from these records of the original Association include the following:

1907 Samuel Henderson lent Association $2,500—group that formed in 1896 with little structure turned over assets of $134.57 to Association;

1908 Association considers buying steamer *Empress* from Mossom Boyd;

1909 Association paid 5% dividend on members' paid up capital—advertisement in Peterborough papers that pavilion can be rented;

1910 Harry W. Stock, new proprietor of Juniper Island store, moved post office to west end of store and built an open-air ice cream parlour and lunch counter. Stock built, with Association's help, "immense boat house" (now Yacht Club) for overnight guests and visitors;

1911 Bowey gas tanks near the dock, newly-extended pavilion gave much more room for "nightly hops" and a "first-class orchestra" of the Misses Doris of Peterborough; the pagoda, constructed by Trent Canal workmen was ready by early June and was an attractive sight with the red roof and decorative ridge ornament; three new regatta cups: J.R. Stratton trophy for the open sailing race; Senator [George] Cox trophy for 14' dinghy race and H.W. Stock cup for the men's single;

1912 painted pavilion for $38—annual meeting held in Toronto in winter.

1914 Felix Brownscombe paid $50/year to act as secretary-treasurer for the Association (a position he held until 1935)—Association's wooden wharf towed to Boschink for winter—three dances per week .25 a person Saturday, but weekday evenings .10 for women and .15 for men—printed dance programs—annual meetings now held in summer—flagpole for property bought by Dr. Willoughby - regatta recommendations: include races for guides, professional canoeists and Indians; prevent motor boats from "fouling" the course;

1915 dividend now 4%—$50 given to H.W. Stock to build a wharf for the boathouse—possibility of forming another association with Clear Lake regarding issues affecting all the lake—pavilion insurance $14 annually;

1916 storekeeper Stock was paid a 10% commission on all annual fees collected—list posted on front of store—Association sent money annually to Sick Children's Hospital in Toronto and the Children's Aid in Peterborough—need for speed boat laws—no regatta held by Association—Stony Lake Red Cross Association not charged usual rental fee of $6 for summer meeting;

1917 bought gas generating plant from Peterborough Curling rink for $50;

1918 storekeeper Wm. H. Fletcher ran regatta—municipal taxes $27.35;

1919 July, peace celebrations held in pavilion;

1920 Annual meeting no longer in Peterborough but first Monday in August at the lake—new pavilion floor $287.72 of clear, dry maple 2" wide, 10' long, provided by Peterborough Canoe Company;

1921 the last year that Association issued shares;

1922   sold small parcel of land to Peterborough Canoe Company for $200—for only boat livery and repairs, shop to sell only their products (not everyone agreed with this venture by the Association);

1923   J.M. Gouinlock offered to rent pavilion and run programmes for five years. This was the beginning of the Stony Lake Aquatics Committee which ran regattas and organized entertainment until 1950;

1929   chemical toilets installed—attempt to sell the property for $6,500.

The 1930s were depressed years for the Association as for many other organizations. There was talk of the cottagers forming their own municipality, and rent payments were falling behind for the store and the church apartment in the boathouse; James E. Lillico of Peterborough who had taken over Fletcher's lease in 1921 was apparently not cleaning the pavilion as required. In 1931, the dances were reduced to two for the season. James (J.M.) Gouinlock and Russell (J.R.) Dodworth were the long-time organizers of these events. For many years the Dodworth family maintained a large, bound volume called the "Stony Lake Register" which was kept in the pavilion for visitors, guests and residents to sign with names, date and their boats' names.

By 1936, the Association was in financial straits, a situation that would not improve for 14 years until the current association was formed in 1950. Through these difficult times the directors held firm to their principle that the two-acre Juniper Island property of the Association must not fall into the hands of one or two individuals, even when they were well-known to cottagers and were familiar with the lake. To prevent this happening, J.M.R. Fairbairn who owned the remainder of Juniper Island bought up all outstanding shares in the Association, plus 446 that J.E. Lillico had purchased. Lillico and former store operator Herbert W. Stock had hoped to buy the property, but when they realized the opposition and possible contravention of the bylaws, they withdrew their proposal.

In January 1937, it was a surprise for J.M.R. Fairbairn to learn that a $1,000 mortgage by the recently deceased Clark Leslie had been placed on the Association property in 1936. B.C. Park of Peterborough, secretary of the Association and lawyer to Leslie's estate, discovered this fact.

Mr. Fairbairn arranged for J.E. Lillico, president of the Association, to take all necessary information including the original charter, transfer book of shares, stock certificate books and duplicate of mortgage, to a Toronto law firm. Fairbairn then took over the mortgage, with an interest rate of 6.5% to be paid off over five years.

The last years of the original Association were difficult because of the depressed economy, the war and finally, in the late 1940s, the need for new ventures. Thanks to J.M.R. Fairbairn and Wm. Richardson, president of the Peterborough Canoe Company at that time, the Association was able to survive several years of no revenue. Without store operators, the post office or a regatta in the latter years of the war, virtually all operations ceased. The directors held annual meetings, but there was little to report except an increasing deficit. In a letter to the directors in 1947, Cephas Guillet made several suggestions including turning the boathouse into a social and education centre; establishing committees for a library, property, safety and health, beautification of the lake (especially eradicating white pine blister rust), regatta (he was not in favour of the former Aquatics Committee), membership and speed regulations.

By the end of the 1940s, the Ladies Pavilion Committee was up and running, netting

24

$112 in 1947 and $243 in 1948. It continued until the late 1970s organizing children's and adults' social and recreational activities. The 1953 *Programme of Events* booklet states: "The aim of the Ladies' Pavilion Committee is to provide social amenities for the cottagers and summer visitors of all ages at the Juniper Island Pavilion. The proceeds from these various endeavours are directly applied to the maintenance and improvement of the Juniper Island Pavilion under the supervision of the directors of the Association. In this connection, during the past several years, the supports of the Pavilion have been greatly strengthened, the shutters have been altered and improved and the building has been painted, the latter having been accomplished largely through the efforts of a willing board of volunteers."[4]

By 1949, the directors of the Association were well on their way to reorganizing. Following a meeting of August 19, 1949 a committee formed of R. Roy McMurtry, Chairman; Lyman M. Crawford-Brown; Herbert H. Webb; Robert K. Slater; and B.K. Johnston recommended "...that a new corporation without share capital be incorporated, upon completion of incorporation the assets of the present limited company to the be transferred to the new corporation which will also assume this company's liabilities. The Provincial Secretary's Department which will not allow the present name to be used by the new corporation have agreed to the, "Association of Stoney Lake Cottagers Inc." which name this committee recommends to the directors for adoption."

On 4 March, 1950, a Memorandum of Agreement was signed by the Provincial Secretary and the following seven directors: Roland Roy McMurtry; James Edwin Ganong; Stanley Braund; William Aubry Richardson; Herbert Hodgson Webb; Robert Kenneth Slater; Lyman Crawford-Brown.

Their aims were virtually the same as those of the original Association, but the significant difference is that this organization is non-profit, without share capital. The 1953 *Programme of Events* summarizes the aims. "The Association, incorporated in 1950 under the Laws of the Province of Ontario as a non-profit corporation without share capital, has as its purpose the improvement of all interests of those who summer at Stony Lake. It owns the store, pavilion and club house on Juniper Island, rents the store to Mr. and Mrs. McColl and the Club House to the Stony Lake Yacht Club. The Ladies' Committee, consisting of all the wives and daughters in the Association, arrange all social activities at the pavilion, and the various Regattas at Juniper Island and Mt. Julian are organized by the Yacht Club."

One of the staunchest supporters of Stony Lake history and activities was the newspaper man, Nick Nickels, whose family roots are imbedded in the Kawarthas. Nick's "Afield" column in the *Peterborough Examiner* of July 31, 1954 depicts well the Association and its importance to cottagers. "Juniper Island is not only a community, it is an institution. The rambling supply store with second-storey apartments, the spacious pavilion with its wavy hardwood flooring and the "Yacht Club" boathouse are owned by the cottagers.

"No summer communities are as well versed in the workings, and pitfalls, of a cottagers' association as theirs. They have tried all combinations over the past 50 years; the adolescent age of associations that are supposed to run themselves, and fall; the limited companies that are controlled by a few; and during the last four an incorporation that is democratic and smooth-running.

"The Institution—the current incorporation has its head office in Toronto's financial district. Officers and directors are: G.F. MacDonnell, president; R.E. Merry, secretary; J.M. Gouinlock , treasurer; directors are A.J.

Sneath Q.C.; Dr. Russell Morgan; L.C. Bonnycastle; J.E. Ganong Q.C.; W.L. McDonald and H.B. Boynton. Yacht club officials are commodore Harold "Keeler" Knapman, vice-commodore Rob Willoughby, secretary Ken Slater and treasurer Karl Duffus.

"The incorporation is organized to the point where it issues a 32-page booklet that lists among many things, church services, programs of events, marketing, transportation and medical services, fire and boating safety rules. Since directors are chosen from Juniper and all other cottage communities roundabout, the booklet incorporates items of interest to cottagers everywhere on the Upper Kawarthas.

"Any weekday after 2 p.m. when the mailboat arrives you will see small boats converging on Juniper Island. They not only call for letters and groceries, hardware, laundry, homemaking but for motorboat gas and oil, repairs and gear, the latter services at the Peterborough Canoe Company Livery that can store and service 25 motorboats and 100 small craft during the closed season. The only objection campers have to the livery is the new name painted across the front wall "PECANO," Peterborough Canoe is an old familiar name to them, they say and ask, why change it?

"Cottagers make a point of bizarre clothing, or the lack of it, and you will find the people of highest standing in the workaday world, the most disreputable looking. That, too, is the way they like to live, dress and play according to individual tastes.

"On this, Civic Holiday, weekend you will see Juniper Islanders at their best. Tonight there will be a community supper and big dance. There will be junior and senior trophy sailing on Sunday and on Monday a junior

Former Peterborough Canoe Company boat (1922-1962). *Courtesy David Carol Collection.*

26

Mel Hunter's sons in a runabout circa 1948. Mel owned that Peterborough Canoe from 1962 to 1972. *Courtesy David Card Collection.*

regatta in the morning and senior events in the afternoon."

By the mid-1950's, as Nick Nickels relates, activities were in full swing at Juniper Island, under the auspices of the new Association. The Yacht Club was developing a comprehensive junior program and more structured adult weekend races. Thus, the last half of the 20th century saw hundreds of children reaching Red Cross swimming levels, hundreds of young sailors meeting recognized standards in sailing skills and racing and, more recently, specific tennis instruction. The Cottagers' Association is committed to water safety as seen in all the programs it sponsors, but it has always encouraged enjoyment of the lake surroundings.

As a community gathering place, the Association continues to draw residents and visitors not only through the on-going activities, but also by the care of the land, shoreline and

buildings. The latter have stood the test of time remarkably well. The general store is the oldest building (1892) and has been undergoing significant repairs to its underpinnings. The Association members were adamant in their support of maintaining the original façade. Inside work is gradually taking place, providing safe upstairs living arrangements for the store operators and adequate display and short-order cooking areas on the main floor.

The operators, as has been noted, originally were area merchants and, in the case of T.W. Robinson and Herbert Stock, avid canoeists and sportsmen. The Lillicos were popular storekeepers from Peterborough who brought some lively dance bands to the pavilion in the 1930s.

By the early 1960s, it was becoming difficult to find operators who would consider a five-year lease of running the store. Ads were placed in Toronto and Peterborough papers and in university placement offices with not

Everett and Ira Lillico, operators of the Juniper Island Store in the 1920s and 1930s. *Courtesy Marnie Young Collection.*

much response. However, 1974 saw the beginning of a most successful youth business venture on Stony Lake which, up to and including the summer of 1999, has seen 28 different young "Stony Lakers" operating the store. The usual tenure for a couple is two years, but some have stayed an extra year, or one member has not been able to return a second year and someone else takes over. In all cases, these young men and women have grown up on the lake, are usually at or beginning university when they apply for the position and have a wide range of skills. So capable are they, it is very difficult to make a choice from all the applicants. They have often volunteered or taught swimming, sailing or tennis; they know the youngsters who swarm into the store throughout the day and they are goodwill ambassadors to visitors at Juniper. Their contract with the Association necessitates appropriate bookkeeping, record management and usually willing parents who have been known to fetch, carry and generally pitch in. Each pair of operators brings new stock and services to the store, which they run from mid-June until mid-September.

The pavilion is a handsome structure that has seen every conceivable social, business and spiritual activity imaginable. Perhaps *Globe and Mail* theatre reviewer, Herbert Whittaker sums it up best in the August 15, 1970 condensed account of a fundraiser for pavilion repairs on the occasion of its 70th anniversary: "Stony Lake Follies: traditions repair a pavilion. In summer, they depart for the lakes. A whole separate life emerges. Summer friends of several generations return to a social life centering on the dock, the boat, the general store and the pavilion where the Saturday dances take place and meeting are held to stop irresponsible drivers of power launches. Admittedly, the aim of the Stony Lake Follies was not cultural. The pavilion at Juniper Island, centrepiece of summer existence, needs a new roof, and a new west wall. Happily, at Stony Lake, one of the old family cottages houses an actress-director, Araby Lockart, and her husband, playwright Jack Gray. Miss Lockart was given charge, and under her drive the Stony Lake Follies took shape. The new roof of the pavilion at Juniper could shelter a treasury of the kind of Canadian life for which Stony Lake has stood for well over a century. Now, it can include one memorable sliver of theatre in its past—a program from the Stony Lake Follies of 1970."

The pavilion has been transformed for wedding receptions and other celebrations. Its latest restoration in 1991 was made possible thanks to the generosity of the Anderson family and also to local cottager/woodlot operator, Tim Sherin, who provided all the lumber for new siding and shutters. Glenn Bolton was the contractor and John Jones supervised the whole operation, including mounting a commemorative plaque. The last structure to be restored was the pagoda, the last steamer waiting station still on the Waterway. Two years ago, Fisheries and Oceans undertook the essential crib replacement. Generous cottager donations of money, time and energy completed the scraping and painting and even a wooden replica of the original metal roof trim. Thanks to the painstaking efforts of Sandy Beatty, Hugh Drake and Jack Matthews, all the wood is now gleaming and resplendent in the pagoda's original colours. Hugh Drake and Kathy Hooke undertook to find vintage photographs and were especially grateful to John Lyon, co-owner of the Roy Studio Collection who unearthed the very early panoramic shots now displayed on the east and west walls. A generous donor paid for special reproduction and preservation for all these images to be safely displayed year round.

A stone cairn commemorates the 1983 "hundredth year anniversary" of the American Canoe Association Meet of 1883, and a store plaque celebrates the 100 year history and restoration of the pavilion (1996).

What have been the key issues of the 50 years of this Association? Some have not changed over the 100 years; the emphasis remains on maintaining boat and water safety, preserving the natural environment and continuing to provide services for the betterment of all cottagers. Specifically, these concerns have focussed on local government's official plans, such as setbacks, severances and other property matters. The natural environment is a major concern as noted earlier. Government regulations are far stricter than they were 100 years ago, and residents are often bewildered by the multiplicity of ministries. However, the Association has been in the forefront of many cottage groups in preserving our fragile habitats, and expects to continue as such.

Some issues came and went; trailer camps and houseboats were major concerns in the 1980s but have faded over time. The Association established a charitable foundation in the mid 1990s which can and does receive funds towards restoration and historic operations. Members have been generous, especially with regard to the Association property. Of the cur-

East end of Juniper Island Store and two young cottagers, 1914. *Courtesy Katharine Hooke Collection.*

Relaxing by the store verandah after morning tennis and fitness in 1995. Left to right: (standing) Angela McCumber and Linda Welsh, (seated) Kathy Nelson, Nancy Davies, Patty Macdonald and Sheila O'Neill. *Courtesy Katharine Hooke Collection.*

rent roster of 13 Association directors, nine are descendants by three or four generations of original Stony Lake families, four are women (none was 100 years ago) and together they represent mainlanders and islanders. Some are welcome newcomers to the lake who are prepared to accept the challenges that the

Steamer waiting station or pagoda at Juniper Island, about 1915.
From the Roy Studio Collection, courtesy John Lyon and Rob Roy.

Association is facing. It is an organization that has always served its people and its environment well. As Blair Mackenzie says: "Our lake is a very special place, strengthened each year by a thousand actions, large and small, some well known and some carefully concealed."[5]

Four

LIVING HERE

ONE OF the great fascinations in reading about the lives of earlier generations is their everyday life. Many current Stony Lakers are fortunate in having written and oral records that have been passed down over time. Out of all those bits and pieces emerges a picture of individuals and families laying down a framework that endures and sustains the generations to come, providing strength to the Stony Lake community. From the first of the cottagers to make the lake their summer home we recognize a commitment to nature, retreat, simplicity and communal family as their guiding principles. Throughout, the underlying focus is the family, regardless of some activities that today may seem quaint.

In stepping back to those earlier times, it helps to know why cottagers originally came to Stony Lake. And there are many reasons. For outdoor enthusiasts, the late 1800s was a time of ample hunting and fishing, especially in the unspoiled wilds of Ontario. The American Canoe Association (ACA) Meet of 1883 at Juniper Island certainly gave the area tremendous publicity and led to the buying of islands and ultimately to the building of cottages. In 1887, the ACA established a northern branch of the organization which included Canada and, again, a canoe meet took place at Juniper Island, now equipped with a primitive supply store.

Camping on the islands was a natural follow-up to these canoeing events. Those campers, generally from Norwood, Lindsay, Lakefield and Peterborough, could be outfitted thoroughly in Peterborough by Turner's Tent, Awning and Sail Factory who supplied the necessary tents, awnings, sails, flags, waterproof clothing and, for land-based activities, waterproof horse cloths. On July 28, 1892 the *Peterborough Examiner* recorded that Messrs. Clegg, Crane, McCallum, Kidd and Fisk, plus some Toronto friends, were amply equipped with five large tents for camping on Juniper Island. Meals were prepared by a John Tremblay, noted as major domo and *chef de cuisine*. This two week-long venture was a serious undertaking! Another group, the Grand River Canoe Club camped on Juniper Island for two weeks in 1893. Their expeditions included Fairy Lake and Eagle Mount for the view and blueberries, Mr. William Church's red cedar workshop on the Mt. Julian road, the Blue Mountain and the Indian River. "Going up the lakes" and travelling to the "back lakes" were the local idioms. If campers needed supplies, Thomas Hull of Upper Stoney made deliveries twice a day in his steam yacht, the *Idle Hour*.

Construction begins from campsite to cottage on Austin Island, 1901. Left to right: Harold Austin, a local lad, William Jones of Eagle Mount, George Austin and Harold East. *Courtesy Carol Ingleton Collection.*

The *Peterborough Examiner* refers, perhaps disparagingly, to these "250–300 lake loiterers" who frequented Stony over the summer of 1889. A letter of September 4, 1889, from Eleanor Douglas to her son George at school in Halifax, gives an interesting picture of would-be campers who treated private property rather casually! "…I came up here a few days for a change and rest. We thought we could get to Tealeaves Island, but when we got up, found it occupied – so Wright's Island having no one on it, we pitched our tent there. The house [cottage] is locked up and I rather wish it wasn't today, for it is raining and it would be jolly to get inside and have a fire…Yesterday we sailed up to Eel's Creek… and didn't get back to the camp until after dark…Then we went to George Strickland's campfire. It was a very small campfire, for really everyone has gone home and the singing is very feeble."[1]

Campers' days were taken up with preparing ample meals, undertaking daily excursions and celebrating the evenings with campfires, rollicking singsongs and undoubtedly some discreet "spooning." It was a period of "muscular Christianity" with many church, youth groups and YMCA camps throughout the islands. But the spiritual tone did not prevent dancing on the rocks to the music of banjoes or harmonized singing in illuminated canoes. The Echo Banjo Club housed at Emerald Isle featured a tiny melodeon, which could be operated from a skiff.[2]

Although camping organized by the YMCA and YWCA continued into the early years of the 20th century, there was a definite move by cottage owners in the late 1880s, encouraging the owning of land and the building of cottages. The *Peterborough Examiner* on August 3, 1889 referred to campers or "lake loiterers" who did not always treat property responsibly. The paper implies a certain prestige to ownership when it states "...year by year Stony Lake is becoming more civilized...with houses [cottages] being put up in a modern style ...like those one sees at fashionable places."

On September 9, 1886, the *Peterborough Review* predicted the results of the completed survey of the Burleigh Township islands: "A number of those islands have been sold, and during the next year or two it is probable that numbers will be up. It has been argued that the islands will be all be sold and that there will be no place for outsiders to camp. But there are, even if the islands are all sold, acres and acres of shore land; and an example as to how campers will be prevented from using the islands is given by stating that at one time this summer there were nearly fifty people camping on Messrs. Edwards & Roger's island, without even asking permission to do so. It will be a decided benefit to sell the lake property. The owners take an interest in their places, and the fires which pass over, leaving an island a blackened waste, will be in a large measure prevented."

Nine years later, the *Daily Evening Review* of August 9, 1895 remarked that the earlier "...rather rough structures have almost disappeared...now we see fresh paint and tasty architecture." The paper also observed a decrease in camping parties and the rise of several boarding houses and some rented abodes such as 'Fairy Lake Villa,' which would be pleased to receive paying guests. Some of those rough structures may well have been hunters' cabins in the wooded hills between the Burleigh Channel and Lovesick Lake.

Turning then to the fairly consistent patterns of the daily life of early cottagers, we are grateful to their memories, logs, diaries and letters for these priceless glimpses into days gone by. Because the cottages were generally simple in design and purpose, their housekeeping chores reflected these structures. Although most early cottaging took place over summer with possible extensions at either end, winter cottaging was not unknown, as will be seen.

An early log entry by a guest at the Buell's 'Shanty' notes that hanging out muslin curtains to air, washing dishes taken down from the open shelves and sweeping out the cobwebs or other winter detritus, was fun on a sunny day with many hands making light work. The Buell's "man", Jim Robinson, from Young's Point, would have dealt with the heavy opening-up chores such as removing shutters, bringing the skiff and canoe down from the rafters, and perhaps laying in some fresh supplies, after taking a block of ice from the ice house and putting it into the kitchen ice box.

August 1904 guests at the 'Shanty' were grateful to the July residents who "...had busied themselves to leave the cottage, rocks, docks and campfire in readiness for inspection by the new hostess." This group summarizes a typical day after the initial shakedown: "...in time expeditions started for McCracken's, Cassidy's, the Store and Mrs. Crane's, combining domestic duties and social pleasures."[3]

Long before that opening day, families prepared in various ways for the halcyon days of the cottage. "Stuff for the cottage" gradually accumulated in boxes, dunnage bags or hampers. Many families ordered supplies from Eaton's, which published *Eaton's Camp and Cottage Book: a helpful reference for camper's comforts*.[4] Peterborough and Lakefield merchants would pack supplies, including furniture, lamps, and bedding, which would be loaded onto steamers in Lakefield. Consider this advertisement in the *Peterborough Morning Times*, August 2, 1900—"The very thing for Stoney Lake cottagers and campers. The Times' Megaphone! It will carry the voice half

Many hands make light work—shelling peas at South Beach, 1909. Left to right: Hubert Stuart, Marion Stuart, Stella Grier, Dorothy Stuart, Geraldine and Helen Brooks from Young's Point. *George Douglas Collection, courtesy Katharine Hooke.*

a mile to a mile and a half. Made in two sizes. Price $1.50; $1. Every cottager should have one." Twenty years later, the Juniper Island store offered cats for rent to catch those pesky rodents at the cottage.

One family walked both to work and to school during the winter months to save money for a summer holiday at the lake. Several people to this day recycle worn sneakers, plaid pants and paint-stained sweaters directly to the cottage. (It is often said that visitors to Stony Lake are the ones in new clothes.) Marion Teamerson sums up the experience of many: "In the early years, we could not wait for the ice to go out each spring, so we could go see if the mice had eaten the mattress during the winter. All during the 'off season,' we fill containers in the garage and basement with 'Things For the Lake' like bleached clothing that's OK for Stony but nowhere else, and half worn-out furniture that has at least eight more summers at the cottage, never mind that none of it matches and heaven only knows whether we'll get it across to the island, as it's too wide for the boat."

Once close to the cottage, cottagers would stop at nearby farms for fresh supplies. As Mar-

ilyn Ott recalls: "Regularly, upon approaching Stony, we stopped at the Tedford farm. He would behead a chicken or two and we took them to the cottage (feathers included) to be cleaned as soon as possible. This was the same Tedford family whose produce boat serviced Clear and Stony lakes on a weekly basis."

Most families did their own opening up which often involved removing shutters and keeping an eye out for bats, and bringing the wharf around from its winter safe haven, always assuming the out-going ice hadn't carried it who knows where. There could be priming of the hand pump and a particularly filthy job of screen preparation—before the days of galvanized screens. Rusty Dodworth remembers his father wiping a mixture of lampblack and linseed oil over 88 screens to prevent rust. Marilyn Ott's recollection of the ice house includes the appearance of large grubs in late summer. Chores weren't always pleasant but, eventually, boats, cottage and surroundings were made ready for the season by tasks that certainly weren't accomplished in a day.

Meals followed a set pattern, at set times. Read what George Greening recalls in his paper, "The old red Boathouse," about meal-times at the Collins Island. Other large families such as the Mackenzies, Guillets and Coles have memories similar to this one... "There was a long table on the verandah, where meals were served, sometimes to unlimited numbers. Mrs. Collins used to bake huge loaves of lovely homemade bread, which vanished in no time. With such large numbers to feed, meal hours had to be regular. Breakfast was at 8 a.m., dinner 12 noon and supper 6 p.m. and if you were not on time that was your look-out. The horn was blown—this implement is still in the kitchen—and everybody came flocking, the kids on the double. After breakfast each morning, Mr. Collins conducted Family Prayers. A good old custom which is not observed by many to-day. Meals taken outside were a great attraction for the wasps. Mr. Collins had a "swatter" of his own construction, a piece of leather on a short stick. I can still visualize him sitting at the head of the table, making shots, right, left and centre. Sometimes a bullseye would be scored in the marmalade, much to the disgust of the girls but to the merriment of the children present."[5]

A later Collins' in-law notes that the prayers involved being on your knees behind your chair, which often led to a certain amount of horseplay among the children. Robin McGraw, a descendant of the early Willoughby family remembers this "table" story: "I have been told at times there were as many as 20 people sitting at the table. Another table had to be built as an extension to the main table. This huge table was covered with a piece of oilcloth and the children, especially Rob Willoughby who was the oldest, took great delight in spilling a little milk and quickly lifting the oilcloth and sending it down the table onto the lap of the first unsuspecting victim."

No one recalls dealing with ice as being particularly pleasant. Tom Cole vividly depicts the ice house and its attendant tasks: "Obviously the ice house was essential in the early days of the camp. Ours, 'Oakleigh's', was double-walled with air space between for nests of wasps, mice, bats and who knows what else. Fish not immediately to be used were placed on the blocks of ice under the sawdust. There also, but not too close, were put the 25 lb. flats of butter I remember us bringing up at the start of each summer holiday. Getting out the ice for the icebox was an arduous chore, especially as [when] the summer wore on, the blocks became one big one and had to be separated with a crosscut saw and splitting equipment—and the blocks never fitted the icebox."

Lois Miller recalls a similar tedious task: "Our refrigeration was a cement ice box built outside the kitchen. It had to be stocked with ice from the ice house which was filled by Dave Brown [nearby farmer who had a small wharf on the shore] in the winter. The ice box had one door on its longest side. The ice went into the ends, which meant that everything had to be removed and then replaced every time we replenished the ice.

"Not every cottage had its own ice house, so a large one often supplied two or three nearby families. For those without their own source of ice at hand, local farmers dutifully made deliveries in those early days. Sometimes the cottager still had to dip the piece of ice into the lake, rinse off the sawdust and lug the slipping beast to the ice box. Emptying the drip pan was some child's daily task. Now these sturdy oak ice boxes are valuable antiques and make fine cabinets. Little did we know! To keep supplies from spoiling, the Cole family built a trap door in the kitchen which opened into a cement-stone walled chamber for cooling or storing items which might suffer by the heat in the hot summer weather."

Following breakfast would be tasks such as cleaning lamp chimneys, trimming wicks, cutting wood, splitting kindling and the daily "milk run." Farmers on all the shorelines around Stony Lake were wonderful sources for milk, butter, cream, garden produce and chickens. The Michael Mackenzies and the Wyly Griers in Mackenzie Bay made twice daily trips to the Cassidy farm, one family in the morning, one after supper. Rob Guillet's evocative memories of this task capture the scene well: "For many years we took turns paddling or rowing to Dunford's each day, to get fresh cream and milk, eggs, and a few vegetables. I remember so clearly the cool scrubbed interior of the milk house and the wonderful stainless steel cream separator that spun when you turned a big handle and gave out an ever-increasing whine as its speed increased. Dad loved thick cream, and ate it on pretty nearly everything. No worries about arteries clogging in those days!" Rusty Dodworth recalls that, to relieve possible tedium of the daily task of going for milk, "...the three Dodworth sons, Russell, Paul and Stanley, would row to the mainland Hamilton farm and fill their porcelain pails with milk fresh from the cows. For the trek back to their stubby, rowing punt, the children would swing the pails from their arms in circular motion, with centrifugal force keeping the uncapped milk in the pails."[6]

Although most of the early lighting was by coal oil lamps, several cottages, namely 'Boscobel,' 'Lochend,' 'The Lodge,' 'Wanakuen' and 'Endiang,' installed gas carbide systems, a volatile heating and lighting service. Pipes threaded throughout the cottage carried the gas, which was generated by water and carbide and pressurized at ten pounds. A tap at each light controlled the flame. Routley's china store in Peterborough made an odourless night glow lamp which provided and consumed its own gas. One pint of kerosene provided light for 20 ten-hour nights. Easier to operate were Coleman lanterns, which produced a bright white light, after you pumped up the tank in the lantern, along with a characteristic hissing.

When motors became available, it was possible to pump water into a large tank, which worked on the gravity principle; once it was full, the water flowed through the pipes into the cottage. The Dodworth cottage, being situated on a fine breezy point, made good use of a windmill to pump water. Delco generators were

Summer ice box in mid-winter, built between two rocks at Point of Rocks, 1915. *George Douglas Collection, courtesy Katharine Hooke.*

36

available from the 1920s. However, until electricity reached the islands in the early 1950s, most cottages used a hand pump or water carried from the lake, and continued to light with coal oil lamps. Some people still rely on propane, rather than use electricity, which is inclined to go out during summer thunderstorms.

Tom Cole comments on these developments over the century, noting that rooms were often dark because of verandahs. The gloom "...was more noticeable where artificial lighting was limited to candles and coal oil wick lamps. The Aladdin mantel type were a great blessing when they came in and, of course, the noisy and frightening Coleman naptha gas lamps and lanterns shed much more light in the days before hydro. A few places were illuminated with carbide and later by electricity from Delco gasoline generators. Juniper Island Store and the Peterborough Canoe Company Boat Livery were those I now recall using carbide lighting, but there were others.

"When [Ontario] Hydro came to Juniper, it was regarded by neighbours as rather a mixed blessing: while bringing refrigeration and better lighting, it permitted canned music louder than the old player piano and excruciating amplification of live music, not always of top quality."

Laundry was certainly time consuming in early days, but inventiveness was the name of the game along with a group effort. Some families relied on battleship grey flannelette sheets, which seemed unaffected by dirty feet or other signs of outdoor activities. In 1890, Eleanor Douglas, while on an early spring walk along the north shore near Mt. Julian, came upon a group of local farm wives rinsing heavy blankets in the cold water. To spread the soap throughout the wool, they would stamp in bare feet over the blankets spread out on the rocks, with their long skirts hiked up around their waists.

Heating water in copper boilers over a cook stove and hefting sheets and towels through a mangle that squeezed out excess water through rotating rollers were chores that involved both sexes and strong backs. In his 1913 diary, Eric Grier describes paddling out to the waiting steamer in mid-Mackenzie Bay to deliver the weekly laundry in a dunnage bag, to be washed at Young's Point. However, by the 1920s laundry pick-up for Fanning's laundry and dry cleaning in Peterborough was available at McCracken's and Kawartha Park. In the 1940s, Marilyn Ott clearly remembers an American Montgomery Ward Sears model washing machine sliding down the *Islinda's* gangplank at Horseshoe Island. Nancy Hunt recalls rinsing the heavy laundry at 'Nakemi' by tying it to the skiff and then rowing it around Cassidy Bay. The Wyly Griers towed canvas for their "burlapia" dining area behind their skiff to soften and shrink it before it was installed. Lois Miller describes the process at her family cottage in the 1920: "We did all of our own wash. There was a low bench with a hand wringer and three wash tubs. We kept the pump and stove busy too on wash day. We ironed with a set of three irons that were heated on the stove. One handle was used for all. It snapped on and off. The ironing board rested on the table edge and a chair back."

What were those clothes that were so arduously washed? By mid-WWI, middies for girls were the fashion along with surge bloomers, stockings and running shoes. City clothes were hung up on arrival and not put on again until the trip home by steamer and train. Bathing suits, before the Olympic Annette Kellerman tank suit of the 1920s, were often handmade. At least one girl's bathing suits were made from her brothers' cast-off flannels.

In our era of environmental sensitivity, we well may shudder at some of the early disposal measures of garbage and other waste. Many over the age of 50 easily recall the weekly bottle and can ritual. One of the children would paddle or row out to a nearby deep part of the lake to sink the containers. Margaret McKibbon recalls that her precise doctor father dug a deep pit for all the flattened tins whose ends he removed with an axe. Paper was burned and, although no one has described early composting, many cottages had a damp, musky "sink hole" for all the kitchen waste. To dispose of tin cans, Jean Mackenzie required her family to remove the labels and the bottoms, squash the [used] cans flat and stuff them into a deep crevice in the rocks. Bottles were washed and reused. She was well ahead of her time. Of course, there was a certain amount of indiscriminate pitching of old bedsteads, stoves and other forlorn castoffs into the lake or back in the bush. It is said that in earlier times cottagers on Eagle Mount had a communal mid-island dump.

Many enterprising cottagers attempted some sort of self-sufficiency on their property, challenging at best on the granite and thin soil. Vegetables, fruit bushes, trees and vines supplemented the bounty of wild raspberries and blueberries. Earth was brought to islands by sleigh or barge, and watering was often tedious especially during hot, dry summers. Some even tried dairying on a small scale with cows or goats brought across for the summer. An added bonus was the prospect of these creatures feasting on the endemic poison ivy. However, cattle grazing on 'Endiang' was short-lived; within 24 hours of their arrival, these disgruntled beasts swam back to a rock in Dunford's Bay where Doug Dunford had to rescue them in the middle of the night, having seen, by flashlight, their great eyes shining in the dark. Goats brought to 'Lochend' in 1940 managed to strip bushes and young trees of tasty bark, but wisely avoided the poison ivy. A few cottagers brought along some unwitting chickens to scratch out their last days before being eaten by the family.

Thanks to ever-helpful farmers and their supplies and, later, the McCracken's market

and professional supply boats, most cottagers had a source of meat and vegetables. Fish was a staple part of cottagers' diets and the art of fishing is a story unto itself.

Drinking water came from many sources; in early days, the lake itself was the main one. It is rumoured that one current cottager still makes ice cubes from lake water, claiming (incorrectly) that freezing makes it pure. For many, the spring between Kawartha Park and Sandy Beach provided a delicious, constant supply of ice-cold water. Pumped well water was available at McCracken's, Mt. Julian and Burleigh as well as Juniper Island. Cottagers may not know that there was a well (unused today, but still there) on Juniper Island, near 'Cordach' which several local cottagers used during the 1930s and likely later. Some families took the added measure of boiling and straining both milk and water. Lois Miller notes that: "Mother pasteurized all our milk and cream and boiled all our drinking water, which came from the lake via the hand pump on the sink."

No account of cottage living is complete without considerable discussion about "facilities." Whether referred to as privies, outhouses or conveniences, this essential "chamber" required regular attention. Most outhouses were easily accessible—especially in the dark—and discreetly located, sometimes one for each sex. In the 1920s, the Amys' property included a chemical outhouse as well as the standard variety. Outhouses varied in size, from one- to four-holers, and were maintained throughout the seasons with liberal doses of lye or chloride of lime and ashes from the stove or fireplace. If those ashes weren't cold when dumped down a wooden outhouse, the inevitable happened! Tom Cole writes about a fire "...in the late thirties which took place as a result of removal in a wooden box, from the stove or fireplace in 'Dingley' to the outhouse, of ashes still hot. It was very embarrassing to my sister and her female guests, there alone, to have to direct those who arrived to help extinguish the flames before the trees suffered. The edifice was quickly replaced with planks from our own pine trees."

Provided the outhouse had a good soil base and was not perched on the edge of an island, drainage was sanitary and acceptable, as it is to this day. Some smaller structures were tipped up over the winter and, by the next season, the only residue was inoffensive ash and earth.

Regarding what we now term "grey water," cottagers who nurtured gardens would dump their dishpans of kitchen water onto flower or vegetable beds. Until recently, many cottagers would bathe and wash their hair in the lake as a matter of course. At least two early cottages had bathing houses, built over the water, so the more genteel ladies could take their ablutions in private.

Generally, mothers of the families organized the daily chores, sometimes with the help of older children, paying guests, or useful nieces and nephews who would supervise young swimmers and provide strong arms and backs for chores. Paid help came in various forms from kitchen girls brought up from the city who sometimes were afraid of the water, or were lonely without friends. Local girls found jobs on the lake, such as Florence Tedford who chose to work for Mrs. Sam Henderson [Emma Sherin] along the Mt. Julian shore in 1930 and '31, instead of going to Normal School. "I cooked, cleaned, filled the cookie jars, served at bridge parties. There was no set time off, just when the work was done. Then I would go to the dances at Viamede or paddle across the lake to visit my cousins in Dummer township.' Florence notes that many north shore cottagers came to the afternoon Sunday service at Holy Trinity at the top of the Mt. Julian road and would join the South

Burleigh library for the summer.[7]

Another example of summer help is that of the nanny. Miss Adeline Roberts was an educated lady of few means but, as a relative of the South Beach Stuarts, she was acceptable to the Griers, Mackenzies and four young Stuarts, and became a most capable companion, guardian and general "dogsbody" for several summers. In a 1915 letter to George Douglas, she describes typical summer activities at 'Camp Ararat' [now 'Nakemi']:

"We have made several expeditions to Perry's Creek to get blueberries which are exceptionally good this year; we got 14 quarts in a few hours. There were two bear cubs caught at Apsley and they have them there on a wire outside the Burleigh Hotel… I wish you would come back and shoot snakes, there is a big beast who divides his attention between our camp and 'Wee Island' I'd give anything to see him shot. We cook on an old camp stove outside and the open fire."

Robin Prince remembers the summer of 1928, when her mother died and her grandmother, Bess Willoughby, "…heard of a young nurse who had a cottage in Upper Stoney. Her name was Clarice Willoughby but she was not related to us. Father hired her to return to Baltimore with us after my summer up here." Clarice was a strong paddler and swimmer and an ideal nanny.

It is likely that most families had their main meal of the day at noon: fish, meat that could be ordered and delivered by steamer, and local vegetables. Before the era of the popular supply boats, at least one gardener made his rounds by skiff. Robert Norgrove Stuart of South Beach, known as "a fine gentleman and keen cricketer for the Peterborough team," grew superb vegetables and lovely flowers. He timed his Saturday call to the Mackenzies for noon hour and generally stayed on for a meal. Jeannie Guillet fondly remembers the evening meal as a picnic, campfire supper on a nearby small island. "Kitty [Van Natta] always had a maid to help run the cottage and prepare the meals. The main meal of the day was at noon, because Kitty wanted the evening free for picnic suppers on Iona, at that time a remote wilderness island in Eight Acre Bay. These [meals] were a family ritual, a time for families and friends to get together in unspoiled nature."

Making your own fizzy drinks or fruit syrup was popular in many families. After picking bush raspberries you could produce tantalizing juices. Homemade drinks, such as those shown, were expected.

Lois Miller's family made root beer at the start of their six-week holiday. We don't know her recipe, but she does recall the result: "We made root beer every year. Since it usually took about six weeks for it to become fizzy we were always trying to speed up the process. Sometimes the hot weather helped, but often we stored it in the kitchen and had to dash madly to rescue it, when the caps began to pop off the bottles."

Not all cottagers were equally successful at brewing or distilling. Blair Mackenzie recalls an early attempt at making wine at the lake: "I 'borrowed' a bottle of Welch's grape juice, added sugar and yeast, and placed it under my

bed to ferment. The hot weather did its job, the bottle exploded and Mother was not at all amused."

Over time cottagers would attempt early interior decorating. Christie Bentham describes the evolving summer house: "Some time after 1888 the sound of hammers hitting square-headed nails was heard, as the old cottage was built. Small inner rooms, a large wood-burning stove, [multi-sectioned for water heating, plate warming, baking and cooking] a huge wrap-around verandah, a variety of paint colours as each occupant added his favourite." Nancy Watson records the efforts made at 'Cairn-Dhu': "At the time of purchase, 1913, the living room floor of this large two storey Victorian cottage was covered with sisal matting and the beams were crowded with paper Japanese lanterns—an invitation to a conflagration should a spark from the fireplace (or my grandfather's pipe) land in the wrong place. The first thing the family did was remove these fire hazards. Also, with the exception of the kitchen and dining room, every room was covered with layer upon layer of wallpaper. My godfather, Jim Lockhart, remarked that there was enough wallpaper paste between the layers to feed all the cockroaches on the lake for 1000

RASPBERRY ACID CONCENTRATE

12	quarts	raspberries
5	oz.	tartaric acid
2	quarts	water

Let stand 36–48 hours
Strain through a sieve, but be careful not to mash the berries. To each pint of juice, add 1 ½ pounds loaf sugar. Stir until sugar is dissolved. Bottle juice and tie muslin over neck of each bottle.

GINGER BEER

1 gallon boiling water poured over ¾ pound of loaf sugar, 2 oz. of bruised ginger and the rind of one lemon. When lukewarm, add the juice of a lemon and a gill of yeast. It should be made in the evening and bottled in the morning.

Exerpt from the diaries of George Douglas.
Courtesy Katharine Hooke.

years! Subsequently my parents, Archie and Louisa Land, 'restored' one room each summer, removing the wallpaper and decorating each of the four bedrooms in a colour scheme to complement its china washstand set."

Some cottages saw few changes. Lois Miller remembers her early married days in the 1920s: "During those years the kitchen was much the same: a sink with hand pump for water from the lake and a small drain board on one wall; the big iron stove, a table with one drawer and a wall of shelves. The pots and pans hung on nails on the walls and everything else was on the shelves. All staples were in tin or glass containers."

Sleeping arrangements at a cottage were varied and often delightful. There were certain advantages to being able to slip in and out without parental knowledge. Children seldom had a bedroom of their own, but fun more than made up for lack of privacy. Many have recollections about sleeping quarters.

George Greening recalls busy summers on Collins Island: "The island was crowded in the summers 1919 to 1925. It was usual to have as many as ten, or more, beds in the Boathouse, ranged along both sides, with a passageway down the centre. The doors in front were opened and replaced by screens, providing a good current of air. Once the crowd settled down for the night, everyone slept soundly. There would be hurried dressing when the horn blew for breakfast at 8 a.m."

Sometimes sleep came a little late when the fellows were full of spirit, as clearly depicted in "The old Red Boathouse" as written by George. "The summer of 1923 stands out in my memory as the last year in which the Boathouse was crowded to capacity, and was a riot most nights. Fred would be ragging Bill one night, and the next night Bill would be trying to get back at him. Others willy nilly would be drawn into the proceedings. The climax was one night when Fred came to bed early, most unusual for him. Grace [Leeming[must have had another date? Fred's bed was next to the door, in the front of the Boathouse. The light was hardly out, before the missiles began to fly, first small articles, increasing in size as time went on. Fred, the old soldier, took cover under his bed, emerging at intervals to do the throwing. Bill, in desperation, hurled a big leather portmanteau, which he used to prop up his bed, in the general direction of Fred. The last object to be thrown was the giant-sized community 'thundermug', this took out one of the side windows. A truce was eventually called, by which time the place was a shambles but, strange to say, no casualties."

Dottie Drake writes that at 'Forest Home', the Knapman children of previous generations had tents: "The cottage only had 2 bedrooms then, a spacious master one and a small helper's room. The children always slept in tents—boys one side girls the other on cedar platforms and metal cots." As Don Cameron remembers, his family sleeping arrangement was different; the parents were in the tent. "The first cottage to be built onto the Livingstone lots was a 16' x 10' cabin, which was the beginning of the 'Patch', in 1928 for the newly married Marg [Livingstone] and Don Cameron. When Norah (my sister) came along in 1930, a sleeping tent was set up for my parents. By the time I came along five years later, a complete camp was in place with the 'Patch' now including a kitchen and two new sleeping cabins."

The Reeds with five children needed two sleeping abodes. As Doug Reed recollects: "The boys [Horace, Doug and friends] had their own large white canvas tent on a wooden platform while a separate two-bedroom structure was added for the girls [Mary, Delight and Becky] and guests. Later, a grand (to us) two bedroom cabin with sleeping porch replaced the boys' tent. A smaller cabin was home for Cecile, our beleaguered mother's

All dressed up and going nowhere on the veranda of 'Kawana', 1915. Jessie Grahame is reclining, wearing a bonnet. *George Douglas Collection, courtesy Katharine Hooke.*

helper from Buffalo, who was afraid of water! When Mary was a teenager, she was pleased to call this cabin her own space. Later it became a tool shed."

The Russells on 'Spree Island' spread the sleeping cabins well around the property, but thanks to Keith's ingenuity all the buildings were linked by an early intercom system. Whether in tent, cabin, boathouse or cottage loft, it is probably safe to say that all sleepers at Stony Lake are soothed by sounds of rippling water and refreshed by breezes wafted in by pines.

Families made their own fun that often included others along their shoreline or on a large family island such as Fairy Lake Island, which was interwoven with paths and trails. Margaret McKibbon recalls the yearly work of clearing paths and painting stakes to mark boundaries. Mothers made good use of these walkways especially in the afternoon for bridge, tea or less abstemious refreshments.

Although the great majority of cottagers were comprised of parents, children and assorted cousins and friends, some people chose the single life for several years. Their habits reflected this choice. Donald Cameron

relates the early exploits of his father, G. Donald Cameron or "Kimmels" as he was usually called: "He first started exploring Stony Lake as a guest of the Alick Mackenzie family at 'Gairloch' during the early to mid 1910s. He was a boarder at the Grove School in Lakefield and had adopted the school and the Mackenzies as a second home. He was quick to acquire a canoe and when the Mackenzie camp was full, which was probably quite often, he would camp on one of the many vacant islands in the lake. For almost two decades from the acquisition of his first canoe in about 1912, through until 1928, my dad's cottage was his canoe and a tent. Most meals were cooked over a campfire. For more substantial fare there were probably frequent rescues from his friends' parents at Crane Island, 'Kawana' or 'Shota'."

Gerry Hill briefly describes his grandfather's property: "The Hill family's presence on Stony Lake goes back to the turn of the century as did a lot of businessmen from Lakefield who owned cottages on the north shore of the lake (west of Mt. Julian). My grandfather, Albert "Tiny" Hill, owned an island in what I call Dunford's bay. As far as I know, he tented and never built a cottage. He sold it around 1909 and bought another island in Katchawanooka from the Rice and Mud Lake Indians, so the deed that I have says. Today it is known as Hill's Island on the charts."

George Douglas wanted a small piece of property so that he, like "Tiny" Hill, could paddle up from Lake Katchawanooka and have a spot on which to pitch a tent and then explore the lake. George camped for two years on Wee Island in Cassidy Bay before building a modest cottage, which then served for winter and summer expeditions.[8]

Robin McGraw recounts living arrangements of one of the many Willoughby clan. "Among this crowd was a relative, Uncle Frank Lacey. He was an 'old' bachelor who did not like children, so he pitched his tent far away where my cottage now stands. Hence, the property is still called 'Uncle Frank's Point.' However, he always turned up at the main cottage for meals!" Lois Miller describes an interesting living arrangement. In the 1920s, her elderly grandparents, Dr. Henry and Amelia Barnes, employed a Native couple, Herb and Katie Beaver, to help with household duties. The Beavers and their two young daughters camped in a tent on the Barnes' land.

Although the Kawartha Lakes do not have a history of organized camping like Algonquin, Temagami or Haliburton, many Stony Lakers remember the Peterborough YMCA and YWCA establishments. The YWCA moved its quarters several times from the Burleigh Channel to central Stony, settling on 'Inglestane' until the late 1940s. The YMCA, which moved from Sandy Point to the east side of Clear Lake, was known locally for years as the Boys' Camp. It currently operates year round as Camp Kawartha, no longer under the auspices of the YMCA. Upper Stoney's boys' camp, Oak Ridge, offered keen competition at the Juniper regatta, particularly under director Don Fitzgerald of Lakefield, a noted canoeist

in the 1930s, and Reg Blomfield who taught canoeing at the camp. Reg competed in Toronto regattas in the 1920s and, while well into his 80s, would also perform canoe stunts at local regattas.

John "Bubs" Macrae recalls an interesting camping experience in the summer of 1940. As a former Grove boy, he was persuaded by Headmaster Winder Smith to forego summer work at Queen's and to undertake a special boys' camp for English boys who couldn't go home during the war. John could not refuse, for, as he says: "Windy exuded kindness so generously that anyone who knew him was bound to be indebted to him. I certainly was, so I reported for duty as ordered. The kids enjoyed the school without bells, without regimentation, but Stony beckoned as far as I was concerned, so at the end of a week we were transported to Mackenzie Bay, never to return until summer's end. The Hugh Mackenzie cottage, 'Lochend,' was spacious enough for us to pack into, including the school matron, 'Polly' Perry and her niece, while outside there was a separate kitchen manned by Chief Petty Officer Lee, the school cadet instructor, and his wife who did the cooking—a splendid arrangement.

"Life for these campers was pretty much like that of all the other young cottagers, in, on and around the waters and rocks. We had only a few canoes, but when it came to an expedition to High Falls or wherever, our neighbours most kindly lent us what more we needed. The kids became sufficiently skilled paddlers to handle these outings and we even had a regatta to stir things up a bit. There was no shortage of enthusiasm.

"There is no doubt that these young Brits absorbed the love of Stony Lake that others take for granted. Now they are a loyal band of Englishmen who form the nucleus of the Old Boys of Britain, having a formal dinner annually and working constantly in ways to serve The Grove [now Lakefield College School]."

43

Just around the corner in Cassidy Bay at 'Nakemi,' Ruth Allen also ran a camp for evacuated English children, primarily girls, who were billeted with friends of hers. Ruth and her husband Stewart also felt that a summer at the lake would be an unforgettable experience, a chance to learn to swim, handle a boat, and enjoy the fellowship of other young people. Besides her own three children, Nancy, Ken and Michael, Ruth convinced nearby girls like Mary Reed, Jane Easson, Kay Grier and even Rose Huycke from Boschink to join the crew. This was not your sophisticated camp of Algonquin Park, but it was fun and organized.

Kathy Hooke remembers her days at camp: "A resident cook, who worked without pay for the privilege of being on an island with her young son for summer, prepared hefty lashings of porridge topped with wartime KLIM (dried milk power). Large containers of oily peanut butter and strawberry jam lined the shelves of the gloomy inner storeroom. We ate off a large table in a screened-in verandah, and slept in a side verandah with orange crate boxes as bedside tables.

"After breakfast, tidying up and chores, Ruth conducted a quiet period in "Cozy Cot", an outside gathering place of cedar benches around an open fireplace. She read us Bible stories while we all knit squares for some obscure war effort. (I am a left-handed klutz and did not enjoy this activity.)

"Swimming, diving, and playing with canoes were all very popular. Ruth taught the children to swim by tying a rope around their middle and pulling them along the wharf as she kept up encouraging non-stop chatter. When we could swim across to and back from George Douglas' 'Wee Island' we were considered water safe.

"Canoes and a punt formed the fleet, so a huge treat was the occasional ride to St. Peter's in the Kawartha Park *Admiral* (the water taxi)—usually only when it rained. We picked berries, or organized paper chases on the old logging roads to Burleigh, ran local regattas and most fun of all, had regular bonfires with hearty singing and toasted marshmallows. Stewart came on weekends only, as he worked long hours at de Havilland. The responsibility lay with Ruth, helped by older local teenagers like Betty Lampman."

These two remarkable camps would be impossible now with today's regulations, sad to say.

Ruth and Stewart Allen's campers on 'Lochend' shoreline, about 1942. The campers range in age from approximately 6 to 15 years. Betty Lampman, here in her late teens wearing the striped bathing suit, was a counsellor. *George Douglas Collection, courtesy Katharine Hooke.*

A Sunday afternoon outing on the Lost Channel, organized by Mother, 1915. *George Douglas Collection, courtesy Katharine Hooke.*

Another group haven resulted from the donation of a cottage as a summer retreat for Roman Catholic sisters. In 1939, the Sisters of St. Joseph's Hospital in Peterborough received an unexpected gift: three islands and the summer home of Peterborough Mayor Thomas Henry (known as Harry) Denne. 'Denholme' was described in the December 8, 1939, *Peterborough Examiner* "...as one of the most spacious in the Kawarthas." This generous act was "...as an appreciation of the Sisters to me and mine."

Not every day was peaceful, of course. Accidents, illness, irritable aunts and cranky infants all had to be coped with. Most families had tried and true recipes for upset stomachs, poison ivy and sunburn, the most common ailments. Marg McKibbon recalls her father, Dr. Williams, finally bringing his medical bag to the lake as he found it easier to take fishhooks out of scalps with his scalpel. He successfully resuscitated Ken Allen who once fell in the lake at the nearby Brewin cottage. One summer he was wakened by Frank Gillespie's water taxi at 3:00 a.m., and called to attend to a serious compound ankle fracture

of the YWCA camp director at 'Inglestane.' She had slipped on the rocks while checking up on noisy pranksters. Dr. Williams called on the culprits and the campers to hold lanterns while he dealt with the fracture.

Lois Miller remembers a natural remedy for asthma: "During one summer Mother ran out of her asthma medicine, a powder which she burned to inhale for relief. Dad gathered mullein leaves, dried and powdered them. When burned they gave the same relief."

Dr. Cooper Cole was always willing to bring aid, as were Dr. Russ Morgan at Kawartha Park, Dr. Tom Currier and Dr. John Cole. Sonny Cook recalls her mother's quick wits in dealing with an emergency: "Mom had put mouse seed out in saucers ("Won't Kill Rats") and I (5 or 6 years old) ate it all. She made me drink mustard and water to throw up. I felt quite triumphant – proved I wasn't a mouse!"

From Kady Denton comes a kaleidoscopic image of the unforgettable days of being a child on Stony Lake: "My earliest memories of Stony are of our cottage 'Kushaqua' in the late 1940s. Thinking back brings isolated images: sharp, golden, exciting times. With my sister Janet, I hitched rides on the supply boat to visit neighbouring islands where we had cousins. We might return that afternoon, or not for days. For years we had just a canoe. If there was an emergency, my mother Flory would lay a white towel on the rocks at the end of the island, and that was the signal for nearby relatives to come in a motor boat."

Visitors and residents of all ages were, and continue to be, enveloped by life in their summer houses at Stony Lake. It is said that the early cottagers honed leisure to a fine art. Certainly the setting and the community embrace all who come to the lake. How they live there reflects that embrace.

While reading of the summer accounts of the early campers and cottagers, and knowing that modern insulation and thermal underwear were far into the future, it may come as a surprise to learn that intrepid folk did experience the lake in fall, winter and spring. In March 1883, officials, laying out the course for the American Canoe Association Meet of August that year, were surprised to see a winter camp on Amys' island. Early in the 1900s, American cottagers would return to the lake in November for the annual deer hunt. The *Stoney Lake* was often chartered, allowing the hunters to both bunk down on board and to shoot from the upper deck.

Here is what Lois Miller recalls of her first time at the lake: "The first we remember of Stony Lake is about 1920. We came in May and stayed into November. Dad had to quit work for six months because of his health, and we spent it at Stony Lake. The black flies and mosquitoes were terrible that year. We slept under mosquito nettings and used a smudge on the porch in the evenings. When it got cold our beds were moved to the living room and all the cracks around the doors were stuffed with newspapers. The big cast iron stove in the kitchen kept it warm, but we had to dash

through a corner of the dining room to get from one warm room to the other. We had our baths in a wash tub in front of the fireplace where it was hot on one side, and freezing on the other."

Thanks to George Douglas's compulsion for calculations, we have a record of his costs for 39 days in the late fall of 1915 and winter of 1916 at 'Wee Island'. This spartan diet, supplemented with a couple of partridge and a rigorous skating and skiing regimen, cured his serious depression and uncertainty about his future.

On Hand Mar 22		Used	Approx. cost
Flour	100 lbs	5	.20
R. Oats	20 lbs	6	.25
Sugar	70 lbs	35	3.50
Bacon	10 lbs	11	3.30
Lard	9 lbs	6	1.80
Fray Bentos	9 lbs	3	1.20
Hard Tack	15 lbs	3	.30
Other	10 lbs	2	.20
Apples	20 lbs	3	.50
Tea	4 lbs	1	.70
Bread			1.30
Tomatos	9 tins	2	.20
Coffee	3 lbs	2	.80
Port wine	½ qts	3	2.00
Candy		4	.80
Gasoline		2	.50
Coal		1	12.00
TOTAL			29.95
Say 40 days cost			$30.00[9]

The challenges of dealing with uncertain ice, cold temperatures and crippling storms adds a challenging dimension to winter lake life. George was invigorated by the conditions on a December 17, 1918 visit to the cottage: "The ice was very good about 5 inches thick.

Some black ice along the Ayotte's shore. A great joy to see this lake stretching out to the North in the pure morning sky. I slept on the verandah and slept heavily till about 6 a.m. when I woke up from the cold. The inside of cottage was fine and warm."[10]

Three years later, on March 25, 1921, Michael Mackenzie, his daughter Kay Douglas and son Hughie made a late winter excursion from Cassidy's boarding house to 'Lochend'. Kay writes in the 'Wee Island' diary: "We tried to cross on the ice which was several inches thick but very rotten; we tried using planks but it was not good enough. Hughie got nearly across but went through twice. The water is very high and the land very wet. We walked by land to Cassidy's Point but could not get any farther—the water was so high. We untied a wharf we found fastened to the shore and with half an hour's hard work got over to 'Wee Island'. The ice tho' rotten was very hard to push a wharf through. Daddy and I poled from behind and Hughie broke the ice from in front. We lit both fires [kitchen and living room] Hughie changed and we tidied up while Daddy went back for a bag or two of rain-coats we had left at Cassidy's. He ran a rope from shore to shore so that the wharf can be pulled across. After lunch of soup and bacon and blueberry jam, Hughie and I tried to get over to Lochend—first by pulling the canoe across the ice, then by working her through the ice and along a lane out of the bay where the ice was strong. Then by land but the water was so high the marsh was impassible. We got the canoe to Miss Roberts' [now 'Nakemi'] made a bridge of logs at the channel. Played three-handed bridge."[11]

A day later was Easter Sunday and Kay and her father sailed the canoe up to St. Peter's. "...a wonderful sail through mist and clear spaces—very heavy mist to the east and up Clear Lake. All clear water except the bays right up to the church and beyond. On the way home by following up a lane in the ice we only had to go through about 50 yards."[12]

Felix Brownscombe of Peterborough was a man of considerable energy, curiosity and skill. Like George Douglas, he was intrigued by the land and lakes in winter. Thanks to his comprehensive record keeping and diaries much of this family's life is on record. Ken Brown [great grandson-in-law of Felix Brownscombe] gathered the following from family accounts and the newspapers of the day: "For many of the Brownscombes, particularly Felix, nothing was as important as getting to the cottage, whatever the time of year. On the kitchen wall of his cottage is a notation of 'first trip to the lakes.' An article in the 1926 *Peterborough Examiner* claimed that '...by his trip this year he has commenced his 64th year at Stoney Lake without missing a year.' If this is correct, it means the Brownscombe family were continual campers on the lake from at least the year he was born, 1863, long prior to purchasing the island in 1886. Felix regularly reported back to the Peterborough newspapers on when the lake was open or almost open. His diaries record many early trips, including, an account written in 1937 at age 74, of a memorable spring visit with his grandson Doug: '...with an ax and an ice chisel we had borrowed from Mrs. Spencely, we chopped an opening for the punt...Douglas kept pulling the punt forward with a pike pole while I stood in front and cut the ice.'

"Felix's son, Minto, also had memorable winter trips to the lake, with two of them recorded in the 1917 *Peterborough Examiner* as follows: ' 'Y' Boys on Snowshoe Tramp to Stoney Lake...Three of the 'Y' boys, Garnet Galley, John Carlisle, and Minto Brownscombe, returned to the city this afternoon from a snow-shoe tramp to Stoney Lake. They started out last Saturday, fully equipped with snowshoes, toboggan, dunnage, etc., in fact everything necessary for a trip to the wilds in the middle of winter. They, however, over-looked one very necessary article, a canoe, as when they awoke this morning, and started for home it was raining like it does in the good old summer time. Nothing daunted, and as provisions were running low, the pangs of hunger prevailed, so they loaded their tobog-gan, put on their snowshoes, and headed for the south. They followed the ice trail from near Burleigh, out around Juniper Island store, and down the centre of Clear Lake to South Beach, where they left the ice and fol-lowed the road to Lakefield and Peterbor-ough. Needless to say they were wet when they reached home, but they did not mind that and they pronounced the outing one of the best they have ever taken, even if they did get wet to the hide. Next time they will remember that sometimes it rains in the winter.'

"This adventure in February 1917 was fol-lowed by another in December that year, also reported in the *Peterborough Examiner*: 'Two Collegiate Boys in Storm: Two Collegiate boys, 'Doc' Young and Minto Brownscombe, skated from Lakefield around to Buckhorn Lake on Saturday in an endeavour to make the circuit to Chemong. They took to the ice at Katchewanooka, and went up through Young's Point to Clear Lake, to Burleigh, where the blizzard overtook them. They had dinner at the Brownscombe cottage, having packed their 'eats.' They struggled through the storm until they reached the Indian village at Curve Lake, where they had supper, and after-wards pushed on through Ennismore to Chemong, where they spent the night, arriving home on Sunday morning. It was a trying experience in its last stretches, but the boys fought the storm where it exercised its full force in the open country places. Other youths of the Collegiate had planned to accompany them, but of those who had talked of the out-ing, only two reported at the G.T.R. station at 7:00 a.m. Saturday.' "

In the 1930s and '40s at least one caretaking couple stayed on into the winter to look after the island. Phyllida Smith relates this account about 'Boscobel': "Behind the main house and over the brow of a little hill, lived Sam and Mil-lie in their own private cottage. This consisted of a bedroom, an ablution area, and a sitting room with a large stove for cooking and heat-ing purposes, for Sam and Millie lived there year round so that, when my grandmother was not in residence, Sam would take care of the island. In winter he walked over the frozen lake to Mt. Julian for supplies and to get the mail, and to this day I have photographs he took of the island and its buildings covered in snow."

Jim and Babe McClelland spent a few win-ters on Rackham's Island, just off Big Island and were very exposed to wind and weather blowing up Clear Lake. Fortunately, they were well prepared for dangerous times with a spe-cially designed boat on skiis, along with warm, inflated wet suits.

Berenice and Harold Knapman at 'Forest Home' were able to spend 18 years cottaging through all the seasons. As their daughter, Dottie Drake notes: "A big change in 1953 when my parents retired to the cottage. Elec-tricity, indoor plumbing, oil heat, enclosed verandahs, etc. They were captivated by the seasons in all moods and the many friendly visitors—both human and wild animals." Dottie and her sister and families spent many Christmases on the island. Harold died, prob-ably as he wished, while chopping a channel in the spring ice at the island.

Jean and Bev Wood are relative newcomers to winter living at Stony. Their story captures the essence of the lake community: "Through the years we visited at 'Shota-Too' we met many of the relaxed, friendly people on Stony Lake. Many of them, we realized, are descen-dants of the original cottage owners, carrying on the traditions of the forefathers. We enjoyed hearing about the congregation of St.

Peter's-on-the-Rock, the summer activities held at Juniper Island and the Association of cottagers, mindful of keeping the lake a healthy place to come while we completely enjoyed the atmosphere we were in.

"During the years we spent part time here in spring, summer and fall, we were invited to winter weekends in mid-February to 'On the Rocks.' There we saw the beauty of the lake when it is frozen: experienced walking, cross country skiing and snowmobiling over the frozen water; saw the islands and mainland covered in snow, and enjoyed the feel and smell of crisp, cold, refreshing air, away from the city.

"Our first purchase in the autumn of 1991 was flotation (survival) suits. The first three winters we tried an 800 pound, eight wheel, six passenger Argo, over a part of frozen Stony Lake, where there are two currents under the ice between our cottage and the mainland. It was a good machine on land and in the lake. We learned, however, that it was like a snow-mobile when it comes to slush...they don't work. Also, it was extremely difficult to get out of water up onto ice that would hold it, should it break through the ice, and it did, even though fitted with ice cleats on the tracks.

"The fourth year we opted to have a light-weight snowmobile that could be more easily managed. When the ice is not thick enough to support it, or there is a lot of slush on top of the ice, or if the lake does not have a covering of snow for the track on the snowmobile, we walk.

"The cottage faces the south shore of the mainland. We have islands to the right and the left of our view towards the mainland and, unless we have very cold temperatures, there is a current of open water within our view as well. (We enjoy watching a bald eagle that often flies down to the edge of the ice there to catch a meal.)

"When very cold temperatures do occur here, we hear booming sounds from the lake

Ice is out! Cassidy Bay, looking east, 1915. *George Douglas Collection, courtesy Katharine Hooke.*

in the mornings, as the expansion of the ice buckles and cracks it. There have been times when we have felt the vibration from that force of nature here on the island. It is inter-esting to see the fissures when out on the lake and hearing those booming sounds.

"There have been other times when the tem-perature has risen high enough for several days to take the ice cover off the two currents in front of us. Then we put a boat into the water to navigate to solid ice between shorelines as we do before total freeze-up, which usually occurs by the beginning of January, and break up, which usually occurs by mid-April."

It is likely that winter visits and year round living will increase. The sights and sounds of the frozen landscape have a special magic.

There is always the promise of spring as the days lengthen and the perennial question is on everyone's lips: when will the ice go out this year?

Five

GOING UP THE LAKES

THE STONY Lake saga of earlier days almost begins like "Once upon a time, there were trains and steamboats, stages pulled by horses and cars with vulnerable tires..." Journeys that now take only a few hours once took two days. As for flying your own seaplane right to the cottage dock or landing a Cessna on a farmer's field—that was inconceivable until the 1930s and even then, a rarity. Perhaps more than any other component of the cottage experience, the "getting there" has undergone a fundamental change since the time our story begins.

By the 1870s, the attractions of Stony Lake and the surrounding waters were being publicized enough to attract sporting enthusiasts, campers and potential cottagers. The settlers and the lumbermen had been making use of the lake, winter and summer. On land, many local railways were working their way across this part of Ontario as the chartered rights for new lines were acquired. Initially, it was enterprise as undertaken by lumbermen, mill operators and farmers that led to steamboat building. As the land and water-based operators coordinated their services and the moving of goods and passengers became the responsibility of the entrepreneurs, the travelling public became the benefactors. However, by the 1930s, when former dusty roads became paved highways and when the outboard engine became a ubiquitous source of power, cottagers travelled as individuals in family cars and family boats rather than by public transport.

Tourist development is said to be fostered by attraction, accessibility, accommodation and advertising.[1] The attractions of the Stony Lake area were well-known from literary writings as well as from tourist pamphlets. Local entrepreneurs advertised their services and made them accessible, particularly their mode of transportation. As well, accommodations attempted to meet the needs of a range of travellers, many of whom eventually became cottage owners. *The Town and County 1876 Directory of Peterborough* claimed how easy it was to travel here. "The favourite route for pleasure seekers is Stoney Lake, which may be arrived at by morning train, thence by steamer *Chippewa* to the Mount Julien Summer Hotel, which was built by a company of Peterborough gentlemen, on the west shore of Stoney Lake; the enterprising firm of Messrs. R.C. Strickland & Co, of Lakefield being the principal proprietors. The scenery of Stoney Lake, studded with its innumerable islands and of the surround stretches of water, is really beautiful, rivalling that of the Thousand Islands itself."

Off to Peterborough. The "stage" at McCracken's Landing, conveniently parked on the wharf, about 1910. *Courtesy Art Cole Collection.*

We are fortunate on Stony Lake to be part of a lovely waterway stretching 148 miles across the province, linking Lake Ontario to Georgian Bay. The story of its 82-year development is complex and fascinating. Here, we can only highlight its key points as a transportation route. Champlain explored theses waters with the invaluable help of the Natives. To the settlers of the 1820s and '30s, Stony Lake was part of a system of lakes that had potential for both inland communication and as a source of power and commerce. However, any work undertaken to develop all the lakes and rivers was, at best, piecemeal and erratic; it was begun by settlers, developed by lumbermen, then undertaken by the province of Ontario, and, finally in the 1890s, by the federal government.

The hamlet of Young's Point at the south-western edge of our area is a microcosm for the waterway development as a whole. When the first Young's Point lock was built by the Trent Canal in 1869, boats could then travel from Lakefield up to Rosedale and down through Lindsay to Port Perry. With both Lakefield and Port Perry having rail connections by then, travellers could be transported considerable distances.

When Francis Young, an Irish engineer of the Peter Robinson emigration of 1825, arrived at the rapids at the east end of Lake Katchawanooka, he allegedly claimed, "Here I will stay."[2] As a widower with nine children, he set to work to build a wooden dam across the rapids and a grist mill (to which Catharine Parr Traill and Susanna Moodie brought their grain) and sawmills on both sides of the water. He also opened up a small aqueduct beside the dam so canoes could pass from Lake Katchawanooka to Clear Lake.

It was no wonder that N. Hugh Baird, surveying engineer for the provincial government, praised Francis's ingenuity in 1835 while he was surveying the water system from Rice Lake to Lake Simcoe in preparation for building a comprehensive canal.[3]

In 1886, Francis's grandson, Patrick Young, decided to expand the family operations by owning and building steamboats. He bought the small 56 foot *Fairy* (1882–1888) on which he had served as mate and apprentice captain under Captain William Scollard in 1883, taking participants and spectators to the American Canoe Association Meet at Juniper Island. Thus began, in modest fashion, the 59 year history of the Stoney Lake Navigation Company (SLNC), which according to Richard Tatley "was the longest lived and most successful steamboat line in the entire history of the Trent Waterway."[4] The fleet included five original vessels. In the typical fashion of wooden steamboats, the Young's boats often burnt or were damaged in storms. They would them be rebuilt from the keel up lengthened or reconfigured. If each vessel is considered individually (reincarnated or not), the SLNC had eight ships in its long and important boating history.

Soon after P.P. Young's fledgling steamboard business began, his one vessel, the *Fairy* with a capacity for only 50 passengers, was facing stiff competition from Roland and Robert Strickland's similar business in Lakefield. Thus, on May 31, 1888, he launched the *Mary Ellen* (1888–1897) 76 feet with capacity for 75 passengers, to supplement the *Fairy*'s capacity. (The *Fairy* disappears from this history by summer's end when she allegedly broke up on the shores of Clear Lake and is not heard from again). In 1890, Mr. Young made structural changes to the *Mary Ellen*, including moving the engines to increase speed. Then, in the fall of 1896 he decided a refit was necessary for his nine-year old ship. He dismantled her, saving only keel, engines and pilot house. On May 5, 1897, the former *Mary Ellen* became the 76-foot *Majestic* (1887–1920) with a capacity for 75 passengers. She was broader, sturdier and

faster, but by the winter of 1909–1920, her owner again undertook another refit, following some fire damage and the *Islinda I* came off the ways in Young's Point in April 1910, 80 feet in keel, licensed to carry 150 passengers. She was fated to last only one season, due to arson late one night at Young's Point. Never daunted, the Youngs then built the *Islinda II* (1911–1945) out of the former vessel's remains. At 80 feet and with a capacity for 211 passengers, she soon became the most familiar and beloved of all the steamers on Stony Lake. As of August 1992, the engine boiler and propeller of the *Islinda II* were installed in the *Bytown Pumper* in Ottawa.

However, besides reincarnating one steamboat, the Youngs added to their fleet. The 93-foot *Empress* (1899–1929) licensed to carry 245 passengers, was built in Lakefield and bought by the Youngs from the competing Trent Valley Navigation Company of Bobcaygeon in 1908. She was another favourite Stony Lake steamer making daily runs to and from various lake landings and Lakefield. In June 1927, she towed a scow to Cornwall, 309 miles—the longest voyage taken by any

The fleet at rest: *Islinda, Empress* and *Stoney Lake* at Young's Point, 1910. *George Douglas Collection, courtesy Katharine Hooke.*

Locking through at the Point. Steamer, yacht, launch and two canoes, early 1920s. *Eric Grier Collection, courtesy Katharine Hooke.*

steamer in the Kawarthas at that time. Her tragic demise by fire at the Mount Julian wharf in 1929 is recounted elsewhere in this book. Although the machinery was salvaged after the fire, it would have cost the Youngs too much to rebuild, and by this time the steamboard era was waning.

The little *Manita* (1900–1938) built in Kingston and licensed for 150 passengers, was only 66 feet in keel, but a sturdy ship that filled in for the SLNC when the *Empress* and *Islinda* were booked. The Youngs bought her in 1914 from the bankrupt Peterborough Navigation Company. She could do dredging and, like all the steamers, carried mail, towed logs and was contracted for fish restocking operations or making the "cheese run" to Lakefield for a cheese factory near Mount Julian. Sadly, she rotted on the way, in Sawmill Bay above the Young's Point locks.

Last, but certainly not least in this account is the SLNC's flagship, the *Stoney Lake* (1904–1944) 92 feet, licensed to carry 295. She was last seen locally in late September, 1944, when she left Young's Point with Captain Pat Young (P.P.'s son) at the helm and a few of the family aboard. The vessel was sold to a Captain Ross Carnegie of Kingston where she was remodelled and strengthened before sailing on to Montreal as the *Island Queen*, a floating cocktail bar and finally ending as scrap in 1972. In her days on the Kawartha lakes, the *Stoney Lake* was a proud and grand lady, designed primarily for excursions. She is well recorded in many postcards and professional photographs.

Thus, Young's Point, the enterprising Young family, steamboat travel and the locks of the Trent Canal are inextricably linked to the Stony Lake story.

While reading the following excerpts, listen for the steamer's whistle; watch for the puff of smoke as she gets underway and hear always the cheery words of Captain Pat, engineer Fred and all the other special folks who made travel on the steamers summer magic. Remember that the steamers provided an inexpensive, picturesque method of travel for visitors to the lake; bring your picnic, travel for one dollar round trip from Lakefield, watch a regatta from the deck and dance to a local band on the return trip. What a delightful way to go to the lake!

George Greening of the Collin's clan provides this overview: "My first introduction to the island was the summer of 1910. I had met Annette [Collins] in Toronto during the previous fall and winter and in the interval had moved to Ottawa, where I had come to know Bob Collins, then in the Molsons Bank. Having been invited to Stony, I enquired how I should get there. The regular route was by CPR to Peterborough, a short run from there to Lakefield on the old Grand Trunk, thence by lakeboat via Young's Point, on through Clear Lake. There was a strike on the Grand Trunk at the time, so I took the boat from Peterborough, over the Liftlock, and up the Trent Valley canal. A wonderful ride, and great value for the money, about $1. The trip took between three or four hours. There was not any hurry, life was at a more even tempo in those days. The boat stopped en route at any cottage wharf, where there were passengers to get off or to be picked up, or where freight had to be delivered. At each island all the inhabitants came down to the wharf. This was the event of the day. In time the roads from Peterborough improved, following the increase in motor traffic, starting with the old Model T Ford. Eventually there was not enough business for the boats. Service was stopped in 1945. The road from Lakefield, up as far as the Mines, was surfaced in 1957. What a change from the old dusty, washboard road. Time to Peterborough is now about half an hour."[5]

Although the captains were very accommodating about dropping off and picking up passengers almost anywhere, there were some shallow properties they could not reach safely. In Mackenzie Bay, for instance, any passenger for a steamer stood at the end of a long pier jutting out from 'Lochend'. Crew and passengers kept their eyes peeled for a stick and white flag, a signal for a steamer stop.

If the boats could land at your shore, the procedure was much as Tom Cole describes it: "In consequence of the usual means of access, nearly everyone built a steamer dock which of course made disembarking from a small boat a real problem while making the steamer's gangplank less formidable. Actually those who ran the steamers were extraordinarily able in their handling of the boats and their contents and they could get giddy ladies in long skirts ashore or aboard at almost any bit of rocky shore. My grandparents used to transport flat silver to and from the lake, in addition to masses of other luggage and supplies."

John Collins relates a family story that is typical of the helpful steamer crews: "While I was there, I have only the memories of my mother who said that the *Islinda* brought the furnishings after dark on a rainy night in late August. The captain would cosy up the ship against the steep rocks on the north side of the cottage, several planks were spanned across from deck to rocks and everybody pitched in to carry all the items to the cottage. With darkness and not many lights, rain, wet rocks and unskilled labour, mother thought it was a miracle that no one was injured."

However, in some situations a captain could be understandably testy. Doreen Foote tells this anecdote: "As was the custom, Harry Foote would go into town on one of the steamers taking with him a grocery list to be filled at Hamilton's store in Peterborough. On one particular day the steamer had left the dock and was proceeding on its way when Ella Foote was observed to be waving frantically. The captain was notified and immediately began backing the boat toward the dock. When the boat was within shouting range, Ella called out to her husband that he should buy two pounds of butter instead of the one pound that she had put on her list. Passengers on the boat later described Harry Foote as being very embarrassed and the Captain was furious."

Captains on the SLNC steamers were justifiably proud of their boat handling skills. (They had three years' apprenticing before they took the wheel alone). Jane Matthews describes the trip from Peterborough to the head of the lake during WW II: "From Peterborough , Father drove to the Lakefield dock to meet the *Islinda*, to bring our family to Stony Lake for the summer. Pat Young ("Captain Pat") was a friend of my father who brought him his beer. With my mother and brother, we embarked, with a cat turning flips in a cage each time the whistle blew. In the hold there was a cargo of lumber along with various supplies to be delivered to cottages and landings along the way. Due to the gas rationing there were few motor boats. White flags were visible at some docks, requesting the Captain to pick up passengers. There were steamy smells emanating from the funnel infused with the tasty baking, of pies being cooked in the galley for the crew. When arriving at Gibson's dock, Uncle Joe [Gibson], an energetic Scot, was gesturing at Capt. Pat for a safe landing through some hazardous rocks. Pat was *not* amused as he knew every hazard, but chewed on his cigar and kept silent." In earlier days, the steamers served meals, "$1 a day" according to a 1905 *Peterborough Examiner* account.

The steamer operators made their money in the off seasons by transporting goods to year-round landings and generally providing any service possible. The canal system has never needed to be a military escape route as originally proposed by the Duke of Wellington in 1819. Nor did it ever become an Erie barge canal carrying emigrants and trade goods as promoted by the mayor of New York City in the early 1800s. But it did serve as a route for transporting local materials. Below is the record of lockages at Young's Point for the 1913 season: "Young's Point, P.P. Young Lockmaster: Steamboats, 1,143; small boats, 735; scows, 253; rafts, 150; lockages, 2,281; passengers, 25,777; ft. lumber, 795,000; cords

wood, 4,789; livestock, 200; shingles, 815,000; 5 scow loads saw logs; 2 scow loads tone; 3 scow loads sand; 2 scow coal; 1 scow load brick; flour and feed, 93 tons; hay and cement, 1,100 bbls; agr. implements, 55 tons; furniture, 63 tons; merchandise, 740 tons."[6]

The *Peterborough Examiner* relates an injury in July 1905 that was treated successfully thanks to the cooperation of steamer and train. A Pennsylvania woman staying at the Burleigh Falls Hotel was wounded, when a boy shooting a crow missed the bird but hit a Mrs. J.A. Pierce in the shoulder. Dr. Alex Fraser of Lakefield who was at the hotel gave her immediate treatment. She was then taken by the *Majestic* to Lakefield and placed on a special train to Peterborough and Nichol's Hospital. Likewise, when Mrs. Cooper Cole fell and broke her leg in the 1920s, she was carried to the steamer dock on a door, placed on the steamer and, once in Lakefield, carried to Jack (usually referred to by initials J.M.R.) Fairbairn's private rail car for travel to Toronto for treatment.

We tend to think of boat captains only on steamers or modern cruise boats, but at least two launch owners on Stony Lake needed a qualified captain to pilot their vessels. Dr. Oscar Race, a dentist from Brooklyn, hired Captain Charles Grylls of Lakefield as his captain. In the winter, Mr. Grylls built canoes for the Lakefield Canoe Company with Thomas Gordon and Edward Rolleston Tate. Nearby Dr. Race's cottage, 'Boscobel,' was William George Morrow's launch *Oakdene*. His chauffeur and boatman, also from Lakefield, was Braden Blewett, a skilled canoeist early in the 20th century.

Another method of travelling on Stony Lake as a business enterprise was initiated by Richard Birdsall Rogers, designer of the Peterborough Lift Lock. As the developer of Kawartha Park, he was in a position to propose a "pooling venture." Owner of a large

56

houseboat, the *Lotus*, Rogers was a familiar sight at regattas and known to all. At some point Mr. Rogers had purchased a yacht, the *Victoria*, to tow the *Lotus*. He wanted a few of his friends to form the Lotus Club; together they would share costs and use of these boats. The costs and expectations of this venture are interesting now, nearly 100 years later. Here is what he proposed:

"Property: The property consists of one houseboat *Lotus* and yacht *Victoria* which are both registered. The houseboat is in first class condition. The hull which is 45 feet x 16 feet was rebuilt in August 1905 with sides of British Columbia fir.

"The yacht *Victoria* is a powerful little boat, and has a first class engine 5 x 6, and a Roberts pipe boiler. The hull is in a fair condition and will last for several years. She was overhauled last season and made an open boat with curtains. She will hold 25 persons and has a speed of about eight and a half miles per hour.

"Proposition: It is proposed to place the outfit at a valuation of $1,200.00 to be divided into shares of $[undetermined] each, with one extra share reserved. The time and manner of occupation of the outfit shall be regulated by the majority vote of the club. The outfit can be rented to outside parties if thought advisable, which would make it self-sustaining and also a dividend earner.

"Cost of Running: When being used, the approximate cost of running will vary from $2.75 per day to $6.00 according to the distance moved and number of crew employed. If it is desired to lay stationary, no expense need be incurred; and if members of the party steer the yacht, which is quite easy to do, only an engineer need be engaged at a wage of $1.75 or $2.00 per day, and wood for fuel will cost an average of about .75 to $1.00 per day, or a total cost of $2.50 to $3.00 per day.

"In renting to outside parties, a profit of bout $9.00 per day can be earned. The daily expense of crew, fuel, waste, &e; would be about $6.00 per day, leaving a profit of $9.00 per day, which for a period of say 30 days the outfit was rented, would leave a profit of $270.00. Valuing the outing at $1,200., and taking $70.00 for repairs and upkeep which would be sufficient, the balance of $100.00 will pay 8% on the capital invested, and also allow $100.00 for depreciation of plant. If the outfit were rented for say two months, a dividend of 30% would be earned after making an allowance of $100.00 for depreciation. There would be very little doubt as to the renting of the outfit for two months, and probably three months each season. Mr. Rogers has the opportunity, at the present time, of renting for two months and a half for the season of 1908."

"The outfit (houseboat *Lotus* and tug *Victoria*) was rented to a party (Standard Oil people) from Pittsburgh for 13 days and to a New York party for 14 days, at a rate of $15.00 per day, or a total of $405.00. The following was provided—the houseboat fully equipped with bedding, men, cutlery, dishes, &e; and the tug with the necessary crew (captain and engineer) and fuel for running the tug."[7]

Not all travel to the lake was by water, of course. As early as 1913, Eric Grier drove an RC Hupmobile, an open touring car from Toronto to Kawartha Park, taking 13 hours and enduring several blown-out tires. Assembly of the Hupmobile in Canada began in 1911. A low-slung angular vehicle with high-perched headlamps, it was built as a runabout for $850 or as a touring car for $1000 (a vast amount in 1913!).[8] By the 1930s, car travel was becoming a little more common. Tom Cole describes an arduous trip on the forced road running from Warsaw to Peterborough. These picturesque, winding roads represent the difficulty that local road builders had in following the usual grid pattern typical in most of the province.[9] In some cases, they had to encroach on private property to avoid some obstacles. "Even after motoring became more popular, it was, for many years, not something to be undertaken lightly. Few were the paved roads, low was the horsepower and capricious were the tires. The cars were loaded to and on the roof, and there were racks on running boards and trunks. I remember one Victoria Day weekend in the early thirties when my father—always keen on exploring – decided to keep straight east on the South Dummer road instead of swinging northeast along the curve of the forced road to Warsaw. Fortunately we had not gone far before the mud was up to the hubcaps and, I guess, the oil pan breached. It was necessary to get a cab from Peterborough to take my mother, five children and a nursemaid on to McCrackens' Landing while father arranged for the salvage of the car.

"Flat tires averaged two each way and on the morning of the day of departure from Stony, there was always an advance party sent to the Landing to check for and repair flats as well as take some luggage. At first the paved route from Toronto as far as Peterborough was #2 and #28; then #12 and/or #7; then #7A and, of course, after the Second War, #115 and then #134 between #7 and the War-

saw Road; it was then known as "the garbage route" because the Peterborough City Dump was on the east side where, at the time of writing, a big industrial subdivision is booming. Of course, to avoid traffic on weekends, many were and are the alternate routes between the Lake and Toronto—a distinct advantage the Kawarthas enjoy over the Muskokas."

Island cottagers would, and still do, often leave a canoe or a skiff on shore for travel in the off season. George Guillet was known to hire a Payne relative to bring him by horse and buggy from the Norwood train station to the shore at McCrackens' Landing from where he would paddle to Horseshoe Island, a good four to five miles.

George Douglas liked to be prepared for any conditions with a variety of methods of transportation. In a letter to his brother Lionel, he describes paddling to Young's Point from his home on Lake Katchawanooka one February morning, tying up to the stern of the *Islinda* tethered below the locks, getting groceries at Ed Young's store and paddling back to Northcote Farm. Later that afternoon, he snowshoed out to the highway, hopped on an old bicycle he always kept at the gate, rode to Ayotte's farm at the top of the Kawartha Park road and skied to the Cassidy Bay shore (he kept his skis at Ayottes). The only difficult

A novel way to come to the lake. Single-engine bi-plane on floats, Juniper Island dock, early 1930s. *Courtesy Marni Young Collection.*

At your service! Train, delivery wagon and steamer at Lakefield dock, 1914. *Eric Grier Collection, courtesy Katharine Hooke.*

part, apparently, was walking through the sticky snow over to 'Wee Island'.

The Brownscombe family seems to have been afflicted with the same desire as George Douglas, a desire to sample the environment by whatever method seems to work. Ken Brown [married to Felix Brownscombe's great-granddaughter], has been caught up in this Stony Lake adaptation of running the ice floes on the St. Lawrence. He describes the procedure graphically: "The 'get to the cottage' disease carried on to the next generation of Brownscombes. Felix's grandson Jack has treated me to many 'spring' boat trips to the Lake, some as early as February. The techniques are straightforward. Sometimes you walk with one foot on the ice and one in the boat, ready to jump into the latter when the ice gives way. Sometimes you run the bow up onto the ice, and run forward in the boat to break through, rocking from side to side if necessary. If not by boat, then skis will do. In the spring 1999, Jack Brownscombe, age 71, and brother Ross had some excuse why they had to get to the island. No matter that they could see open water in places, and occasionally their poles went right through..'as long as you kept moving you were OK.' "

American cottagers and visitors like the Buells from the Rochester area counted on two days of travel if they came across the lake. First they took the streetcar to the car ferry docks on the American side of Lake Ontario. When they landed in the morning at Cobourg, they took the train to Port Hope, Peterborough and Lakefield. (The ill-fated Cobourg-Peterborough line to Rice Lake was never reinstated after the ice carried away the railway bridge in 1854). Prior to the final few hundred yards of track being laid to the steamer dock in Lakefield, Billy Stabler, the venerable Lakefield baggage carter, loaded

On land and water. Cars at Mount Julian, beside freight shed. *Stoney Lake* steaming by with an excursion on board, early 1930s. *Courtesy Michael Fowler Collection.*

Top: William Thompson (with Gladstone bag) and daugher, Bessie, waiting for the steamer at Mt. Julian, circa 1920s. *Courtesy Michael Fower Collection.*
Bottom: Mackenzies and neighbours and all their impedimentia, 1915. *Eric Grier Collection, courtesy Katharine Hooke.*
Right: Michael Mackenzie with flag to alert steamer. *Eric Grier collection, courtesy Katharine Hooke.*

and unloaded supplies at the station and dock.

In 1925, the Stoney Lake Navigation Company advertised that its "...steamer would arrive in Lakefield in time for the motor bus, arriving in Peterborough at 12 o'clock. Steamer will leave Lakefield on arrival of noon train, for the Lakes."

In spite of positive statements about "...excellent motor roads direct to hotel and high test gas and oils," as described in the "Guided Tourist Map of the County of Peterborough and Part of the Kawartha Lakes," (1925), these were not the driving conditions we now experience 75 years later. If one did drive to the lake, it was likely to be as Jean Wood describes: "In the 1920s, cars became the more popular form of transportation. However, their tires and the existing roads were not compatible. Car tires on the new vehicles were made of single ply rubber, each using approximately 80 pounds of air pressure, [today they are four ply and use approximately 26 to 28 pounds of air pressure], and they were ready to rapidly deflate going over the rock winding roads to the lake. Many a flat tire had to be repaired before arriving here. In fact, on those early cars two spare tires were carried rather than one. These added to the loads of luggage and necessities being carried along with families and pets. The trip would be a long slow one with all the weight being propelled by low speed engines."

A recurring concern, observation, criticism —call it what you will—about the lake concerns water levels. This factor significantly affects transportation as all those who have hit bottom know from experience. "That rock wasn't there last year." "Why don't you mark your shoal?" The comments are endless. In 1906, by order-in-council, the federal government was given control of all the feeder lakes that drain into the Trent Canal. Traditionally these had been the responsibility of the lumbermen whose primary concern was enough water to float their logs. Since that date the Trent Canal authorities have been able to maintain a reasonably constant level. Today's charts for Stony Lake record the water level at 768.1 feet above sea level. This is approximately three feet higher than was prevalent in the early 1900s.

The last dam to affect Stony Lake was constructed at Young's Point. Cottagers who obviously lost land when the water rose by at least three feet were compensated by the federal government, as remembered by the Sonleys, Brooks-Hills and Walters. The south shore residents had to deal with the problem of deadheads, as much of this original shoreline was farm and wooded land. Jack Gouinlock recalls teams of horses hauling out stumps of flooded trees. Tom Cole notes that when "...lake level was raised some four feet, it was said that the area of Grandfather's island was reduced by an acre or two and one part separated by a new channel. He was offered compensation of, I was told, $72—being $1 per pine tree lost (no relation to acreage). He declined, so I assume his heirs and assigns still own the flooded land and could technically decline to permit trespassers to anchor in less than 4 feet of water off the shore."

Water taxis have always been a service provided by the various landings and are discussed more fully in the next section. One particular story serves as a reminder of their pre-serverance. Tom Cole recalls one particular vessel and its operator: "Water taxis became available and vital as motor travel became the norm. Robert Hamilton of McCracken's Landing advanced from an outboard to an open inboard, *Maryann*, a Port Carling Seabird, I believe, of which, however, he did not take the most particular of care. Eventually gas in the bilge blew up and Bob was lucky to be unhurt and without passengers at the time." This boat was beached following the mishap on 'Singkettle,' the Hooke's island, in the early 1930s. When George Douglas bought the island in 1935, he found the keel and ribs rotting on the island.

Now, as we come and go to the lake only faint reminders of those early days remain. No more tracks are to be seen on the Lakefield to Peterborough rail line where the "Bullet" puffed along the Otonabee shore. Today the rail bed is a walking trail and the station is restored as a fine antiquarian bookshop. The wooden steamers are no more, but cruise boats are increasingly common on many waterways. Stony's *Chippewa II*, operating as a popular excursion vessel, recalls those early days by carrying visitors around the lake. The tug *Ajax* no longer pulls booms of logs or scows through the waterway. William Thompson's *Naiad*, a former fisheries patrol boat, reincarnated as a passenger, cargo and mail carrier vessel, will never again head out at dawn to pick up passengers and mail at Glenwood Hotel. Who now remembers those odd hybrids, the alligators, that worked the log drives on land and water? What about the once-proud *Bessie Butler*, flagship of the Trent Canal's work boats, with the flats of geraniums to stock the window boxes at various lock stations?

Getting to the lake no longer depends on train and steamer schedules. When we come in the off-seasons, we know the highways are ploughed and bridges have not washed out.

What have we gained and what have we lost over the century? Earlier travellers to the lake often came for the season so the journey to and from was a memorable expedition as has been noted. What we have gained with modern transportation is, of course, the ability to come and go as we wish with the result that many trips have little impact. But perhaps what is more significant for everyone at the lake is the season in which we see it, year after year: the first stretch of open water after winter, the sparkle of a perfect summer day, the hint of red as fall approaches. The essence of the lake and its surroundings remains.

Six

ENTERPRISES AND ENTREPRENEURS

LIVING AND working in the back townships was difficult in the mid to late 19th century, and especially so in the five townships surrounding Stony Lake. On the south side of the lake, settlement had begun in Douro with the large government-assisted Peter Robinson emigration from Ireland in 1825. Dummer began to be settled in 1831, only eight years after Richard Birdsall's survey, with many English settlers paying their own way, along with several half-pay military men of little agricultural background and a large group of Chelsea Pensioners, retired soldiers who had exchanged their pensions for free sea passage and land in Canada.[1] Few of these people possessed any skills for living in the Canadian bush. In fact, one of the first set of instructions from Charles Rubidge, the government Emigration Agent in Peterborough, was "How to build a shanty." Across the lake on the north shore, life was harder as here was the Shield country with little arable soil over the granite rock. The Burleigh Colonization (sometimes called Communication) Road was not finished until the late 1860s and, for several years wooden bridges were washed out regularly with the high spring run-off, or were destroyed by forest fires.[2]

The population of Burleigh was so sparse that the township was attached to Dummer for municipal purposes until 1865. Then, as settlers straggled in, it united with Chandos and Anstruther townships to the north. Once a township registered 100 adult residents it could separate, which all of these did by the end of the 19th century.

Jobs were related to the rugged environment. Lumbering was a major employer for the families of settlers. Men would head into the bush for the winter, returning with the drives that came down Eel's Creek and Jack's Creek and on through Stony, to Young's Point, Lakefield and beyond. By 1850, a slide had been built at Burleigh Rapids (as it was known then). Note the abrupt, forthright message of lumberman Mossom Boyd to local settler Joseph Amiotte on the Burleigh Road:

"Peterborough Oct 18th 1859
Mr. Joseph Amiotte
Dear Jo
    I am told that there is considerable repairs required at Burleigh Slide. Townsend's dam requires some repair sufficient to strengthen it so as it will not be carried away. The Slide wants some patching and bracing. Booms to be repaired and stop logs got for Big Burleigh. I want you to do all this and do it well let the cost be what it will you shall be paid. Send me words to say

that you will do it and I may depend upon you.

Yours, M. Boyd."[3]

Presumably Mr. Amiotte was glad to have the work, in spite of Mr. Boyd's peremptory tone. In 1857, the Park Hotel at Burleigh opened to meet the needs of lumbermen and survey crews in the area. Within another 20 years, tourist booklets were extolling the bountiful hunting and fishing in the area.

Even earlier, in the 1840s, employees of a pencil-making business, possibly from Norwood, had made forays onto Stony Lake especially on Otter Island. Their mission was the cutting of all the cedar trees, the preferred wood for this product.

Logging and lumbering led to mills along the waterway, one of which had a spectacular beginning. In 1838, following the Mackenzie Rebellion of 1837, Thomas Choate of Warsaw blasted an opening in the narrow ridge of rock between Gilchrist Bay and White (now Dummer) Lake. This picturesque setting has long been part of a favourite canoeing destination, but its purpose in the 1830s days was financial. Simply raising the water level with a dam at Young's Point would not provide a sufficient overflow from Gilchrist Bay into White Lake for Choate, who had rounded up 25 or 30 men to do the blasting. Although he was charged as a rebel supporter because of his possession of a large amount of dynamite, the case was dropped and never came to trial. His somewhat illegal initiative was successful for the channel was now deep enough to float logs. In time, lumber mills were established all the way to Rice Lake. Edward Payne was one of those mill operators northeast of Warsaw on the Indian River and his descendants, who are Guillet relatives, operate a mill to this day.

Lumbering was the first major commercial enterprise to involve Stony Lake on both water and land. Environmentally it was a mixed blessing, as noted earlier. Lumbermen, boat operators, farmers and ultimately cottagers viewed the area from different perspectives, and feelings ran high with appeals to politicians about water levels and traffic flow. The following recollections describe the scene well:

"At times all the water north of the Collins Island was filled with logs so that boating on that side of the island was impossible for a day or two. Even today the rings used for tying up on the log booms can be found about three feet underwater on that side of the island," writes John Collins. His cousin Jim Collins adds, "As log drivers worked their way through Hell's Gate the loggers would tie the floating cookhouse, the catamaran, to the Collins Island at a place now named 'Catamaran'." Tom Cole's father, Dr. Cooper Cole, describes how "...big rafts of logs were drawn across Stony by horses walking around a capstan on a platform to wind in a cable attached to an anchor which had been rowed out in a punt and dropped. Bark was forever dropping off logs, and some of the logs became waterlogged and sank to become deadheads. The water was often brown from the bark." However, many cottagers made friends of the log drivers and owners. Burritt (E.B.) Edwards and George Roger of Juniper Island would rent the shanties from the lumbermen in the late 1880s for trips to Eels' Creek. Log booms travelled through Stony until the early 1930s and the square cribs of concrete to which boom chains were attached, marked the boating channel in Lake Katchawanooka until the 1940s.

In an attempt to make it easier for potential settlers to reach Burleigh, Dummer township in 1864 wrung an agreement from the Commissioner of Crown Lands to pay half the cost of a bridge across Stony Lake Narrows (now Boschink), if Peterborough County and the other townships would pay the rest. But, because of all the on-going costs of repairing

Tranquil view of former quarry site, the west slope of Eagle Mount. *Courtesy Marni Young Collection.*

roads and replacing burned or swept-away bridges, it was impossible to raise the tax base, already stretched to the limit. An appeal to the Lieutenant Governor for $1,500 fell on deaf ears, even though it stressed how future settlement of Crown lands along the Burleigh Road would be enhanced. Although that bridge was never built, pressure for a rail line continued throughout the railway era. For example, in 1889, the *Peterborough Examiner* reported the possibility of a CPR spur line from Indian River Station to White Lake and Gilchrist Bay. The last of these schemes was a proposed railway link, again from Indian River Station, over Boschink and through the hinterland to Algonquin Park. It also died on the drawing board.

Mining was another late 19th century venture, which became well developed in the Madoc and Marmora area. A letter in 1889, sent to J.B. McWilliams of 'Tecumseh' in the Burleigh Channel, optimistically predicts that if the copper lode in Stony Lake materializes, one of the richest, if not the richest mine in Canada is possible, "...leading to the creation of a plant for the reduction of ore."[4] This, like so many similar dreams at that time, did not materialize.

However, the granite quarry on Eagle Mount was a successful enterprise for about 17 years. According to land registers, in September 1889 the entire island of Eagle Mount, except that part occupied by cottages, was purchased from the Crown for $510.25 by Thomas Murray. This sale was made with the approval of the Superintendent-General of Indian Affairs. The property then was sold in December to William McCoomb Jones for $5,000 along with "...lands, tools and machinery used in connection with the Quarry." The quarry, established on Lots 2 and 5, included a two-storey wooden building housing a mess hall, office and sleeping area. On the north half of Lot 7, a 24' by 40' bunk house was erected, which is now Doreen and Hugh Jones' cottage, 'Roxie'.

All the Peterborough newspapers of the time described the operation. According to the description in the *Peterborough Examiner* of July 3, 1889, "...immense rocks drilled off in large pieces broken by cutters into pieces twice the size of a bush." However, the breaks were smooth and easily made, "...with a tap so the stone fell apart like cutting cheese." The same issue of the paper continues: "Granite from

Eagle Mount is said to be the best in Canada." From a wharf at the base of the west-facing bare slope of the island, the rock was piled, loaded onto barges and towed to Lakefield to the railway spur which ran to the docks.

So enthusiastic were the owners they began work before the sale was registered. The *Peterborough Examiner* continued by noting that "...a gang of thirty carpenters are now employed erecting houses and preparing the island for the reception of a large staff of men it is intended to place at work in the quarries." Perhaps 75 to 100 men would find jobs here for, as the paper states, "...this will be a good opening for competent workmen, as for young men wishing to learn a good trade at high wages."

In 1906, the quarry closed as it was deemed unprofitable. However, over its productive years, tons of pinkish gray granite were used locally for St. Aidan's Church at Young's Point, which opened on New Year's Day 1900, and in Toronto for the roadbed for the Spadina street car tracks, part of an 1889 contract for $44,000.[5]

Hugh Jones, great-grandson of William Jones, has been vigilant in retrieving artifacts from the quarry site and in saving written and pictorial records through his extensive postcard collections. Alf Cole recalled seeing the cables running down the rock face and noted that the Hauth's cottage is on the site of the former quarry blacksmith shop.

Another raw resource in the local landscape led to mining of nepheline syenite,[6] discovered in the Blue Mountain area at the head of Upper Stoney Lake. This mine, which opened in 1935, was the first commercial development of this deposit in Ontario. It still operates two plants, employing 142 people in the dry milling process of crushing, magnetic separation, and particle sizing. The *Wauketa*, an oil-fired steamboat with her barges loaded with white nepheline rock, was a familiar sight on the lake in the 1940s and '50s. After 1946, as the South Stony Lake Road was improved, the company began to truck the ore and cottagers finally lost an old friend. Interestingly, the *Wauketa* had started life as the pleasure yacht of Sir Wilfred Laurier!

The high ridge separating townships and lakes at the east end of Stony has long been an attraction for canoeists, rock hounds and nature enthusiasts. Locals in the 1930s used the idiom "the Mines" which may well have referred to several small mines near Blue Mountain that had been worked since the turn of the 20th century for sheet mica and corundum. In the 1880s, tourists on the lake undertook expeditions in this area, often looking for interesting mineral bits and pieces.

How did the name Blue Mountain come about? No one knows for sure but, because

Rescue mission of grounded *S. S. Wauketa* on round side of the red buoy, south of Big Island, 1942. The Trent tug *Bessie Butler* eventually came to her aid. *George Douglas Collection, courtesy Katharine Hooke.*

this geological feature stands 300 feet above Stony and Kashabog lakes, it is certainly obvious on the horizon. It was also famous for its ample crops of blueberries, a reason for many expeditions.

When prospector Bill Morrison bought a few hundred acres of the Blue Mountain from a Douro man in 1934, he convinced the Dominion Glass Company to use nepheline rock in their process. The result was favourable and, from that first customer, developed a small but highly successful mining operation. Locals still refer to the area as "the Mines," or the Nephton mine, though much of the townsite is gone. Since 1990, the company's name has been Unimin Canada Limited. As Rob Guillet notes: "...the company actively supports environmental projects...to reclaim old mining acres and promote wildlife. The potential reserves are enormous...and in years to come the social and economic benefits will be continued."

As a year-round operation, the Mt. Julian Hotel served the needs of the Gilmour Lumber Company of Trenton which had acquired a large tract of land north of the lake in 1851. Before it was built, the lumbermen had brought sleigh loads of pine logs to the shoreline. These were made into booms for the spring drives. Mt. Julian was the landing place for supplies coming by water in summer, and the starting point for crossing Stony Lake in the winter months. In fact, until the Burleigh Road was widened and paved as a Depression project in the 1930s, many locals continued to use the frozen lake as their winter highway, crossing to McCracken's Landing, travelling south from Hall's Glen to Warsaw and hence to Peterborough.

Steamers ran from break-up to freeze-up, bringing supplies and passengers to and from the lumber camp north of Mt. Julian. The trip from Apsley to Peterborough would take two days, so passengers often broke it by staying overnight at the Mt. Julian Hotel. This large frame building, containing dining room, kitchen and a bar, with rooms for rent on the second floor, commanded a beautiful view of the lake to the south. To the north of the hotel were a large barn and drive sheds to accommodate the guests' horses and rigs. To aid the settlers, local land owner, Alex Reid, operated a grain elevator, butcher shop and slaughterhouse nearby. The *Sportsman Gazetteer and Guide of 1877* writes glowingly about the hotel's charms: "The Mount Julien Hotel, on the very shore of Stony Lake, for the especial comfort of tourists and sportsmen, has accommodation for sixty guests, with every luxury that could reasonably be looked for in the backwoods of Canada. Terms $2 per day, $10.50 per week. Sailboats, row boats, and canoes, guides, and dogs are always at hand."[7] The bar was an especially convivial attraction, particularly during the years of Prohibition. Many stories are told of ingenious ways used to foil the authorities. It is said that beer, at a time of strict Ontario temperance laws, was shipped out of Quebec in ginger ale bottles to a bottling plant in Peterborough and thence to Mt. Julian.

In winter, travellers to and from Apsley used a "winter road" which cut across the fields to the northeast from Mt. Julian to Haultain on the Burleigh Road. Sleighs carried lanterns to light the way, while passengers bundled up in fur lap robes.

From 1891 until 1903, Charles Armstrong managed the hotel during which time enthusiastic canoeists could load their canoes onto a farmer's wagon, and then accompany it on foot along a trail about 1½ miles north to Julian Lake, then known as Little Cedar Lake. About 1890, local setter William Church bought the general store just north of the hotel on land belonging to Roland and Robert Strickland of Lakefield, who had optimistically laid out a town site of six named streets and two commercial blocks of land in 1873.

The year 1903 brought William and Mary

Thompson to the Mount Julian hotel. They were former cheesemakers in Otonabee township but now began a long career as hotel operators. The Thompsons also bought Church's store which now included a post office. The latter was run for nearly 40 years by Miss Melissa Kidd of Lakefield who boarded with the Thompsons.

Just prior to the Thompson's arrival at Mount Julian, the telephone link from Apsley to Burleigh Falls was completed. The Bell Telephone Company laid out the following conditions:

"Whereas it is proposed to establish at "Mount Julian on the shores of Stony Lake an office an agency of the Bell Telephone Company, and Whereas such an agency would be a great Convenience for the property owners on the lake and to all summer visitors and tourists, and Whereas for the purpose of establishing such an agency it will be necessary to run a line of wire and poles from the company's present office at Burleigh Falls Hotel to Mount Julian situated as above mentioned.

"And Whereas the Bell Telephone Company have agreed that if a line of poles properly erected all to come up to necessary specifications as required by said Company, and properly placed in the ground at equal distances and as resubscription, said Bell Telephone Company will properly wire said poles and maintain the line so wired from the said office at Burleigh Falls Hotel to the Mount Julian Hotel at Julian's Landing or Strickland Village, and in the Township of Burleigh, in the County of Peterborough.

"Now therefore, we the undersigned for the purpose of paying for the poles and the erection of same from Burleigh Falls Hotel to the present Hotel known as Armstrong's or Mount Julian Hotel at Mount Julian all in the Township of Burleigh aforesaid, respectively agree each for themselves to give the amount set opposite on respective names whenever called upon so to do."

A hand-written account records names, addresses and pay for both poles and work, in amounts from fifty cents to a dollar or two.

G. Booth	10	Poles	Paid
J.C. Stone	20	Poles	Paid ½
Wm. Sanderson	2 days	Work	None
W. Spence	2 days	Work	None
Arthur Dugen	2 days	Work	None
W.J. Hicks	2 days	Work	Paid
P. Shewen	2 days	Work	None

Nearly 100 subscribers signed, including George (G.M.) Roger of Juniper Island, J.B. McWilliams of the Burleigh Channel and the Honorary James R. Stratton, owner of the *Peterborough Examiner*. The original telephone booth remained in the Mt. Julian Hotel long after modern equipment was installed.

To successfully operate a hotel, store, post office, and to provide a water taxi service along with boat repairs and ice cutting, would have required such stamina and ingenuity that it is almost impossible to comprehend. So often the daily ledgers disappear, but fortunately the Thompsons kept extensive records which are now preserved by their grandson, Michael Fowler. Some sample entries from the ledger list the following purchases by William Northey, a nearby farmer and customer.

"Oct 1st 1903—Wm. Northey,
  soap 5c.
  cloves, 5 c.
  currants, 25c
  sugar 18c
  8 plugs tobacco, 80c
  1 lb. Pepper 30c
Jan 1904—Wm Windsor
  3 gal. Coal oil, 30c
  writing paper, 5c
  ink, 5c
  rubbers 70c

An account with the crew of the Otonabee Navigation Company's *Water Lily* notes five dinners at $1.25 each. Cryptic notes from Thompson's diaries show plans for a busy April 24, 1916:

"get wharves tied up
put pipe in lake to get pump engine started
and pump couple gallons into tank
take engineer out in launch to pile wood
until 25th
fix old hen house…"

A hotelkeeper's lot was not an idle one. Some daily jobs were less pleasant than others —such as cleaning spittoons in the lake.

In 1932 after William Thompson died, his widow, Mary and their daughter, Annie, and her husband, Don Fowler, took over the hotel, and later built a new store on the shore in the early '60s. The old general store closed when Annie died in 1973. Their son and daughter-in-law, Mike and Joyce Fowler took over the business in the 1970s.

From then until the fall of 1999, the Fowlers concentrated their efforts on a May to mid-October operation, catering particularly to families and anglers who returned for many seasons, staying in the modest cottages on site and enjoying hearty meals in the hotel. Although many American fishermen trailered their specially equipped boats to the hotel, the Fowlers provided small runabouts, canoes and sailboats for their guests. Like Mike's father and grandfather, they also had an amicable working agreement with several nearby islanders regarding boat and car parking. Their sons, Roy and Timothy, were actively involved with the Junior Sailing program at the Stony Lake Yacht Club. The Fowlers closed the small convenience store at the shore and in the mid 1990s removed the gas pumps.

When Mike and Joyce decided to sell the business in 1999, they were able to negotiate a heritage easement agreement for the wall of primitive paintings in the hotel parlour. Thanks to the cooperation of the new owner, Don Bennett of Viamede Resort, the township of North Kawartha (formerly Burleigh Chandos Anstruther) and several Peterborough heritage organizations, those paintings are now protected.[8]

Next door to Mt. Julian is Viamede Resort, now an up-scale four season operation. Robert and Betty Graham of Lakefield were the original owners in the 1890s when a modest building called Viamede Cottage boasted six rooms, at a rate of one dollar a day, all meals. However, a devastating fire in 1907 destroyed much of the hotel's facilities including seven cottages, a water tower and a boathouse. Early postcards depict the replacement as a new grand summer resort, described by the *Peterborough Daily Review* in February 1908: "The new building will by 160 feet long by 140 feet wide, fronting on the lake. An immense kitchen and servants' quarters will be erected at the rear 24 by 44 feet. The bedrooms, thirty-six in number, will be large, light and airy. The house will be fitted with the most modern improvements in the line of plumbing and will be lighted with gas. The new building will have room for about 100 persons."

William Thompson steaming to winter quarters in late fall before freeze-up in motor vessel *Niaid* with his cold crew huddling in the bow, 1920s. *Courtesy Michael Fowler Collection.*

Typical tourist advertising from David Breeze's Glenwood Hotel, looking south. *Courtesy Katharine Hooke Collection.*

Mr. Graham took guests on tours in his large launch and Fred Brooks-Hill remembers acting for him as line boy in 1919. In 1920, Eva and Les Ianson bought Viamede. "There was hardly a road, but there was a trail up to Viamede," quotes Mrs. Eva Ianson. "There wasn't a bedroom finished, just the bare 2 x 4s and the outside boards. But the situation was grand." Mrs. Ianson ran the hotel for 50 years, six years with her husband, and then alone for 44 years after he died. "Mrs Ianson did all the cooking for many years. Fire was always her great fear, " writes her granddaughter Susan Lumsden. "She saw to it that the hotel was equipped with buckets and a water supply pumped by windmill from the lake. The closest call came during an August night in 1929 when the steamboat *Empress*, berthed at the nearby Mt. Julian government dock, caught fire and drifted aflame downwind towards her boathouse. She bossed a bucket brigade and saved her building. The steamer burned to the water-line and sank." Truly she was an indomitable woman. Eva's son Bill, and later his widow Bea, ran the resort and built attractive shoreline cottages.

For at least 25 years, Viamede ran a regatta, including one of the early power boat events. It also operated a small boat livery from the Brown Canoe Company of Lakefield. The resort was purchased in 1985 by Don Bennett, a Peterborough businessman, who has modernized the business considerably. With changes come discussion and, ideally, compromises with which everyone can live.

Along the north shore, in the cluster of islands near Boschink, is the site of Breeze's Hotel, built in the 1890s and operated by the David Breeze family until the 1920s when it was taken over by a nephew and his wife, Alex and Hattie Lowe. They renamed it Glenwood Hotel. Legend has it that lying in wait for "sticky fingers" in the cash box at Glenwood tuck shop was a resident snake! When Alex drowned in 1930, the next owners were Messrs. Cameron and Ferguson of the Peterborough Streetcar Company. Breeze's Hotel was William Thompson's first stop on his early morning mail run from Mt. Julian, picking up and leaving mail at 5 a.m. This hotel was a steamer stop as well, as depicted on early Roy Studio coloured postcards. The fact that David Breeze was freight and passenger agent for the

The beloved *Empress*, August 1929, after the disastrous fire at Mt. Julian. *George Douglas Collection, courtesy Katharine Hooke.*

steamer *Golden City* that plied the lake probably increased publicity for the hotel.

Just beyond our boundaries, but important to all those who have ever broken a propeller (is there anyone who hasn't?), is a small repair operation, Bayview Marina, at the foot of Northey's Bay. Art and Evelyn Johnson tore down the cottages and built first a storage shed and then a new large shop in 1987. This marina is noted for its propeller repair business, with parts shipped all over the world. The largest propeller ever repaired there came from a Hamilton, Ontario, tug. It was over ten feet in diameter and weighed over 7400 lbs. In 1999, that same tug was working in Greenland, raising two bombers that went down in World War II.

Swinging back to a southeast arm of the lake, a canoeist can always enjoy the peace and beauty of Gilchrist Bay. When poking along through wetlands and in and out of narrow channels, it is difficult to imagine the thriving former businesses at the end of the bay. As noted earlier, this arm leads into the Indian River system and ultimately Rice Lake, so it was an important lumber route that bypassed many rapids and miles of the Otonabee River.

Bill Armstrong ran a small supply store at Gilchrist Bay in the early 1900s. Like so many early structures, it burned. A little later three nearby sawmills ceased operations causing a little community to dwindle even more. However, Percy Little now maintains a busy, viable enterprise. When the bay was dredged near their farm property, Percy and Jean built a new store and later added cottages and a marina. Next door is Pine Vista Resort, owned and operated by Vernon and Bonnie Hamilton.

The Hamilton family is a good example of successive generations of an enterprising family. The first Hamiltons, Joseph and Lucinda with baby Robert, arrived from Ireland in 1879 and lived in a log cabin on property bordering Hamilton Bay. After Joseph died in

1886, Lucinda married George Little and had a son, Art. Joseph and Lucinda's grandson, Bill, and his wife Marguerite started Birch Cliff Cottages in 1945 on the McCracken's shore. These six housekeeeping cottages are now managed by Marguerite and her son David. Another grandson, Ralph, and his wife Florence, bought a farm on the west side of Hamilton Bay in 1938. When Ralph was 65 in 1970, they opened Hamilton Bay Golf, a nine-hole par 35 course with convenient access for cottagers arriving by boat or car. Today, it is managed by Harry and Art Hamilton. An earlier operation on this site was Brown's farm, a supplier of many early cottagers.

Every community has its characters, but few on Stony could rival Alex "Peg-leg" Sharpe, termed the "lunge hunter," by newspaperman Nick Nickels. Alex was an indomitable entrepreneur who always found work. In brief, Alex lost his right leg in a lumbering accident in Apsley in 1880, but that did not prevent him from managing on an artificial leg of his own making. He recuperated at his island house with his wife Elizabeth and their children. Tragedy struck the following year when she died in childbirth. Alex later married young Susan Harper in 1896. During an especially mild February in 1901, Alex came home early from the lumber camp to discover Susan had gone – to the home of her lover, William Hull, in South Bay. Taking his gun, Alex headed immediately to Hull's house and shot the young man. Next day Alex gave himself up to the magistrate. Alex served seven of his 15 year sentence and returned to Gilchrist Bay in 1908 to pick up his life of guiding and fishing. With his children grown, he moved into a house next to the abandoned general store in the Bay. The Dodworth family, in particular, were very supportive of Alex. He is still remembered for his handmade two-wheel carts that he would rent for 50 cents to anyone needing to portage a canoe from Stony to White Lake. He was an expert, if eccentric, guide. An intrepid survivor, Alex Sharpe died at 91 in 1937.

Dummer township as noted earlier was settled in 1831, so McCracken's Landing has as early a history as Mt. Julian. It has been well recorded in the annals of Sam Hunter, a shoreline cottager who worked for the *Toronto World* and *Toronto Star* as writer and cartoonist in the early 1900s. According to Hunter, the settlement was once known as Tom's Landing after a Native who pitched a wigwam at the top of the hill, wore a bright sash and sword, and on moonlit nights would walk up and down the steep hill, disclaiming, "stand back and keep off." It is said either he had killed his brother over a woman, or he had been a pirate chief. This tale has probably grown with the ages. It is known that Native Peoples did camp on the shore in the early 1800s and also at Boschink Narrows. All who are familiar with the area realize that Hunter aptly describes the McCracken's Road as "plunging down hill with suicidal desperation into the water."

By the 1880s, W.R. McCracken, who owned at least a mile of shoreline on either side of the landing, claimed that any citizen of Dummer township could camp on Eagle Mount, under an agreement with the Crown. Another claim was that the spring at McCracken's had the best drinking water between Eel's Creek and Lakefield. It is still a source of good water.

The community developed in a somewhat haphazard fashion because of the steep hill. Of all the landings on Stony Lake, McCracken's probably evokes the most memories for cottagers because of its wide range of services and its attractive setting. It was also a government steamer landing and a Ferguson bus lines destination from Peterborough. In the August 7, 1895 edition of the *Peterborough Examiner*, Sam Hunter described the landing as an "...irregular cluster of frame buildings, balanced on boulders which look as if they had come down in a mud slide or been pushed in during a nor-easter." These buildings included the large red brick McCracken house, Choate's store, a boathouse, ice house and several garages.

Choate's store, which celebrated 100 years in 1997, has a memorable history. Opened by Arthur Choate, son of Thomas and Hannah who ran a similar venture in Warsaw, this operation stayed in the family until 1949. In its early days when Art was ill with smallpox, Natives of the vicinity brought him food and Indian treatment for the disease. The store began simply enough as a single cabin, then gradually expanded.

Tom Cole remembers: "At one time the store was wired up for receiving money and making change through little containers which by a spring, shot from the counter to a cashier in a little office up by the ceiling, and gravity brought them back. This was at about the same time that it was being done in the big stores in town. The cashier must have been pretty warm at times. Mr. Choate never accepted Daylight Saving Time and we used to engage him in philosophical arguments on the subject. He was never without a cigar in his mouth, but I don't recall ever seeing it lit or more than 2 inches long. In those days there would be a few mainland residents and perhaps unengaged Native fishing guides taking their ease on the wide verandah across the store. Father reported that on one occasion Mr. Choate had actually sprung for a fresh cigar and lit it. Some wag, feigning great alarm, cried out, 'Mr. Choate, your chaw's caught fire.' "

When Arthur died in 1931, the store was managed by his wife Vida, and then by his daughter Bessie Bell until it was sold out of the family in 1949. The new proprietors were a kindly couple, "grey-haired Mary and no-haired Lorne Morrison," as Cecily Morrow remembers them. "These two people were my

A venerable institution at the McCracken's Landing. The Choate Supply Store. Left to right: Vida Choate, Lorne and Mary Morrison, Bessie Bell, 1942. *Courtesy David Card Collection.*

adopted grandparents. Year after year they stood behind the counter, ready to wrap our milk and butter. Mary expertly pulled the light brown paper from a huge roll on a rack next to the counter. The yard-long blade, which cut the paper from the roll, was flat-edged and sharp. This blade made a clean-sounding cut across the paper. I loved to watch Mary wrap the milk. She took the triangle of paper, which formed and rolled it tightly over the carton until the sides could be folded in. Then, with one tug, just enough string fell down from the spool overhead for Mary's wrinkled hands to wrap and secure the paper in place. Then she snapped the string in two between her fingers! I watched intently as each parcel was artistically placed by Lorne into the box to be carried down to the boat."

In 1967, the Morrisons sold the property, which changed hands twice before Ned and Jean Skead, the present owners, bought it in 1974. In addition to running the store, they provide boat and car parking space and operate a marina. They have provided invaluable help to the Cottagers' Association over the years and have rescued many a cottager and visitor in distress. For years, the Skeads have been especially helpful to the student opera-

tors of the Juniper Island Store. During power failures on the island, they have rescued supplies from the freezer. Ned maintains the swimming docks at Juniper and, in many unobtrusive ways, he has been a faithful friend of the Cottagers' Association.

Jean Skead remembers a rather harrowing evening in the late 1980s. It began with a call from the Coast Guard at 7 p.m. saying they'd had a call about a ship in distress. Although directions were vague, Ned located the "ship" near Eagle Mount and started to tow it back. Meanwhile, Jean was coping with an emergency on the dock, where a man had collapsed. She called an ambulance and, while the attendants were reviving the man, Ned arrived with boat and its occupants in tow. Because their motor needed repairs and they had no way of getting home, Jean and Ned drove them all the way to Washago, a two-hour drive, then turned around and drove home again. A lot of excitement for one night.

Another drawing card to McCracken's Landing was the farmers' market every Tuesday and Friday morning. Set up alongside the road from the store to the wharf were tables with vegetables, eggs, cheeses, fresh baked pies, cakes, cookies, and handknitted goods, quilts and handicrafts. Two butchers came, Macauley from Warsaw and Jopling from Peterborough. They had chopping blocks at the back of their trucks and cut the roasts and chops to order. A barber from Warsaw cut hair for customers seated in a barber chair under the verandah of Choate's store. Raffles were held and Louisa Land was delighted to win a beautiful patchwork quilt, which still adorns one of the beds at 'Cairn Dhu.' " Sadly, the advent of faster boats and better roads reduced attendance at market. Gradually it dwindled to one or two tables and then was no more.[9] Some of the people who worked at Choate's and went on to similar work were O.B. Earle who became a buyer of "foreign goods" for Eaton's and A.C. Hawthorne who became a Vancouver merchant. Richard F. Choate became a skilled Toronto newspaper man as editorial writer and arts critic for the Toronto *Globe and Mail*. His papers are now housed in the Trent University archives.

On the hillside next to McCracken's is Wantasa Inn, formerly the Victorian House, built in 1894 by John Morgan of Warsaw. In its heyday as a turn-of-the-century establishment, the groundskeeper, Mr. Picken, was known for his fine gardens and his attractive curved driveway bordered by young trees. The lobby was adorned with "two black bears and a porcupine stuffed and mounted in a natural manner by Mr. Picken," who was a taxidermist as well. In 1923, Jack and Cholmondely Strickland of Lakefield bought the hotel, giving it its present name. The Wantasa Inn was purchased in 1937 by Clarwin Cherry of Lakefield and later operated by his wife Helen and their daughters until 1973. The Cherrys built the log cabin on the property and a row of sleeping cabins along the shore. Cecily Morrow remembers dining at Wantasa with her mother and brother: "From our island I could hear the dinner bell ring out across the water at 5:30 p.m. to call the fishermen guests in for the evening meal. Wantasa

had a very grand appearance. The banisters in the entry foyer were rubbed to the softest shine. The dining room had the most highly polished floors imaginable."

When Erik and Ruth Erdmann purchased the property in 1973, they renovated the fourteen housekeeping cottages, but could not make the many changes required in the main building to pass safety codes. Finally, in 1987, the Erdmanns sold to Ian and Pat McLeod, the present owners.

Equally well known on the same shoreline is Carveth's Marina, a thriving boat storage, repair, rental and water taxi operation. Like so many of the lake businesses, it began simply, the dream of a skilled entrepreneur. Starting in 1928, Walter Carveth opened a carpentry and marina business. He built cottages and pews for St. Peter's on-the-Rock, and provided boat storage and rental. Walter then started a much needed taxi service. His son Russell worked with him and took over the business in 1942 after the death of his father. Jim Collins worked at the marina for two years and recounts: "There was an oil-soaked rolltop desk where the bills were prepared. Customers would sit on it to visit, and generally got in the way. A part-timer named Nick placed a coil from a Model T Ford in the desk and a connecting battery and switch in the drawer. Two flat head screws were fastened on the desk where people sat. Opening the drawer trigged the mechanism. The resulting electrical jolt made the unsuspecting victim feel as if spikes were going up his behind and he shot off the desk, landing several feet away."

By 1960, a new boathouse had been built. Russ Carveth and his wife Pearl put in long hard hours serving their growing number of customers. As a child of nine, Russ ran the interesting business of delivering 200 copies of the *Saturday Evening Post* around the lake. With a 4-horse power engine, he managed to navigate the channels, learning about the rocks because he "hit every one of them." Today's cottagers are delighted with the early morning delivery of the *Globe and Mail* by local teenagers. Those adept boathandlers probably encounter all the rocks known by Russ.

In 1967, Ed Benetin bought the marina business and sold it to the Hauth family in 1976. Rick Hauth, the present owner, brought with him experience in teaching sailing and running dances and much else besides—a schoolteacher, a singer—a man of many talents, as well as being talented in marina work. Rick, who grew up on Stony Lake and always dreamed of owning the marina, left his teaching career to run it. Ed Benetin stayed on as the service manager. Rick believes Carveth's Marina is the second oldest Outboard Marine Corporation (OMC) marina in Canada, the Sudbury Canoe Company being the oldest. Rick has been a tremendous to help to many Stony Lakers, rescuing people and dogs, docking the fireboat, as well as transporting musicians, books and equipment for events at Juniper. His commitment to the community is evident in many practical and caring forms. While taking his son Adam to swimming lessons at Juniper, Rick saw that waiting parents were perched on rocks and logs. It wasn't long before he built and unobtrusively delivered six or seven comfortable benches for their use. Carveth's water taxi business often operates without a charge; for example, the barge which transports books and equipment for the annual book fair; a power boat to protect the mile swim participants from fast boats; the transporter of Pam Hooke and her bridal attendants to St. Peter's on-the-Rock as Rick's present to the bride.

Thankfully, fire services or winter rescue equipment are not often called upon, but it is reassuring to know that since 1978 three equipped fire boats are available at Carveth's, Crowe's Landing and Little's in Gilchrist Bay. Thanks to well-trained Rick Hauth in his role

of organizational fire chief with Dummer for eight years, cottagers and permanent residents know that emergency service on the lake is up-to-date. The ice rescue boat which is kept near Little's Landing is stocked with winter flotation devices for the rescuers. The money for this equipment comes from proceeds from the annual OMC fishing tournament hosted by Carveth's Marina. Rick notes: "I get turfed out of bed a lot for emergencies. Ambulances, police, even helicopters come to the marina." He has had several cottagers "die in his arms."

A small nearby business involved the legendary Gary Braund. From the late 1930s to the early 1970s, Bill and Elizabeth Pearl operated a store at the west end of the Carveth's Marina property. They sold ice in 50 lb. blocks which were delivered by Gary Braund from 1944 to 1948. The tales told are similar to this one. "Depending on how hot the day was and how fast the iceman worked, taking his socializing into account, you were lucky to get a 20lb block. Not understanding why it took so long to make the deliveries, Mrs. Pearl decided one day to accompany Gary. Now Gary had a dilemma which he attempted to solve by making a lot of calls on cottagers who weren't even customers. It was evening by the time they returned to the store and that was the last time Mrs. Pearl ever joined Gary on his route. Whether Mrs. Pearl was fooled we'll never *know*."[10] It has been said of the ever-genial Gary as he made his rounds, "ice in, beer out."

Also on the south shore is Howard Hamilton who began his career in May 1930, working for ten years as a contractor's helper for his uncle, Joe Hamilton, before going out on his own as a contractor and building supplies dealer. Howard and his family were in business for many years, constructing cottages, docks and septic systems. Howard kept meticulous accounts in small black notebooks, which he kindly donated to the St. Peter's -on-the-Rock archives after the church's 75th anniversary. Besides recording labour costs, dimensions, hours worked and other typical builder's details, he also wrote brief descriptions of the jobs and their purpose. His 1953 notebook includes this sampling: "Sept. 11 Mr. [Barclay] Vineyard—take out pipes, clean toilet and close in back with screening to make sure flies cannot get in. Sept. 13 Mr. [Page] Wadsworth —make floating wharf approximately 6' x 20' to act as a breakwater from east end of present slip wharf."

The following spring, Howard began various seasonal chores, such as building a boathouse for George Baird "...as soon as the water becomes low enough." After a phone call from Mr. [Arthur] Walter on the long weekend in May, his tasks were to take off shutters, have the house cleaned thoroughly, arrange for Russ Carveth to start the stove and refrigerator and refill fire extinguishers. Like all the skilled versatile workmen around Stony Lake, Howard always had work ahead. The year 1954 ends with references to letters received and answered, including one about the possibility of a cottager renting a wharf for the next summer.

It would be difficult to be a cottager on Stony Lake and not know the whereabouts of Juniper Island. As noted earlier, the headquarters for the Cottagers' Association, on the north tip of the island, has been the focus for virtually all lake activities. Sadly, a much-appreciated operation run there by the Peterborough Canoe Company no longer exists. This boat livery and repair shop was clearly identified by a large PECANO sign. In 1922, the Association sold a small parcel of fairly level shoreline at the western edge of its property to the Canoe Company "...for the express purpose of storing, repairing, and selling products manufactured by the company."[11] From its inception, the Cottagers' Association recognized the principle of providing a community service for cottagers and visitors and

it ensured that the Canoe Company Livery would do the same.

For 53 years, this business provided untold services to cottagers and passing boaters. Gas was brought to the livery in 45-gallon drums lashed to rafts. It was the only island livery on the lake and was the biggest in its day. As in so many of these accounts, it is the people who leave the lasting memories.

Frank Gillespie's tenure as operator ran from 1923, when the building opened, until he retired in 1955. His former assistant, Mel Hunter, took over managing the business and then bought it in 1962 when the Peterborough Canoe Company went bankrupt. In the days before electricity and telephones, Mel worked 12 hours a day, seven days a week and also provided taxi and telephone service to cottagers. A kindly man, he helped many. One of Westel Willoughby's youthful mishaps resulted in a hole in the bottom of his father's boat. Wes took the boat to Mel, who repaired it the same day, never sending a bill. Father was never the wiser.

By 1970, there was strong competition on the lake, so Mel sold the boat livery to Jim Fox in 1971 who ran it until 1973. Its days, however, were numbered and the derelict building became a dangerous eyesore. After some legal disputations regarding the terms of the original 1922 agreement, the Cottagers' Association was able to have the building torn down safely. Jane McMynn notes that "...when the building came down, the wood was offered to the cottagers and a number of us have decks etc. made from those historic planks." Barb and Phil Rimmer bought the property, which they continued to clean up by removing oily residue. Through their care and maintenance of much of the Association's property during their roles as directors, the Rimmers illustrate how deeply the cottagers care about their role as custodians of the lake.

Memories are precious. Here is what Jean

Gillespie Graham recalls about living in a boathouse: "I have many fond memories of the Peterborough Canoe Boat Livery at Juniper Island as I spent all my summers as a child there. We lived upstairs in the west end of the boat house for several years. One day a boat down below caught fire and my mother refused to live above the boats any longer! The Company then agreed to build the green cottage to the west of the Livery for our family to live in. This green cottage still stands in the same location to this day.

"Usually a college student was employed to help my father and mother during the summer months. My mother ran the post office during the War years. Many of the cottagers stored their boats in the boat house during the winter. The larger boats were downstairs and the smaller boats upstairs. It was a sad day when I saw the Boat Livery torn down after spending many happy holidays there."

The Cole family could probably write a book just about the Livery. "Frank Gillespie was a vital part of Stony Lake for almost everyone," writes Tom Cole. "He was kind and reliable and had a never-failing sense of humour. He was an immensely practical man who helped people out of all sorts of cottage predicaments, not just boat related. Frank would refer sick or injured people to my father, Dr. Cooper Cole. When asked, 'What is your fee, Doctor?' Father usually said, 'There's no charge. I'm on holidays.' "

Berenice Knapman recalled a hot day when Frank was hard at work with a pair of pincers in his hand. When a chap came charging into the wharf with a fishing plug in his back, Frank sent him across the channel to Dr. Cole, but he said, "Here, better take these cutters as Dr. Cole won't have any." The man looked at him incredulously and said, "What, and ruin my new plug?" Soon, however, he hove into sight again, as Dr. Cole sent him right back over to the Livery to get the pincers. Berenice

also related how a visitor warned Frank who was hard at work soldering a gas tank. "Frank, you should be careful. It might blow up." "Don't worry," replied Frank, "It's not my tank anyway."

Frank had a nice turn of phrase. Of someone with whom he didn't like dealing, he said "I can't swing on his gate." Another was his saying, 'God darned' to avoid profanity. On a rough day Frank was transporting a coffin from Dunford's Landing to St. Peter's for a funeral. The anxious undertaker asked, " What will we do if we swamp?" Unperturbed, Frank replied, "I don't know about you, but I'm going to grab that wooden box and hold on." When Frank retired in 1955, he and Mabel moved to a cottage on the McCracken's shore.

From these accounts, it is obvious that the busiest communities of central Stony Lake were those at McCracken's, Carveth's, Mt. Julian and Juniper Island. Settlers and cottagers forged important links here that have continued until the present day. However, other sites were also notable in the less populated areas of Stony.

Travelling south from Carveth's, boaters can work their way along the Indian Channel behind Davis Island and among small rocky islets until the large open expanse of Clear Lake appears in the distance. Here, at the boundary of Douro and Dummer townships lies Bryson's Bay, site of a large farm which met the needs of cottagers for many years. Archie Tedford, with two partners, bought 500 acres stretching from Camp Kawartha to the third line of Dummer. This property was known in the family as 'The Ranch'. In the late 1930s, their milk run began in the evening with a pick-up at Kawartha Park and deliveries to the Boys' Camp by 10 p.m. In the morning Archie and son Rodger loaded their goods, meat that had been previously ordered, milk and butter into the lead boat. The ice boat, travelling behind, was wider, deeper and 18 feet long. Their route took them through the central islands, with the final stop at [Joe] Yelland's in the Burleigh Channel.[12]

Kawartha Park Marina, now a bustling yacht harbour, began quite humbly in 1906 as Bertha Brown's Boarding House. Miss Brown was a grand-niece of Peterborough pioneer, Thomas A. Stewart. It is likely that Bertha gained some business experience working with her brother, Charles, in his flour and feed store in Peterborough. She would also have known that vigorous enterprising businessman, Richard Birdsall Rogers, superintending engineer of the Trent Canal. Mr. Rogers, who originally cottaged at Chemong Park, was caught up with the beauty of Stony and Clear lakes. In 1901, he arranged to lease from the Canada Company with option to buy, some 126 acres of shoreline along the Kawartha shore. In 1906, when Rogers divided the property into lots which he put up for sale, Miss Brown seized the opportunity for her own business and within a few years was operating a post office, modest store, commodious boarding house and an extra cottage.

By 1911, the Clear Lake (now Kawartha Park) Cottagers' Association was formed, running regattas throughout Miss Brown's tenure, which lasted through 1912. The *Peter-borough Examiner* of June 20, 1913 reports that "...Mr. Thomas Kennedy, a Peterborough grocer will run the Kawartha Park store and Frank Adams, the Woodside boarding house." They lasted only one season, leading to the 40 year successful tenure of David and Mary Charlton of Lakefield (1914–1954).

Mr. Charlton was familiar with the area from running a concession on one of the steamers. Like so many of the hardworking family operations around the lake, this husband and wife team had many skills. Mary ran Woodside as her own business, keeping the books, hiring staff (including daughters Doris and Madeline) and ordering all supplies. Dave ran the store, boat livery and performed the myriad tasks of a land and water-based operation. In mid-September each year, they returned to Lakefield where Dave worked at the family feed mill and managed the old Lakefield rink. From 1921 to 1934, dances were held in a pavilion next to the store and, in 1934, the store was torn down to build a larger one. Besides the usual items that one might purchase in a general store, there were also worms, coal oil, vegetables from the root cellar and Indian baskets. People used to come to the back to borrow tools or weigh fish. Drinking water was available from a pump behind Woodside

Nicholson and Pelton supply boat, from Burleigh Falls, at 'Cairn-Dhu', 1942. Nancy Land is the girl on the dock and Jimmy Land is the boy on the boat. *Courtesy Nancy Watson Collection.*

and also from a natural spring a few hundred yards up the shore.

Jill Trennum remembers "...the fun of being in Dave Charlton's old store at Kawartha. To buy your goods you had to line up behind his huge old counter and point to what you wanted on his shelf, then he would reach it down and hand it to you over the counter. Imagine a grocery store today using that method. Plus, there was a pinball machine that my brother loved."

In 1955, Mike and Aileen Dean bought the property which they continued to improve and expand, culminating in 1959 with the opening of a marina with an indoor wetslip, a boat lift and a large steel building for boat storage. The Deans also had a tea room and antique shop for seven years.

Bill Harris bought the business in 1976 which he ran for several years. After a few years of uncertain operation by several owners in the early 1990s, Kawartha Park Marina is now once again a successful enterprise under the capable, cheery guidance of Ron Vine. As a family concern, Ron and his wife, Maggie, live year round on the site of the former Woodside.

A little-known modest hotel on the west shore of Cassidy Bay was the Maple Leaf Hotel. This was the farm site of brothers Jim and John Cassidy and their sister Biddy. The brothers were able carpenters who built 'Woodside,' 'Lochend,' 'Woodonga' and St. Peter's-on-the-Rock. The hotel met the needs of fishermen with accommodation for thirty people, plus a fish storage ice house. It was bought in 1935 by Mr. and Mrs. York who retired from the business about ten years later. Four more couples ran the hotel until the late 1980s. The property has since been subdivided into cottage lots, but much of the original main building is still evident.

Two other short-lived commercial ventures were the Dulce Domum Resort and the Davis

Island Manor. The former was operated for a short time by Mrs. William Cox on an island near Dunford's Landing. An 1897 map of Stony Lake District printed by the Department of Agriculture noted that "...the medical experts declare the air in this region to have wonderful curative powers." Like most resorts of that period, it was open May to October, catering especially to fishermen. Davis Island Manor's checkered history includes that of a hotel off and on for 30 years until the early 1960s. A 1957 brochure calls it "the Show Place of Beautiful Stony Lake."

Mention has been made of the supply boats, which represented a much-appreciated service to cottagers, especially before electricity was common throughout the lake. As Nancy Watson notes from her research and recollections: "Many of us have wonderful memories of the supply boats on the lake. Gerald Tedford operated an orange boat with an awning roof in the 1930s with produce from his store on Highway 28, now managed by his son Keith Tedford." In the 1940s, Randall Nicholson and Cecil Pelton from Young's Point began delivering in their floating grocery store, which was, as John Collins recalls "...about 25 feet long, with a vegetable counter down the middle and a display shelf along the port side. There was a large icebox near the stern, a steering wheel at the front, a solid rounded roof supported on spindly pipes, and moveable curtains along both sides and across the stern. An airhorn blast signalled the boat's arrival, and all gathered to buy fresh vegetables and get the roast that had been ordered the previous week. The kids, however, were interested in the really good stuff like Cracker Jacks and chocolate bars. Since allowances and paying jobs for children were still in the future, the mother controlled purchases with ruthless fiscal policies."

The following account of the Spencley family operation at Burleigh Falls by Doreen

Foote skillfully captures its history, vigor and enterprise. She writes: "Spencley's Landing at Burleigh Falls is no longer on the map and that is unfortunate because it honoured a family that made a contribution for three generations to life on the lake.

"William Spencley, in the 1880s, bought 200 acres of land that extended west from the old Burleigh Road (the original road site) to the shores of Lovesick Lake. He developed a quarry on the property with the intention of mining limestone. While there was an abundance of limestone, it was of such poor quality that he was forced to give up. The quarry remained for many years and indeed, when the dam at Burleigh was put in, the quarry provided the limestone.

"William's grandson Bill Spencley and his wife Violet worked full time on the lake. Each year they started early in the spring, cleaning cottages and doing all the necessities for their clients to get the season started. Once people arrived, Bill was a familiar and daily sight on the lake in his green boat delivering ice. Indeed, he brought the ice right up to the icebox. After a visit, always a treat for the customer because he always brought news from other cottagers, he would be on his way. Bill was a special man, always happy and his many acts of kindness are legendary."

It is impossible to recount all the many undertakings over a century on the lake. So many of the people who were skilled and helpful took their work for granted. It was all part of their daily life and, for the most part, they enjoyed what they did. It was a time of few regulations and little bureaucracy. One of these self-taught skillful individuals was Austen Walsh, known as the "Minnow King of the Kawarthas." He was a familiar sight delivering his wares from Young's Point in his launch, the *Widgeon*. His other talent was beekeeping, which he did for over 60 years. As Aileen Young notes, "...his minnow catching

technique was to sprinkle dry bread pieces soaked in milk on top of a net-like cage cover to tempt the minnows. After he caught then, he'd bring them home and put them in cans. They needed daily fresh water."[13]

Then there was the summer travelling salesman, Fred Maddox, a great-uncle of Hugh Jones. Fred made his rounds to the resorts early in the season with his suitcase of felt banners, ash trays and decorated plates of scenes like the view from Eagle Mount. He made many postcards from his own photographs and sold these for five cents.

Many teenagers found summer work at the lake. Art Dobson recalls that in the summer of 1947 and '48 he was employed by Mrs. David Pitcairn at 'Kenjocketty' on Eagle Mount. Her late husband had been president of Pittsburgh Plate Glass, so she was accustomed to a certain style of living, even at the cottage. Her hired help were expected to maintain her standards. The summer job began with Art taking the Toronto Hamilton and Buffalo train to Pittsburgh after Mrs. Pitcairn sent him money for the fare, which included a berth. He helped load her Cadillac once he reached her house and together they drove to the lake, stopping the first night at a bed and breakfast on Hamilton Beach. When they arrived at McCracken's, the launch *Alejada* would be waiting. After a day of unpacking, settling in and meager meals, as Mrs. Pitcairn was not a cook, Art drove to the Peterborough train station to pick up Rebecca, Mrs. Pitcairn's cook and domestic help from Pittsburgh. Rebecca's focus was the kitchen, meal preparation and housework. As was the custom in some households of the day, she ate by herself. Art, as boat boy, ranked somewhat higher and ate with his employer. For several years, Mrs. Pitcairn invited Mrs. Patterson, a widowed friend to stay for several weeks. Art and his contemporaries referred to these two as "Pitty" and "Patty."

Art's major duty as boat boy was to have

the kitchen range good and hot by 8:00 a.m. and to keep the kitchen wood pile well stocked from the large supply on shore. In the afternoons and on McCracken's market days, he would drive Mrs. Pitcairn in her fine 30 foot Peterborough Canoe Company launch to the mainland. She and Mrs. Patterson sat on wicker chairs or on the transom bench in the stern. Art was given the odd day off to join friends on sailing or canoeing expeditions, and late afternoons were usually his own. There would be regular car trips to Peterborough. Although Art maintained the *Alejada* well, he was not allowed to take the launch out alone. Mrs. Pitcairn knew where all the rocks were, she said. However, Art could use the cedar canoe. Rebecca's quarters were a tiny cabin by the lake and Art's the boat house. Meals, outings and leisure activities followed a set pattern. It was a measured, predictable summer, but one that Art enjoyed. When they closed up at the end of the summer, Art took Rebecca to the train in Peterborough; he and Mrs. Pitcairn followed a day later in the Cadillac. Then Art came back from Pittsburgh on TH&B Railway. Different times, different styles!

Of all the activities and daily tasks that Stony Lakers remember, anything to do with ice, the ice house and ice deliveries, tops the list. We know "the iceman cometh" but how those innocuous blocks came out of the frozen lake was something many took for granted, if they thought about it all. This was one of the most arduous jobs for the farmers and other locals, one that could only be accomplished when the ice was thick and firm, usually in late February. Ice cutting took place in Dunford's Bay, Shewen's Bay, near Mt. Julian, near Kawartha Park and along the Dummer shore at Bryson's Bay. There are varying accounts of the size and weight of these ice blocks. Orval Bolton reckons their weight was equal to that of a man. Both temperature and lake location affected ice size. There is no doubt that ice cutting was hard work. Orval explains that to make the task somewhat easier, he would slide the ice tongs into the water on an angle and haul the block out on the same angle. Hard as this was, Orval claims that after working in the bush for a few weeks with a Swede saw, cutting ice with a five-foot one-handled ice saw was easier.

In the 1930s, during a cold spell, Stewart

In the late 1980s, aquatic weed growth increased in the Kawartha Lakes, due in part to an invasion of Eurasian mifoil. Weed harvesting became an annual control requirement, 1978. *Courtesy Miels Family Collection.*

and Russell Tedford had a contract with James Everett Lillico at Juniper Island to fill the store ice house with 1,000 blocks. During the first few days of cutting, the ice thickened from 18 to 22 inches. After they were cut, the blocks were loaded onto a sleigh and packed in sawdust in an ice house. The Tedfords contrived a chute to slide the blocks into the Juniper store ice house. This procedure involved wire cable, a square hook and often a strong work horse as the source of power. Farmers on the winter lake were always wary of dangerous ice ridges and weak ice, due to currents near some of the islands or the notoriously treacherous Hell's Gate. Losing a load of ice or cord wood was one thing, but to have your horses drown was a tragedy. A driver would fashion a slip-hitch on the horses so if a sleigh did begin to sink, he could pull a rope so the horses would break free and not be dragged under. Operators respected the sixth sense of their horses that would balk at crossing thin ice.

The farmer who organized the ice cutting probably made little money on this operation. One source says that the price charged to the customer ranged from twenty-five to fifty cents a block delivered. Another source claims ten cents a block for hand-cut ice. The farmer then paid three cents a block to the cutter, two cents to the teamster and the remaining four cents was the operator's profit. He would collect sawdust from a nearby mill, such as Shewen's near Mt. Julian, usually at no cost.

Earl Shewen, a venerable man of many skills, recalls his ice cutting days. "I supplied ice to Viamede, Mt. Julian and 15 or more cottages nearby. I used an old Model T Ford chassis and engine and rigged up an ice saw on one side of the rear axle. It was adjustable according to the thickness of the ice. We cut until refrigerators took over from the ice boxes."

Car buff Stan MacLeod has given the chassis of one such ice-cutting car a new life as the frame of a restored Model T. That Model T began its ice cutting career with the Dunford family operations. Wellie Dunford also devised a special chisel to determine the thickness of the ice, a crucial criterion in this business.

No matter how ingenious the local inhabitants were, they suffered during the Great Depression of the 1930s like people everywhere. One of the make-work projects of those days was road building. Effie Shewen recalls her husband Earl working at one of the road camps on Highway 28. Camp One was located at Burleigh Falls where Effie's brother bunked down. His pay was ten dollars a month, with free room and board. Earl, as a married man, was allowed to go home at night and because he provided a team of horses, he was paid more. This was hard slow work; horses, dynamite, hand tools and your own strength were what you worked with. Camp Two was located opposite the present-day Woodview General Store, and further camps were built up the highway about every eight to ten miles.

Canoeists, birders and anglers have always treasured a particular stretch of the Burleigh shoreline stretching from Dunford's Landing west to the former Gordon Knapman Fraser property. Because this quiet weed-covered bottom is a haven for a variety of fish species, it was not surprising that in 1951 the Ontario Department of Game and Fisheries approached Doug Dunford about a spawning operation for muskies, considered the oldest species of fish in northern North America. The Native Peoples referred to it as *mask-in-onje*, the crooked pike. Today's official spelling is maskinonge; locally it is either 'lunge or muskie. "This sport fish is hunted, not fished," in the words of local Nick Nickels. Once the ice is out in the spring, the larger female (hen) fish and smaller male (jack) swim in pairs in shallow, weedy waters often with their caudal fins just above the surface.

Marg Dunford continues the story about harvesting the lunge eggs: "Doug helped the fisheries men put in a series of nets held in place by long poles into the mud. He was taught how to milk the eggs from the female and then recognize a jack and use him for fertilization. This operation continued under the Department of Lands and Forests and later the Ministry of Natural Resources until 1990 when it was discontinued.

"There were eleven sets of nets, many behind Horseshoe Island and few near Acton's and Reed's. When pulled up, the bass and pickerel were released, carp killed, and catfish kept for a future meal! All muskies were milked and released. Because of the cold temperatures, all fish were very docile and easy to handle.

"The eggs, collected in pails, were handled gently. In fact, on the rough road to Havelock, they rested on a bed-spring to cushion the ride! All unfertilized eggs, recognized by their white colour, were removed in Havelock at the hatchery."

Jobs on and around the lake at the end of the 21st century will obviously be different in many respects from jobs of today. Regulations inhibit the jack-of-all trades artisan of earlier times. However, ingenuity is never dead. Consider the various craft that undertook weed harvesting in the 1980s. Many young people have made a niche for themselves providing services and products, such as painting, repairing, and safeguarding property. What underlines these accounts of earlier folks is their sense of caring for others and, in many cases, having fun doing their job. Whatever the task, they usually did it well. Those principles work well in any century.

Seven

BUILDING AND REBUILDING

THE JOY of owning a cottage is exceeded only by the pleasure of planning its construction or making improvements. Many a frustrated architect lives in the mind of a city dweller of different profession, and who of us has not lain awake of a cold January night planning next summer's building project? For over a hundred years cottagers at Stony Lake have schemed, built, torn down and rebuilt with zest and imagination.

Late in the nineteenth century, the idea of spending peaceful hours on the shores of a picturesque lake took hold with rapid enthusiasm. The Crown sold parcels of island land on behalf of the Mud Lake Indians, often for very little money. In 1887, $22.00 purchased the two Elliott (Sonley) islands.

Some landowners hired a builder to complete a sizeable structure, though often the ice house and privy were to be built. Other islanders made do with a small building to use as a hunting cabin, for winter storage of boats and tents, or as a basic summer cottage. An accompanying tent platform might later serve as the floor for a sleeping cabin. All construction was done with hand tools.

A feature of early cottage architecture was rather small windows, designed to keep out the hot sun and the cold wind found on these granite islands with little tree cover, the result

of recent lumbering. Extensive verandahs also contributed to the interior darkness. However, several of the early buildings had some fascinating construction features. At 'Endiang,' built in 1905, huge logs cut from trees on the island formed the lower portion of the cottage. An upstairs bathroom drained into a cement septic tank, probably the first such indoor facility on an island. At 'Lochend' in Mackenzie Bay, visiting divinity students were drafted to build two discreetly placed outhouses. One was always wobbly and was named after a disliked Anglican bishop.

'Westaway' was erected in 1891 in Victorian style, sporting a false gable with elaborate sunburst trim, painted in the cheerful colours of the day. In the 1920s, it was painted dark brown and the fancy gable removed. Huge logs replaced porch railings to achieve an Adironack look. However, in the late 1980s, 'Westaway' was restored as a Victorian cottage with its original façade and colours. 'Tarbox Island' has also been restored, though it is now much bigger than the original 20' x 30' cottage of 1903. Kathy Dembroski writes: "The original widow's peak, where a lantern was hung at night to give directions to the cottage, is still intact. The beautiful old red and blue glass throws a lovely reflection of light into the upper hallway."

'Headlands' on Fairy Lake Island, built in 1892 by E.R. Tate, was bought in 1904 by a lumber baron, Bill Irwin. From the vantage point high on the hill, Mr. Irwin could watch his log booms headed for the Peterborough sawmills. He named Hell's Gate and Devil's Elbow because those log booms had such a difficult time getting around the sharp bends in the waterway. When George Baird bought 'Headlands' in 1953, he spent three years of hard labour getting the old long-neglected building back into shape. Using two 12-ton hydraulic lifts, he levelled the house, as the kitchen had sagged a foot. Forty-five gallons of paint were needed to paint the exterior. A creosote post foundation, an aluminum roof and a replacement beam under the verandah made the old place solid, top and bottom once more.

The stone wall around 'Falls View' on Brownscombe Island was constructed from rocks scavenged from the shore before dawn by the owner. Each morning he rowed home with such a heavy load that he seemed to be sitting in the water, rowing without a boat. His family asserts that he bought one island and stole another! In 1910, the swampy areas of 'Spree Island' were laboriously filled with bucket-loads of small stones rowed from the mainland by the chatelaine of the island. Then the island was known as Kozy Island.

Smaller, more economical cottages were frequently erected by the owners themselves. Felix Brownscombe and his wife Carrie built their first cottage, 15 feet square, for $99.84. Many cottages, like 'Deer Rocks' and 'Anchorage,' were of post and beam construction with board and batten siding and a hip roof which could be raised almost single-handedly. In early buildings, square hand-forged nails were used. Foundations were cedar logs and stones found on the property. Unfortunately, present-day owners have found that cedar log foundations rot over time and floors slope. A unique touch is found at

The Guillets at their cotttage, 'Westaway,' on Horseshoe Island, 1891. *Courtesy Rob Guillet Collection.*

'Sand Haven' where stumps from the nearby bay formed the porch railings.

The two cottages on Grassy Island have different construction. The 1885 west cottage has a layer of vertical siding and a layer of horizontal siding with tarpaper between. Later, cedar shingles were added to the exterior and basswood panelling to the interior. The 1900 east cottage is of typical barn construction, with walls of vertical tongue and groove pine boards and no studs, and a roof of one-inch pine boards with no supporting rafters. 'Shota' and 'Cedar Lodge' are similarly constructed.

The lumber for these buildings was brought to the islands in several ways. The local builders had sizeable boats for hauling boards and materials. Earl Shewen remembers: "In the early days I built flat-bottomed punts about 15 feet long. We rowed these until we got an outboard motor in the late 40s."[1] Some landowners towed punts from Lakefield. Lumber destined for 'Sandakan' was dumped when a punt capsized in the middle of Clear Lake, but retrieved piece by piece by the owner. As well, the *Islinda* also delivered construction materials. An entire cottage dismantled on a farm on

Top: 'Tarbox Island,' 1903. Bottom: 'Tarbox Island' as it looks today. *Courtesy Kathy Dembroski Collection.*

Lake Katchawanooka arrived on the deck of the *Islinda* for assembly at 'Lochcroft' in Cassidy Bay.

Some lumber came from pine and cedar logs milled at a sawmill on Norman Bolton's farm, where he also had a blacksmith shop. His son Orval remembers the lean 1930s when one could buy land and build a cottage for $500, with $100 extra for a stone fireplace.[2] George Guillet built fireplaces at 'Sandakan' and 'Westaway.' At Grassy Island the stonemasons used Eagle Mount quarry granite; at 'Spree

Island' they used stones from the Indian River.

Many buildings were not insulated and had single-thickness flooring; however, this lumber was three-quarters of an inch thick and thus more rigid. Some cottages had inventive types of insulation. 'Cairn Dhu' had sisal matting on the floor and layer upon layer of wallpaper, while 'Deer Rocks' had cedar bark strips on the exterior, later replaced by cedar shingles. The walls at 'Twin Bluffs' had an unusual form of insulation - a substantial stash of liquor, hidden from Grandfather by the youth of the household, and discovered by electricians installing wiring in the '50s.

Most structures had screened porches. At 'Headlands' the original copper screening still functions. The kitchen was often separate from the main cottage because the heat of the wood stove was undesirable in summer, and there was the ever-present fear of fire. At 'Deer Rocks' the outdoor kitchen, "...while campy, made doing dishes a running battle with the mosquitoes. It also meant constructing clever devices to try to outwit the raccoons from getting into the icebox, garbage cans and open food shelves. We humans did not always win," writes Delight Dann. "The old dining room was an incredible 6 feet by 7 feet with built-in benches around three sides. How did five children, parents and guests fit in? The first one seated never had to clear or serve because he or she couldn't budge." At 'Woodonga' the screened and canvassed dining hall was termed "Burlapia."

To cottagers using wood stoves for cooking, water heating and comfort, fire was a constant threat. Before Jill Farrow's parents bought Bare Island, the cottage had burned to the ground when a rusty stove chimney ignited the roof inside. The bucket brigade could save only the boathouse at the northeast end of the island. On neighbouring 'Hove-To', now owned by Susan Chapman, one of the two cottages previously owned by the Sheehy family also burned.

Connie Wahl remembers that: "...at the 'Shanty' ten buckets were under the table in the breezeway in case the inevitable occurred. When I was five, it did. The outhouse was a pillar of flames. My mother stood on the point, ringing and ringing the big mud-coloured bell. Canoes arrived, everyone falling out, carrying more buckets. The bucket brigades' water, it seemed, was thrown miles in the air. The 'Shanty' was saved, the icehouse and woodhouse even closer to the fire only singed. A young English boy, staying in Canada during the war, had put warm ashes in the wooden bucket in the outhouse."

Guests who were cottage-sitting at 'Spree Island' were confronted with a roof fire when loose ceiling paper got too close to the stove pipe. They sprayed the kitchen with fire extinguisher foam and spent the next three days scrubbing it off.

Lightning caused the fire on 'Laristan' in May 1940 which destroyed many trees as well as the cottage. After the fire, the owner planted 400 small trees provided by the government. Marj and Bruce Sonley, the present owners, have built their cottage on the site of the old one in 1973. At nearby Grassy Island, lightning welded a spoon to the stove right

Fire at 'Bare Island', 1949. *Courtesy Tom Cole Collection.*

through the bottom of a pot.

In September 1997, the boathouse at 'Cordach' on Juniper Island was struck by lightning and burned to the ground. The fire was contained by volunteer firefighters just as it began to spread to the surrounding trees. Only the massive concrete foundation, poured in 1920, survived. A large flotilla of boats turned out to watch the spectacle. Jack (J.M.R.) Fairbairn, who owned the cottage for many years, had had a bronze bell installed as a fire alarm in 1931. It came from a steam locomotive that had been decommissioned shortly before. Succeeding generations of youngsters at 'Cordach' were forbidden to ring it for fear that it would create a false alarm. Blair Mackenzie, the current owner and Mr. Fairbairn's grandson, is still annoyed that he failed completely in the confusion of the boathouse fire to ring the 'Cordach' fire bell—not that he is in any hurry to be presented with such an opportunity again.

Fire destroyed the Viamede Hotel in 1907 and, in 1929, the steamer *Empress* caught fire at the Mt. Julian dock. Mike Fowler's Aunt Betsy Thompson dove into the water, seized the hawser, and towed the burning craft away from the gas pump on the dock, thus avoiding a greater conflagration.

Even today, with faster boats and fireboats on the lake, care must be taken with campfires, stovepipes and cigarettes. A scene reported in the *Peterborough Examiner* in September 1908 is not wanted as a repeat. "Persons who returned from Stony Lake today say that the smoke was so dense at the lakes that the captains on the boats had to run them very slowly to avoid accident. It was impossible to see more than 20 to 30 feet ahead."

Local builders have served the Stony community for years. Wellie Dunford, with the help of his sons, built 'Treetops,' 'Kerrywood,' 'West Wind,' 'Cashel' and 'Spree Island.' His son Doug has continued to construct and repair cottages, deliver ice and firewood, and provide transportation and help to cottagers on the north shore. On the south shore, Howard Hamilton and family were in business for many years, constructing cottages, docks and septic systems. Earl Shewen began building cottages on Stony Lake in 1939 and has never stopped: "I am a self-taught builder and can do almost all the jobs required from carpentry to plumbing. I've never had an inspector reject any of my buildings and I am proud of my work. One day I was helping a fellow build his cabin and he asked me what he would need to build a boathouse. When we sat down for lunch he got paper and pencil, and I told him how many floor joists, the number of 2 x 4s, the lumber for the floor and roof and how many nails. He was astonished that I could rattle off the list like that and said, 'You must have a slide rule in your head because I teach math and I couldn't do that.' "[3] Grant Shewen carries on that family tradition.

Three generations in the Bolton family (Norm, Orval and now Glenn) have built on Stony Lake. Since 1981, Glenn has averaged 5000 square feet of new cottage construction each year, along with renovations and repairs to old ones. In the towering trees beside the original Bolton home, built by Norm and enlarged by Glenn, a three-level tree house made from scrap lumber is constantly improved by Glenn's four sons. No doubt there will be a fourth generation Bolton on Stony Lake.

Recently, the Shewens and the Drain Brothers have been installing countless septic systems. What a sight to see trucks travelling across the lake on barges in midsummer! Barges have also hauled well-drilling rigs to 'Falls View', 'Horseshoe' and even to Sheila Gallagher's tiny island. These folks have no algae or zebra mussel problems with their water systems.

The ingenuity of Stony Lake cottagers is legendary. The first cottage at 'Oberland' was an 1889 barn which was moved closer to the water: the second was a log cabin constructed by Dr. Henry Barnes with logs from the original farmhouse on Little's farm. An entire two-storey cottage built (by mistake) on Elephant Rock in the Burleigh Channel was slid across the winter ice to Swastika on Horseshoe Island. At the Walter island, the old cottage, built 1886, was, in 1926, rolled uphill on logs to a different location to make room for a new cottage. A dispute between two owners on Bare Island was resolved when one owner moved his cottage to Little Otter. The icehouse on the east Elliott island was moved to the west island and used as a small dwelling.

Blair Mackenzie adds: "...the ingenuity is not restricted to cottagers. When repairs were made to the foundations of the boathouse at 'Cordach' after the fire, the contractor, Tom Collins of Kawartha Utilities, worked well into December. Ice would form overnight around his barge, parked at McCracken's Landing. To get across to Juniper, a mechanical shovel on the front of the barge was used to bash a route ahead through the ice—a veritable Stony Lake icebreaker."

At 'Cairn Dhu,' hydro was not available because Ontario Hydro felt that it was impractical and expensive to lay underwater cable, so young Jim Land got permission to install his own cable from Park Island. He had, in his teens, sewn himself a canvas jacket to hold an air tank and created a diving mask out of a war surplus gas mask. He brought the cable on a huge wooden spool on a trailer and transferred it to a barge for the trip across the lake. Then he laid the cable, dug the necessary trenches at each end, wired the cottage, boathouse and sleeping cabin and received Hydro approval. There is no doubt that this paved the way for the use of underwater cable on Stony Lake.

In 1972, a cement holding tank was constructed at 'Shota.' "This entailed moulding eight layers of chicken wire and various other

Ready for the move, 1926. The Lech cottage on its way to a new site. *Courtesy Margaret Walter Collection.*

bits and pieces into a tank shape approximately 2000 gallons in size, a feat in itself," writes Janet Smith. "The big job of cementing this large shape in was scheduled to start at 8 a.m. but, through unforeseen circumstances, was delayed until 2 p.m. Finally, the willing crew of family, friends and neighbours began work and gradually the tank grew. People came and went—the beer and booze just went." A steam jenny used to condition the cement had to be tended by an all-night watchcrew. Janet concludes: "The holding tank pulled through the whole experience, but I have grave doubts about some of the workers." However, that tank was still in use in 1999.

When the McKerracher family bought Match Point in 1968, it was largely a swamp, which made the family's judgement suspect. However, in 1977, the last of 140 barge loads of sand was unloaded onto the uneven ground, a wheelbarrow at a time, and a tennis court emerged. Most of the construction of the large cottage and a boathouse was the work of the owners, Helen and Keith McKerracher.

The earliest report of architectural expertise was at 'Shota,' built in 1891 by John (J.D.) Baptie, at a cost of $100. Sandford Fleming

Smith, a first-year architectural student, designed the cottage. Just two years later, an architect was hired to design 'Oakleigh', which was expected to be ready for habitation in July. However, when the whole huge family arrived, along with all their provisions and two maids, the lumber still lay on the ground. The house was begun July 12 and finished so that part could be inhabited by July 18, 1893.

Jim Guillet's cottage, designed in 1959 by a young architect friend, has a roofline to make the most of winter sun. But, when the family arrived from Tennessee that summer, with four children aged 4, 2½, 1½ and 2 months, construction was not finished. There was no running water, electricity, fireplace, finished flooring or partitions between the rooms – and no motor boat!

'Ziggurat' in Mackenzie Bay, a distinctive cabin designed with Arizona inspiration by budding architect Andrew Binnie, was later completed by local builders who could not keep the northern rain and snow out. Other dwellings, including the church, have suffered

Luxury living at 'Shota' in the early days. *Courtesy Janet Smith Collection.*

'Oakleigh,' designed and built by the Coles in 1893, is still occupied by descendents of this same family. *Courtesy Art Cole Collection.*

roof damage from heavy snowfalls.

The following account was written in 1999 by Bernie Morin on behalf of Emma Jane Davis (1867–1943). 'Davis Island Manor' was designed in 1904 by "...the noted Frank Darling, as this could be no ordinary residence. We wanted a most modern house in the Arts and Crafts style with all the most up-to-date conveniences and rooms for several guests. There were to be six principal structures in all—the main house, a boathouse, the men's pavilion, a caretaker's cottage, a pump house and a most extraordinary stone tower, which would supply us with water under pressure and afford us a commanding view from atop the observation deck."

Recently, several architecturally designed homes have been built on Stony, some on islands, some on the south shore near Burleigh and several on the north shore near Boschink. Perhaps the most renowned is the beautifully landscaped Wandich home. Known locally as the "Glass House", it has recently sold. Frequently used for a television series, it is admired from the water by tourists on the *Chippewa II* and by cottagers showing their guests the sights of the lake.

Over the years, land for cottages has been acquired in various ways. In the late nineteenth century Queen Victoria sold lands "of which we are seized by right of our Crown" on behalf of the Mud Lake Indians"...that the proceeds may be applied to the benefit, support and advantage of the said Indians in such a manner as we shall be pleased to direct from time to time."[4]

Juniper Island was purchased in 1887 by three partners, who agreed that the survivor would get the island. George M. Roger won the longevity contest. In another scenario, the Knapman family discovered in 1905 that they had built on the wrong island so had to purchase the occupied one in addition to the empty back island. In 1907, an auction divided the Walter's island which had been held "in common" by two Peterborough merchants.

'Singkettle' was purchased in 1935 from the Department of Indian Affairs for $25 as a safe anchorage for George Douglas's sailboat and because it reminded him of Great Slave Lake, which he loved. When Jim Gouinlock first saw the 'Sandhaven' property, it was covered with deadheads and stumps but had a natural beach. Rackham's Island was won in a poker game, and the "pile of rocks" next to it purchased for $34 in back taxes. Both now belong to the Dutton family. 'Nakemi' in Cassidy Bay cost $1000 in 1936, to be paid at the

Sandhaven Bay, 1904. Logs and stumps clog the lagoon, the legacy of lumbering. *Courtesy Jack Gouinlock Collection.*

rate of $100 for ten years with no interest. When the Huycke family purchased 'Boschink' from the George Morrow estate in the 1940s, they did not know that the deal included several miles of shoreline.

In 1947, Ken Slater bought his property with the following stipulation. "As for the boathouse on the shore, perhaps I didn't make it quite clear when we were discussing it. I have the use of half the boathouse, though I don't own it, and I will turn over to you my privileges and will personally guarantee your unrestricted use," as recounted by Judy Finch. 'Majestic' was acquired from the YWCA by Jack Townsend in 1949 because he thought it would be like living on a boat. 'Plum Pudding' was purchased for back taxes, but the cement dock cost more than the cottage.

When Blair Mackenzie is asked the meaning of his cottage's name, 'Cordach,' he says that it is an ancient Gaelic word meaning "never-ending maintenance." The early owner of 'Spree Island' labelled her keys, "the keys to heaven." Many of us today feel that way.

Eight

WATER, WIND AND WAVES

THE COMMUNITY of Stony Lake is water-borne, whether by canoe, kayak, sailboat, rowboat or motorboat. Today, the lake is so motorized that many think like cottager Wes Willoughby:

Not to this peaceful, lovely place
Do they paddle, sail or grace
The water with canoer's pace.
Nor do they waft with billowy sail
To meet their pals and get the mail;
But rather rent the aqua fair
With tin tub and tupperware.
Clanking boats spewing smoke,
Bought by wealthy modern folk.[1]

Birchbark canoes were a major means of transportation for Native Peoples and essential to early cottagers. For previous generations, canoes and skiffs were the only way to get around the lake. Getting from the landing to the cottage, going to local farms for milk and vegetables, making trips to Eel's and Perry's creeks, attending church or just visiting—all was done by canoe; even courting! As a young man, Russell Dodworth would paddle his wide 18 ft. trapper's canoe, with an oriental carpet on the floor, all the way from Gilchrist Bay to see Elizabeth Buell who lived near Kawartha Park. After his marriage, he

and his wife Dorothy paddled to Georgian Bay in that same canoe.

This poem, written by Dot Easson, shows her preference for canoeing:

And as for transportation, it's
No effort, it's sublime.
You go by outboard everywhere
And go there all the time.
Not only does it get you there
But has this added boon
It drowns the tedious racket made
By whippoorwill and loon.
The bad old days and bad old ways
Are changing fast, it's true
But Hiawatha Easson still
Is paddling her canoe.[2]

Joan Townsend senior kept that same tradition, paddling herself to church in the last year of her long life.

Although canoes now come in aluminum, fibreglass and Kevlar, wooden canoes are still the smoothest to paddle. Antique cedar strip, cedar plank or basswood canoes are treasured. George Douglas, a cottager and canoe collector, sold a flush batten canoe to Jack Ryder "only on the condition that the boys don't ever go in it." Tim Sherin still uses his "Star" canoe built by Thomas Gordon in

A beauty of a canoe, *Clytie*, an 18-foot basswood, paddled by Betty Lampman. The canoe is now in the Canadian Canoe Museum.
George Douglas Collection, courtesy Katharine Hooke.

Lakefield in 1876. He has donated a 20 ft. freighter and a 10 ft. folding canoe, which his father acquired from Kay Douglas, to the Canadian Canoe Museum in Peterborough. A Douglas 13 ft. canoe resided at the Reed cottage until Doug gave it to Will Bentham as a boat for the growing of plants. Instead, that little craft is undergoing restoration in the Benthams' boat shed. Christie Bentham's favourite canoe is a Strickland with alternate cedar and mahogany strips, restored several years ago by neighbour Art Teamerson.

The early history of canoe building in Lakefield is complicated because of the several players involved, not to mention fires, lost records, numerous locations in the village and the many boat rental operations on Stony Lake. Partnerships dissolved and realigned. It was the period of what Ken Brown calls the first generation of canoe builders: individuals in boatsheds and barns, before the era of substantial factories and corporations.[3]

Many of the early names of the builders are still well-known in the Kawarthas because of cherished family canoes and skiffs. The mandate of the Canadian Canoe Museum includes unearthing and maintaining the history of these builders, as well as collecting the artifacts.

It is likely that Thomas Gordon (1833-1916) of Lakefield was building some of the earliest carpentered canoes, heavy and cumbersome by today's standards, but certainly distinguishable from the even earlier dugouts. In the period of world's fairs, scientific expositions and a keen interest in exploration, it is understandable that, by the late 1870s, the Thomas Gordon Company (established 1855) and the Richardson and Grylls Company (established 1875) were shipping 16-foot canoes to England. Even earlier, in 1860, Sam Strickland and his sons presented the Prince of Wales with a finely crafted 18 ft. racing dugout, on the occasion of the royal visit to the Peterborough area. Thomas Gordon, typical of the early entrepreneurs, turned his hand to building one of Lakefield's first steamers, the *Cruiser*, as well as several fine houses in the village.

George Strickland and James Brown, who had started with Thomas Gordon, formed the Strickland Canoe Company in 1892. The boatshop burned in 1893, but soon rose from the ashes with separate buildings for a showroom and a paint shop. These were all close to the railway station, the waterfront and Queen Street in Lakefield.[4]

A Stony Lake ketch, with Llewelyn Robertson in stern, 1916. *Courtesy Nancy Watson Collection.*

In July 1904, the Gordon and Strickland companies amalgamated, taking in Edward R. Tate as a partner to form the Lakefield Canoe Building and Manufacturing Company. Meanwhile, the James Brown Boat Company continued operations until the mid 1940s, primarily as a rental business, including a small rental fleet at Mt. Julian.

Fire struck Strickland and his partners again in 1910, destroying many canoe moulds and other equipment. This building was replaced by a larger brick structure under the foremanship of Gilbert Gordon, Thomas' son. Canoe building continued in Lakefield throughout the 20th century, almost dying out when wooden boat construction gave way to man-made materials. However, what goes around, comes around. Now the individual canoe builders are back in the forefront: Walter Walker of Lakefield (now in his early 90s), Ron Squires of Burleigh Falls and Ted Moores of Peterborough.[5]

Canoe sailing was also popular in those early days, both for racing and pleasure. A canoe might be fitted with two sails. Early regattas always had canoe sailing races; on the wall at 'Spree Island' hangs a pennant won in a canoe sailing race in 1910. Many long-time cottagers, including Jim Collins, Derry Smith and Jack Matthews, learned to sail in canoes.

Early in the century an enterprising group of young men constructed a catamaran "...by lashing two canoes together, topped with a platform for the crew. Large sails provided the motive power and ensured a wet sheet and a flowing sea. The stormier the day the better, as the home-rigged craft scudded over the waves carrying its drenched mariners to all parts of the lake."[6]

Rowboats provided transportation in former times. Bill Irwin's rowboat had a special gear mechanism which allowed him to row frontwards to see where he was heading. There is also a hoist in the 'Headland's' boathouse, which assisted Mr. Irwin, who was called "Big Bill" for good reason, to disembark. Lois Miller's father rowed or sailed a skiff from the south shore to Mt. Julian for supplies when the family with two small children stayed at the cottage until November. His wife dyed the sail orange for greater visibility.

Tom Cole and his brother John set off in their skiff for the east shore of Clear Lake to get a few flat pieces of limestone for the amateur construction of paths and steps. He recounts: "With sail, leeboards and rudder we tacked our way there in a gentle breeze, but on the return trip, loaded, we had two or three inches of freeboard and the south wind had risen substantially. Several craft detoured for a closer inspection because all that was visible from a distance was a sail and the upper parts of two boys. The momentum was tremendous and, although we lowered the sail as we passed the boat livery on Juniper, we didn't have to row a stroke to get right to the dock at 'Dingley' on Big Otter. It was fortunate the skiff was watertight even well above the level of normal use. We would certainly have foundered if we had taken in more than a few drops because we hadn't thought to take a bailing can."

Nowadays it is difficult to find a skiff, and new ones are prohibitively expensive. At regattas, the tandem rowing race is still popular, but the crews for the seven-in-a-skiff often have to use a large canoe. The canoeing instruction program at Juniper and the regattas help to create enthusiasm for canoeing in today's mechanized world. Wil Tranter's promotion has helped kayaking, but, sadly, for the skiff there is seemingly no such support. Will the tradition of small boats on Stony Lake be able to be maintained?

Chris Greening writes about "...changes in the boating department. Somehow as a child we managed to get by with a small outboard motorboat and a canoe. Now it seems we must maintain a small fleet of watercraft in order to keep everyone happy and content. This consists of a number of motorized boats of various shapes and sizes, canoes, kayaks, sailboats, windsurfers and an assortment of inflatable craft for towing children when they become bored with water skiing. My brother and I used to ride on a old ironing board. I have no idea how we managed back then, but I do know that it was fun."

In spite of being a relatively small lake in comparison with the Muskokas or the Adirondacks, Stony Lake has been home to a wide range of vessels powered by various sources of energy. The vagaries of steam and the early gasoline launches are graphically described in this chapter. Although these boats are generally remembered with great affection, often the family "captain" was the only one who really understood their temperamental innards.

Launch is the most commonly used term which Maynard Bray defines "...as (usually) a small powerboat having little or no cabin, that goes slowly *through* instead of rapidly *over* the water."[7] These daytime vessels travelled at a leisurely pace, usually on smooth inland waters, and were built with transom sterns or

as elegant double-enders. Some were raced as will be noted.

Steam launches required a boiler and a ready supply of fuel: wood, coal or oil. The Canadian Canoe Company catalogue (1894) describes a 20 foot vessel "...so simple that they will not require a practical engineer to run or take care of....something that can be placed on a wagon or on the train and taken to where you want to spend your holiday."[8] Three Stony Lake cottagers were the major owners of this company: Homer Fisk of 'Fern Rock', Felix Brownscombe of the Burleigh Channel and Thomas Barrie, near Juniper Island. It is likely they influenced fellow cottagers into considering buying one of their models which ranged from 20 to 40 feet, could be fitted with a cabin if over 25 feet, and could seat up to 20 persons. According to the catalogue, the cheapest launch was $250, the most expensive $710.

In this overview of powerboats a brief flurry of interest in electric power is to be noted, but batteries were heavy and even the boats were heavier and more expensive. By

The Cole children off 'Little Otter,' 1920s. Every cottage had a punt, used for transport of lumber, groceries and mothers and children who could not swim. *Courtesy Art Cole Collection.*

95

1887, Gottlieb Daimler's internal combustion engine was adapted for boat propulsion and, by 1905, the American engineer, Cameron Waterman, had patented the first commercially viable outboard engine. Even though these were heavy cast iron, he still managed to sell 15,000 by 1915. But Ole Evinrude's lightweight aluminum engine of 1910 ultimately became the Model T of the boating world.

The move from steam-powered launches to gasoline led to the term "explosive engine" which was quickly changed to "internal combustion" for obvious reasons. The only really explosive vessel of this period was the little known naphtha-powered launch, which attained some popularity in the Adirondacks, in spite of the potentially volatile fuel.

Inboard power boats were followed by inexpensive outboard engines, often attached to outriggers on canoes or to the transom of a popular Peterborough Canoe Co. model, such as the "Speedboat," a 16 foot, V-bottom, "...a good boat in heavy seas or shallow places," as described in the company's 1929 catalogue.

Racing powerboats were so popular on local lakes by the 1920s that the Peterborough Canoe Co. became the Canadian agent for the American Boyd-Martin Company whose boat had set the world's speed record in 1928. In the 1930s, Terry Hall of Syndicate Island would demonstrate the newest, fastest Peterborough boat on the local lakes. These planing hulls were light in comparison to other displacement hulls and had a V bottom that split and threw aside oncoming waves.

Even cabin cruisers and the sleek Muskoka launches, whose features often matched those of cars, were seen on Stony Lake. Often the earliest models were called auto launches because of the steering wheel, windshield and convertible tops. Greavette of Gravenhurst, Gidley of Penetanguishene and Minette of Bracebridge were familiar names, even on the Kawartha lakes.[9] The Ditchburn Disappear-

ing Propeller Boat, built in the 1930s in Gravenhurst and Lindsay, has a strong following of Dispro Owners Association members who meet each year for a rally on different Ontario lakes. Hydroplanes, which appeared after the Second World War, were especially fast racing boats with a stepped bottom to reduce planing resistance. They were raced near Viamede in the late 1940s and '50s but soon lost their appeal.

In looking at some past examples, it is seen that the first powerboat race between two 25-foot steam launches, J.W. Donnell's *Mayflower* and David Breeze's *Flash*, was held at the Juniper Regatta, 17 August, 1900. The course was around 'Bare Island' and back to Juniper with each boat going in opposite directions. J.W. Donnell's daughter, May, the first woman captain on Stony Lake, was at the wheel. A diminutive 5 foot, 86 pound woman, she was sometimes seen towing a quarter-mile long string of canoes to the church at Juniper. Other launches of the early 1900s were Fred Tully's *Tramp,* George Guillet's *Nut,* McBain's *Mollie* and a series of launches belonging to Dr. Varney Barnes, who named them all *Senrab* as a reverse of his surname. In 1915, he travelled from Cleveland for his sister's wedding at 'Buckeye' cottage. "Mother had picked wildflowers for her bouquet and for the living room," reports her daughter Lois Miller. "She baked a cake. When Uncle Varney arrived and found no other decorations he brought all of his boat flags to drape around the living room. For their honeymoon Mother and Dad used Uncle Varney's launch and camped in Upper Stoney Lake."

Jack Gouinlock remembers a trip in one of the *Senrab*s, a Chris Craft, all the way to Cleveland via the Trent Canal, Lake Ontario, the Welland Canal and Lake Erie. Later in the 1930s, Dr. Barnes graduated to a 50 foot cruiser, *Alandi.*

The crew of the Gouinlocks' *Sunny Jim,* a

wood-fired steam launch, could always stop and chop more fuel if necessary. The engineer owner, Jim Gouinlock, sat in the middle of the boat, often very warm because of the larger boiler, while the skipper was in the bow and the passengers around the sides, protected by a canopy top with drop curtains.

Early pleasure boats were sometimes a trial, as this 1909 account from Felix Brownscombe's logbook shows: "On May 2, a cold and windy day, the ground white with snow flurries, I went to Toronto to see the launch I had ordered. They had the launch in the water and Mr. Shaw took me for a run, but told me that it was not making the 10 miles per hour as guaranteed. We was [sic] out in it for a couple of hours, but it did not run satisfactory. One of the cylinders was not working right. When he stopped the engine it would not start so he sent a man from the works who soon had it going again. When returning to the docks the steering device broke. He then took me out in a similar boat but the clutch in it was always going wrong and he said he would not go far from the dock. On returning to shore I told him that I was disappointed at the way the trial turned out."

Later, the boat, christened the *Minto*, arrived via the Grand Trunk Railway. It was 20 ft. 4 in. long by 4 ft. 9 in. wide with planking of cypress ½ in. thick above the waterline and ⅝ in. below, decks mahogany and butternut, the engines 2 cylinders of 4 h.p. each. In the account book, the price is shown as $500. In August the launch was deemed reliable enough to make a 7-day trip to Beaverton and Orillia. "Slept in launch. Expenses include gasoline, $14.20" was recorded in the logbook.

In May 1911 the engine was exchanged for a new one, but on June 4 the account book reads, "...new cylinder head from Toronto 35c to Canadian Express" and on June 29 "Osborne, trying to start engine, $8.75."

Some of the launches pictured in early

Top: *Sunny Jim*, 'Sand Haven's' steam launch, sits gracefully in front of the gas lamp on the dock, 1910. *Courtesy Jack Gouinlock Collection.*
Centre: Her owner, John Gouinlock, stands ready to depart, 1913. Courtesy *Jack Gouinlock Collection.*
Bottom: The engineer, Jim Gouinlock, prepared to "stoke her up," 1910. *Courtesy Jack Gouinlock Collection.*

regatta postcards were luxurious. During the early 1900s, Mr. Bill Irwin toured the lake in grand style in his steam launch, the *Stoney Lake*. Just after the First World War, Hugh Porter's father Fred was proud of his two inboards, *Adelaide I* and *II*. In the 1920s, Gordon K. Fraser had a 100 ft. ocean-going yacht, *Wanderer*, with luxury fittings, lifeboats and a captain and crew. His later boat, a 40 ft. twin-engine cabin cruiser named *Dauntless*, had such a wide beam that she tipped every canoe in the channel, but she met a sad fate, catching fire in the boathouse. Mr. Fraser and his daughter June saved the boathouse by pushing the boat out onto the lake, where it burned and sank.

Tom Cole remembers Sam Henderson's boat *Kanatha* "...almost double pointed with a roof over the undecked portion with striped roller awnings that could be lowered if necessary. The wheel was at the bow, manned by Mr. Henderson wearing always a boater, blazer and white ducks. Immediately astern of him was an enormous gasoline engine, tended by his chauffeur suitably attired for contact with oil and grease. The guests sat in wicker chairs toward the stern. Mr. Henderson would signal for half-speed, stop or reverse by a bell although his engineer was only about two feet away.

"Mr. Morrow's chauffeur-driven launch *Oakdene* was also white but had a convertible top, wicker chairs and lots of polished brass. It was V-bottomed with square stern and a powerful six-cylinder engine. While *Kanatha* was almost noiseless, from Otter Island we could hear *Oakdene* leaving her boathouse in the Boschink Narrows. As she threw a huge swell, we would rush to don bathing suits and scurry down to the water to enjoy the waves. This lemming-like performance might be repeated several times a day as other V-bottomed power plants came down the lake— Harry Sutherland's *Roamer* from 'Inglestane', the *Elizabeths* of the Dodworth family, Waddell's *Condor*, and Fairbairn Smith's *Redbird* from 'Boscobel', a high speed mahogany launch with a rear engine and a sloping stern."

The *Oakdene* would often accompany the steamer *Islinda* on her passenger cruises. Mr. Morrow chose an unfortunate time to graduate to a large cabin cruiser, also named *Oakdene*, for in 1940 gasoline rationing came into effect. During the Second World War he gave the cruiser to the Toronto Harbour Commission, where it was used for many years.

J.M.R. (Jack) Fairbairn had a mahogany Chris Craft runabout named *Nancy* that could turn on a dime, and therefore win races against Crawford Brown's *Popeye*, a high speed torpedo-shaped inboard.[10]

Dottie Scullin remembers a trip through the

Minto at the Regatta. Originally published by the Roy Studio of Peterborough. *Courtesy David Card Collection.*

Trent and Rideau canals to Ottawa in the *The Elizabeth*, built by the Lakefield Canoe Company. Her father had the temerity and skill to cut into the boat's mahogany bow to make extra seating for the lengthy trip. *The Elizabeth* was 28 feet long and 4 feet wide but had only an 18 inch draft, surely an advantage in Stony Lake waters.[11]

The "D.P." or disappearing-propeller boat had a similar advantage, "...because its propeller has a skeg underneath which retracts if it hits a shoal, swinging the propeller shaft up into a metal box near the rear of the craft. The D.P. is just a nice, homey, comfortable, large-sized rowboat, with a presumably docile and quietly behaved engine in its midriff. However, we are doubtful if we have ever seen so small an engine that can throw around quite so much oil and grease and gasoline."[12] One wonders if present-day owners of a dispro, Jane and Jack Matthews, Jill and Grant Farrow and Colin Kinnear have similar problems. In attempting to restore a 1919 dispro with a 2 h.p. Kingfisher engine, Grant has paid more for a muffler than he did for the boat and the engine together.

The Gouinlocks had several dispros, the last named the *Lily Pad* because its lapstreak hull was painted light green inside and dark green outside. With low fuel consumption, it was used all during the Second World War, kept functioning by the mechanical skills of Uncle James Muir. Finally, the oak hull rotted out and the engine was given to Frank Gillespie.

Don Corner's uncle worked at the Greavette boat works in Port Carling and helped build 1800 dispros until they were discontinued in 1958. One boat signed with his name still operates on Clear Lake.

Other families had unpretentious craft. Art and Tom Cole remember that Aunt Freda's *Sputter* "...an old clinker–built sailing dinghy which had been converted to power by installation of a two-cylinder St. Lawrence gasoline

A group of Veterans attending a reunion in 1946, shown in the dispro *Lily Pad*. Left to right: Bill Phair R.C.A.M.C.; Gord Cardy R.C.A.; Jack Gouinlock R.C.A.F.; Frank Hazlewood R.C.A.S.C.; Mick Phair R.C.A.; Ralph Hunter R.C.O.C. *Courtesy Jack Gouinlock.*

engine. Because Grandfather disapproved of powerboats, Freda was not allowed to moor it by the boathouse dock but kept it pulled part way up on the sand farther along the shore, tied to a stump. That boat and engine were extraordinarily durable, possibly because they were never operated by anyone except Aunt Freda [Cole] or Aunt Tave [Cole], who kept things going with the aid of hairpins, vaseline and Frank Gillespie. On one occasion the coils had to be dried out in the wood stove oven. They were then replaced in the engine and away she went."

Today Blair Mackenzie wonders what his grandparents would think of his battered aluminum runabout, which "...they would rightly consider as more a floating farm pickup truck than a proper boat."

Even these little craft are remembered with affection. Michael Allen hopes to restore a 1.6 h.p Viking engine that he was given by Aileen Grier, his former neighbour in Cassidy Bay. He loved the little dory and its engine when he was a child. He also recalls the thrill of being asked to run his Uncle Keith Russell's launch *Whirl-*

larger edition, could plane even when carrying several passengers. The last *Water Baby*, powered by a Chevrolet engine, had a home-designed V-drive and competed successfully in regattas in the '30s."

After the Second World War, the motor boat races were included in the Juniper regatta, as the *Globe and Mail* recounts in 1948: "The Stony Lake Power Boat championship race was postponed until Monday due to difficulties with one of the 225 class hydroplanes which sank at its moorings. The race, late in the afternoon, was won by Lyman Crawford-Brown in *Falcon*. This boat has a 160 h.p. engine and is the 3 point suspension 225 type. It was clocked at 33.2 m.p.h. in the straightaway. Dr. Stanley Braund driving the *Eight Ball* was second. He had a severe handicap due to several reasons. Firstly, his boat sank at her moorings and, secondly, his motor, a new 175 h.p. monster, was only installed prior to the race and was not tuned up."

John Brewin remarks: "Despite the nearly universal view that motorboats races had no place at a Juniper Regatta, the powerboat races were a sight to behold, careening around Elephant Rock before heading toward Viamede."

But for other Stony Lakers, motorboats were a challenge. Don Cameron recalls their 16 foot runabout with a 9.8 h.p. engine: "This was a large machine for that time and quite difficult to master. I remember Grandfather Livingstone, who had only one eye, and was quite a big man, starting this contrary machine and terrifying all aboard with his efforts. He stood in the back of the boat, wrapped the starting cord around the flywheel, and then vigorously pulled the rope. The machine started with a surge, (there were no gears or neutral) knocking him off balance. With no hand on the steering handle, the motor started to twist, sending the boat back towards the shore. After that, Grandfather was persuaded to let younger members of the

Seated beside the 2-cylinder engine of her boat, *Sputter*, is Alfreda Cooper Cole, lecturer in French, and a mechanic par excellence. *Courtesy Art Cole Collection.*

wego back and forth across the lake to create wake. The Grumman Goose aircraft Keith was piloting could not take off in a flat calm.

One talented Stony Laker, George Guillet, designed and built his own boats, all named *Water Baby*. His daughter, Marilyn Ott writes: "The first was just a small punt used mainly for sailing, but *Water Baby II* was a sizeable outboard. A Caille engine with an almost horizontal drive shaft powered *Water Baby III*, a sturdy punt. With rocks in its bow it could travel through thin ice. To get through weeds the operator just elevated the propeller shaft and the weeds were flung off into the air. *Water Baby IV* was a 1927 'speed' boat designed with a step in the stern to give an air cushion. Skimming over the water, it won motor boat races in regattas. *Water Baby V*, a family learn how to operate the motorboat."

When Robin Merry acquired a new outboard, he drove over from Mackenzie Bay to 'Nakemi' for a neighbourly visit. Michael Allen remembers Robin driving frantically around Cassidy Bay calling out, "How do you stop it?"

Lately, some Stony Lakers, including Harriet Fear, Colin Kinnear, Heather and Don Elliott, John Jones and Jill and Grant Farrow have acquired antique launches which, unlike the noisy "cigarette boats" roaring from Young's Point to Boschink and back and the irritating jet-skis buzzing into the back bays, ply the waters with dignity and grace.

Sailing, in boats large and small, has long been a part of the Stony Lake story. Few people know that the hull of a 60 foot sailing craft, the *Mull*, lies scuttled on the lake bottom behind the Collins Island, her cabin removed for use as a home on the shore. Another unusual craft anchored at McCracken's was a Dutch canal boat given to Basil Hall by the grateful Dutch people after World War II. With carved sides and red sails, she was a handsome sight, but it took a hurricane to move her, and she leaked so much that she had to be caulked with rolls of toilet paper.

Other long-gone sailing craft live on in the hearts of their owners. "For the Knapman family, Stony was sailing," writes Dottie Drake. "Once arrived, the food put in the icebox, the kitchen pump primed, all hands tackled the launch of the *Cygnet*. Block and tackle on pine trees, planks under her dolly wheels and she emerged from under the cottage to be placed in her position of honour at the front dock. She was daily transport to Mount Julian for supplies, to visit friends or to explore and picnic. The soft slap of the waves on a wooden hull is still my favourite sound. A less happy sound was the grind of the centreboard on a lurking rock. Several skippers have boasted about knowing every rock, only to land hard aground."

A 1906 Roy photograph on the Drake's verandah shows a Juniper sailing race with three Lake Ontario 16s, one 18 ft. sloop and nine 14 ft. catboats. In those days there were no strict classes. In 1906, Harold "Keeler" Knapman's father brought the *Cygnet*, one of the 16s, from Toronto, where these boats were very popular. They varied in length from 24 to 28 feet but all were 16 ft. on the waterline. Keeler and Jack Matthews' father, Gordon, often sailed the *Cygnet* as youngsters. Then Gordon Matthews asked Keeler to design a boat like her, and Frank Gillespie of the Peterborough Canoe Company built *Skidley* in 1922.

Christie Bentham tells *Spree*'s story: "*Spree* was built in the winter of 1944–45 for my father by his friend, Keeler Knapman. In the fall Keeler carefully measured his own boat, the *Cygnet*, built in 1903, and his wife Berenice wrote the measurements on a brown paper bag. Such were *Spree*'s plans. All winter she grew in Keeler's barn in Picton, with neighbours constantly dropping in to gawk and give advice. Berenice used to say that any profit from the venture was dissipated in the countless cups of coffee she provided for *Spree*'s visitors. People ask how *Spree* got her

Mull with lots of canvas. *Courtesy Collins Family Collection.*

Catboats in the 1930s. *Courtesy David Card Collection.*

name and her sail marking, a cocktail glass. I don't know why Dad chose the martini glass, but I guess I understand the name. Our dictionary says 'spree' is derived from the Irish word for 'spirit' and means a carefree, lively frolic. She is indeed the spirit of our island, and, for me, of all Stony Lake."

Gull was originally a shorter sloop with a bowsprit, owned by Tom Van Natta, and often sailed by Fred Brooks-Hill. In the 1940s, Keeler removed the bowsprit and lengthened the boat to 26 ft. for Harry Huff. *Gull* was recently given to the Hunt family by their uncle, Ken Allen, who had restored both the *Spree* and the *Gull.*

Another venerable boat on Stony Lake is the Ryder's *Yankee,* a Chesapeake 20. Robbie Willoughby's *Pixie,* of the same class, was sold to the Teamerson family and afterwards to Peter Fisher, who attempted to restore her, but her elderly planking defeated him.

The 14 ft. catboat was a means of transportation, especially during wartime gas rationing. Frank Crouse recalls frequently returning home late because the wind dropped. John Brewin writes about the family catboat: "The Brewins were avid sailors and won their share of silverware by crafty seamanship and significant handicaps. They did not exhibit a smiliar propensity for fine-tuning their boats. Andy could sail through a tornado. When a thunderstorm hit, he was often the only boat left standing when the storm passed on towards Upper Stoney."

In 1922, Granny [Mildred] Cumberland told her family that she had a secret which was not revealed until the spring when they arrived at the cottage to find a 14 ft. catboat, subsequently named *Secret.* The Wotherspoon family sailed it for years before it went to the Townsends. From there it went to Tam Matthews who has had a great sailing record, and finally to Hugh Drake and total restoration.

A recent catboat revival, spearheaded by Hugh Drake, has given us not only annual Aykroyd catboat regattas but also the joy of seeing one or two of these graceful craft on the lake on any good sailing day. Although the *Oriole* has survived, other catboats have not been restored. Tony Lockhart's marconi-rigged *Calypso* was known as the "Collapso" because it dumped frequently. Kathy Hooke's *Green Frog* was so named because of its colour, and Dottie Scullin's was the *Flying Sieve* for obvious reasons.

The catboats were slowly displaced by the

International 14s, which George Cook helped design. "After the war he became the catalyst for the rapid growth of the class on Stony Lake, with as many as 15 to 20 boats on the starting line. Robin and I bought *Flame* from Ted Welsh about 1947," wrote Jim Collins. "We inadvertently burned it a short time later!" Asked how this happened, Jim said a cigarette ignited the varnish remover used on the hull. The shed burned to the ground. Fred Brooks-Hill bought three Internationals, one for himself, one for Heather and one for Rick.

Judy Finch recalls: "In 1951, my dad, Ken Slater, and Karl Duffus organized the Canadian Dinghy Association (CDA) regatta at Stony. One hundred 14 foot International dinghies came from various yacht clubs in Canada. To have dock space for all these boats, sections of the old causeway at Chemong were towed to Stony. A letter from the President of the Cottagers' Association to prospective donors tells the story. Dad and George Cook heard that the old floating bridge was being broken up to be sold. They hurried over, and found a section about 115 feet long. It was in splendid condition but it drew a lot of water. They made a deal for it,

finally getting it for $200. Then they pitched a tent on it and rigged up a place for a fire.

"It must have made a strange sight, sloshing out across the lake with two borrowed outboard motors mounted astern. If you have ever tried to propel a 20-foot raft in a stiff breeze, you can guess the determination and skill it required to get this ungainly floating dock through the zig-zag channels and into the locks. After two days and two nights, the weird object rounded Hurricane Point and headed for Juniper Island, where the docks were used for the junior sailing program for the next 34 years."

The International regatta was a great success and the CDA was held at Stony again in 1984 and 1985. Sailing Internationals was energetic; at times the Smith brothers hiked so hard to keep their craft upright that they were in danger of losing their pants!

Another class of boats which appeared at Stony in the '50s and '60s were scows with double rudders and bilge boards rather than centreboards, flat bottoms and a freeboard of 12 inches. *Bootlegger* was owned by Gordon Matthews, *Cutty Sark* by Sir Ellsworth Flavelle, *Kestrel* by Lyman Crawford-Brown and *Habitant* by Art Teamerson Sr.

To keep her from excess speeds, Jim Collins claimed that he tied a bucket under *Kestrel's* bottom. Sailing solo, Bob Teamerson was caught in a storm in *Habitant* and barreled down the entire length of the lake before finding a sheltered cove.

Alan Weatherstone was always tinkering and experimenting with his 24 ft. scow *Mimi*. His daughter, Jennifer, remembers telling her father that the boat was actually going sideways in a race. "Well, my dear," he replied, "I just pulled the leeboards up too much."

Races were rather informal in the 1940s. David Smith would put a shotgun in his dinghy, sail to Juniper and try to find someone to fire the gun, plus someone to crew. The triangular

Gull, Skidley and *Spree*. Designed before 1900, they are still sailing in the new millenium. *Courtesy Martha Hunt Collection.*

Top: Lyman Crawford-Brown's *Bluebird* towing sailboats to Chemong in 1949. *Katharine Hooke Collection.*
Bottom: Once in the lock, how do we get out? *Courtesy Katharine Hooke Collection.*

course was usually Juniper-Viamede-black buoy off 'Anchorage' then back to Juniper. Rounding the buoys port or starboard was the only variation. Channel markers were used as buoys with occasional problems with nearby rocks. Later, Jack Guillet and Art Teamerson Sr. were patient starters, enduring long afternoons on the Juniper wharf in the hot sun, necessitated by the practice of starting the slower boats long before the faster ones. Michael Allen

hoped for a win when he was allowed to start an hour early in their 16 ft. dinghy, dubbed the *PC* for "Pregnant Cow" by his scornful uncle. "I got about as far as 'Plum Pudding' when the other boats caught up to me," he says. Derry Smith recalls crewing for Gary Braund in a Cruising Race. By the time they arrived at the turning mark in Clear Lake, the committee boat had left in order to be at the finish line for timing the lead boats.

The Cottagers' Association used to run the races, but in 1947 a group of young people drew up a constitution for the Stony Lake Yacht Club. Fees were $2.00 a year and it cost $1.00 to register a boat. David Smith was the first Commodore. That group did not continue and in 1951 the Stony Lake Yacht Club was formed, with Ken Slater as first Commodore, to take over the regatta, sailing races and motorboat races. In 1976, the club was incorporated, with the first directors being John Fisher, Marion Collins and Kenzie Dickson, the purpose of the club being "to maintain a yacht club and tennis club."

One of the sailors' great events was the annual tow to Chemong, reviving an older tradition when a logging boat was used to tow boats from Chemong to Stony in the '20s and '30s. In the '50s, sailboats of various sizes assembled at Juniper at 7:30 a.m. Saturday and were placed in long tows with scows in front and dinghys at the rear. Lyman Crawford Brown, Leo Dorfman and Dr. Stanley Braund valiantly supplied the tow boats. In addition to the fun of racing and congregating at the Matthews' cottage at Chemong, it was a challenge to manoeuvre one's boat to avoid the cascade of water erupting from the old locks. A comfort stop was provided by slowing the tow in the middle of the lake to allow the boys to jump into the water on one side of the boats and the girls on the other.

A 1960 article by Dick Faryon in the *Peterborough Examiner* noted: "Tom Guillet of the

Stony Lake Yacht Club is building small prams for learning sailors, a worthwhile endeavour." Tom built twelve 10 ft. fibreglass boats, sloop rigged marconi, and *very* tippy. Joan Townsend was the first instructor, her chief qualification, according to Joan, being that her parents had never allowed her to accept a tow to the races, so she had to sail. Young sailors were also encouraged by the Spoon Races for skippers and crew 18 and under. The spoons were originally donated in memory of David Russell, then afterwards by Frank Crouse because, "his best memories were of the Spoon Races."

Then there were the Egg Cup races, impromptu challenge races with a magnificently battered egg cup as the trophy. These races were revived in 1999 and should continue into the millennium.

Egg Cup Rules:

Rule 1 Races can be held any time and place at the convenience of entrants. They, the Races, can be held over any course and no person can be stopped from entering.

Rule 2 To get up a Race, all that is needed is a challenger.

Rule 3 A defender cannot refuse a reasonable challenge. If he tries, he forfeits possession.

Rule 4 Any *Person* winning egg cup *nine* (9) times in *succession* can have the darn thing.

Rule 5 Races should be held fairly according to the sailing conscience (if any) of the individuals and no one is to be disqualified unless he believes himself guilty of fouling or unfairness. *Note: if entrants have no 'sailing conscience' the race is no good and if the race is sailed with strict rules it loses half the fun. Hence, leave it, the Race, in the hands of conscience. If there is no such thing, it's just too bad.*

Rule 6 This cup is for any boats whatsoever and the races should be arranged (as to handicaps, etc.) by the contestants. It is, however, primarily for 14 ft Dinghies.

Rule 7 It is the defender's moral duty to keep this cup in a conspicuous place (along with these rules) so that others may easily challenge him. *Note: If defender has no morals may this rule haunt his conscience, (if any) and if none of the latter, "nuts" to him.*

Rule 8 The rules along with a list of the winners' names should be kept with the cup.

Rule 9 THESE RULES MUST NOT BE ALTERED IN ANY RESPECT. Being a true and faithful copy of the 1931 rules.

Note: Original rules are on Horseshoe Island West.

Y-flyers came on the lake in the 1950s, and Flying Scots were introduced by Kenzie Dickson and Robin Collins in 1967. Stony Lake

Can boating be much simpler? Can you identify boy, dog or date? *Courtesy Katharine Hooke Collection.*

had at one time 16 Scots participating in races and has hosted several Scot regattas.

From Stony Lake have come several Olympic sailors: Tam Matthews in 470s and Brian and David Sweeney in Tornados. In recent years, the Stony Yacht Club has placed third out of 33 clubs in Ontario participating in junior racing. In 1999, a total of 113 juniors participated in 437 student weeks of sailing instruction.

The sailing world really took to the Laser and over 100 are said to be on the lake. The Junior Yacht Club now uses Laser IIs and Echoes for instruction and competition. Sailboards occasionally appear like butterflies on the water and catamarans zoom by in a strong wind. In 1972, Peter Chittick produced an issue of the *Stony Lake News* describing a race in Flippers between junior sailors and their parents. Peter had heard unfavourable comments from some of the instructors about "...the ability, mobility and even dependability of the parents' sailing capability." The junior team was composed of some of the instructors and top juniors, plus "...a ringer from the RCYC named Matthews—if he can get to the lake on time." Needless to say, the junior team handily defeated the seniors.

A part of sailing no longer with us is night sailing—a bright moon and a flashlight were all that was needed for an evening of sheer delight, the empty lake sparkling, the islands silhouetted, and the stars by the millions to keep you company. Even now the Big Dipper pours its magic onto our tallest pines and will charm future generations as it has charmed the past.

Nine

HAVING FUN

FOR MORE than a century Juniper Island has been a centre for a variety of organized recreational activities, something for all ages. Sparked by the enthusiasm for canoeing after the American Canoe Association Meet at Stony in 1883, regattas became a regular occurrence at Juniper. Large steamboats brought crowds from Lakefield and Peterborough; paddlers, rowers and swimmers crowded the docks. Cruisers and launches moored by Big and Little Otter while the regatta executive ran the races from the floating dock. The Cottagers' Association program for the 1909 regatta lists sailing, paddling, swimming, rowing and launch races. The prizes varied, with Ernie Brownscombe winning first prize in the canoe sailing race in 1919—an oiled raincoat.

The first children's regatta at Juniper was in 1926. During the Second World War, the official regatta was discontinued and so a group of teenagers ran a regatta on their own. There also were private regattas, such as those at 'Rasquelle' and Collins Island, as well as at McCracken's Landing and Viamede. The tradition of the Juniper regatta continues. As a girl, Marilyn Ott won the junior championship, and her son Keith won it thirty years later. Marian Teamerson recalls that when Art and Will Bentham were "young," maybe 32,

and in a tandem race some years ago, Will accidentally hit Art with his paddle and knocked him backwards into the water. He didn't know that Art was out of the canoe, and continued down the course alone, berating his teammate for not paddling enough and not steering at all. Regattas today still provide thrills, spills and laughs as well as the thrill of competition.

A long distance competitive swim is first mentioned in the 1923 program, with boxes of chocolates as prizes. The 1925 race was won by Don Fitzgerald even though he had just finished paddling the long distance race around Juniper Island, while Ann Van Natta came fourth, the first woman ever to swim the course.

In 1960, the Mile Swim was started again by Gord Minty and Bill Lech, whose father Cyril had organized earlier swims.[1] The course for the swim is from the Juniper dock to Lech Island. While in the early years there were about 50 entrants, in 1999 there were 129, ranging in age from 5 to 80. As each swimmer has an accompanying skiff, canoe or kayak, a mini-evacuation appears to be taking place each Civic holiday Sunday morning.

At the awards presentation held in the pavilion following the race every finisher gets a crest, and the winners receive prizes. There

Top: America Canoe Association Regatta, 1883 or 1887. *Courtesy Barbara Harris Collection.*
Bottom: Watching the 1887 Regatta—same old rocks, different clothes. *George Douglas Collection, courtesy Katharine Hooke.*

is even a special Granny trophy, made of tin cans, for the fastest grandmother in the swim. The Corner trophies are presented to the youngest boy and girl to finish the race. In 1981, Kathy Richardson set a course record of 13:50, a record that still holds.

Today the annual event, known as the William Lech Memorial Swim, is a memorial to Bill Lech who organized the swim for 32 years until his death in 1992. Now the Corner and Lech families, along with their friends and guests, act as timers, runners and recorders. Over the years the weatherman has been kind to the Mile Swim. Only once has it rained, and the paddlers found themselves as wet as the swimmers, a remarkable record for forty years.

Dances and parties were very much part of the social scene. An effusive three-column account in the *Peterborough Examiner* of August 18, 1905 describes an "At Home" hosted at the Juniper pavilion by the Hon. James R. and Mrs. Stratton of 'Strathbormond': "A charming sight met the eyes of the Peterborough guests who arrived about eight o'clock on the steamer *Stoney Lake*. Streamers and flags from J.J. Turner & Sons were strung across the promenade in front of the pavilion, a large 'Welcome'sign hung above the entrance, and the countless coloured lights provided many-hued reflections which danced in the ripple of the waters.

"The 57th Regiment Band furnished exquisite music at Lakefield, on the trip up the lake, and in the pavilion for dancing, which was interspersed with a number of vocal solos accompanied with sympathetic taste by Miss Alice Rogers.

"The hostess who wore a charming gown of pale blue embroidered muslin, with lace collar, and carried a bouquet of white asters, received upon a raised platform over which was hung a floral decoration in the form of a canoe banked with roses and ferns. Delightful refreshments were catered by Mr. Long who excelled himself in the completeness of his arrangements and the daintiness of the menu.

"After three cheers for Mr. and Mrs. Stratton, the Peterborough guests departed on the steamer about twelve o'clock and after a perfect trip in the glorious moonlight, boarded the special train which was waiting at Lakefield and reached home with delightful recollections of one of the most elaborate and social reunions which Stony Lake has ever witnessed."

The Stratton invitation. *Courtesy Connie Wahl Collection.*

Before the First World War, there were impromptu dances in the pavilion almost every evening, with a wind-up victrola or someone playing a piano. The *Evening Review* in 1907 reports: "...the Juniper Island pavilion, the delight of the youth and maidens, is again open for the season. On Saturday evening the usual number was attracted to that popular spot, where music was provided by some of the young people." Another article in the *Peterborough Examiner* describes musical evenings at the turn of the century:

Mile swimmers take off from Juniper. *Courtesy Mary Jane Dickson Collection.*

Ferdy Mowry's orchestra, 1931, possibly photographed near McCracken's Landing. *Courtesy Marni Young Collection.*

"...the girls were abundantly capable of taking part in a crowd which made its own fun in its own way. Several of them could take a turn at the piano with grace and musicianly skill. None was more constantly in demand than Helen Hall, of the jolly houseful, which constantly summered each year at the island of her father, Sheriff Hall. Who that heard the 'Washington Post' or 'At a Georgia Camp-Meetin,' with its cake-walk syncopation, as they bounced from the fingers of Helen Hall and ricocheted across the water, will ever forget the verve and compelling rhythms of the one-steps, two-steps, and marches? Breathes there a man with soul so dead that his pulse-beat will not be quickened by memories of 'the Teddy Bears' Picnic' or 'Whistling Rufus'?"[2]

There were also cottage parties where no imported musicians were necessary. As Richard Choate writes: "The Echo Banjo club was equally at home at a hilltop campfire musicale, a shore service or an impromptu concert, anywhere, anytime. A further instrumental novelty was introduced in the form of a tiny melodeon, which could be carried about in a skiff. The 'organist' was really hot as he pumped 'Hot Time in the Old Time' from the innards of his lilliputian instrument."[3]

The annual summer masquerade was an important event on the adult social calendar, and "Granny Fairbairn made a convincing and imposing Queen Victoria with her tiara, fan, flowing cape, sash and various decorations," writes Blair Mackenzie. Other participants were three men dressed as Faith, Hope and Charity—Hope being pregnant. Jack and Flo Ryder were Adam and Eve, and Jim Lockhart, who had lost his leg in the First World War, was Long John Silver. One year, a corn cob costume of yellow crepe paper disintegrated in the rain; another year, the best carving knife in the cottage was lost in the lake by a would-be pirate. One cottager, now a senior, went to his first masquerade in a basket—as Moses in the bulrushes.

In later years square dancing, sometimes in bare feet, was fun for both adults and teenagers. Ruth Allen recruited Norm Bolton, an accomplished local fiddler, to provide the music. Ruth's son Michael recalls his fascination with Norm's ability to retain a lengthy ash at the end of his cigarette until it fell into the opening of his violin. Jim Byrne, who called for square dances at Peterborough Collegiate in the late 1940s, was persuaded by Kathy Hooke to call and instruct the youngsters. Today, the Wednesday square dances, with music from the now famous Leahys who live near Lakefield and calling by Scott Teamerson,

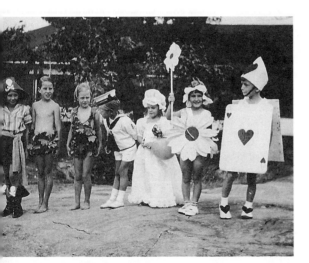

Clockwise from top left: The masquerade, 1936, an important event for the younger set as well, left to right: Robin McGraw, Araby Lockhart, Mary Hope, Tony Lockhart, Jeannie Bennett and Jim Land, 1936. *Courtesy Nancy Watson Collection*; Cousins celebrate the masquerade in 1959. Left to right: Hilary, Parker, Becca and Peter Collins; Collin Smith; Kevin Smith. *Courtesy Mary Jane Dickson Collection*; Mary and Jim Gouinlock, 1924. *Courtesy Jack Gouinlock Collection*; Winner of the 1922 Boat Flotilla Contest with Mary Gouinlock as the Queen of Sheba, Lew Thomas and Charlie Fountain. *Jack Gouinlock collection*; Masquerade, early 1900s. Faith, Hope & Charity with Bill Hamilton, as a pregnant Hope and Tom Barrie as Charity. Can you identify Faith? *Courtesy Jane McMyn Collection*; Alice Thomas (a Sandhaven guest) as a firefly at the 1924 masquerade. *Courtesy Jack Gouinlock Collection*.

Stony Lake Follies in mid-song, 1970. Left to right: Felix Gray, Mabel Grant, Winnie Weatherstone, Jack Guillet, Gerry Loweth, Christie Bentham. *Courtesy Jill Farrow Collection.*

Scott Handler and Bronwyn Perks, are enjoyed by parents and children alike. The masquerade, convened by Carol Corner, is now an annual delight for small children and their parents. A recent masquerade was described by Dianne Ferguson in the 1998 Fall edition of *The Islander:* "A wonderful parade of princesses and creatures had a grand march past the judges. Among those participants were a dragonfly, a bumblebee, a dashing young pirate and a soccer team combining families. Everyone went home a winner receiving prizes and ribbons in various categories."

In 1970, the Stony Lake Follies, directed by Araby Lockhart, involved a large cast of cottagers in skits and songs. Nowadays, the pavilion is home to the Friday night movies where the sound track is punctuated with loud mosquito-slapping from the audience, and the screen is sometimes a backdrop for the antics of bats.

Also in the pavilion, an enthusiastic group striving to keep fit during the summer enjoy fitness classes three times a week. A lending library organized by Joanne Ling and Sue Dutton is located in a room in the Juniper store, improving on a start made years ago by Cephas Guillet. All day long there are swimming classes, from Parents and Tots to Royal Life Saving; in the afternoons are the Safe Boating courses and canoeing lessons. On Canada Day weekend a community barbeque traditionally opens the season, while the Yacht club dinner closes it on Labour Day weekend.

Stony Lake has always had a strong tradition in the visual arts. Research historian Edwin C. Guillet knew of an early painter named Thomas Workman, who travelled about Ontario making paintings and selling them to nearby residents. His painting of Perry's Creek dates from 1895. Even earlier, from 1836 to 1894, Catharine Parr Traill published books with beautiful illustrations of local plants and flowers. Other artists enjoyed Stony Lake in the past, including William Cruickshank (1848–1922) whose sketches include fishing camps and canoeing expeditions.[4] Before the Second World War, Corinne Ringel Bailey and her husband Bill carried on their art careers in a studio near their cottage on the south shore.

A letter written in 1923 by the Bailey's maid

Daisy was found recently in the cottage wall: "Just a few lines to let you know I am alive and kicking and I hope you are the same. well I have put in one week. I can't say I am in love with the lakes. The people are very nice to work for...they seem to appreciate everything you do for them but I don't think that one will get me up here again. It is lovely for people that don't have to work. They can go and have a good time but if you come to work that is all they want you for.

"They have all gone off for a picnic and let me here with the kid...he is a dear little fellow but inclined to be spoiled. They tell me they leave him to me to make him mind. It is nice to leave your kiddie to somebody else to train. I would not like to leave mine to anyone if I had any but, of course, they are too busy making money. They are both artists and they say they don't have to go after work, it come to them. They seem to take it for granted that I will go back to Cleveland with them. Of course the housework is not much but they certainly eat and make quite a bit of washing. I seem to have got very easy back to cooking...they have told me they have enjoyed the meals. We have had company once and I have been left with the boy three times so you see, they are having a good time."[5]

Probably many of the servants working for families on the lake in earlier times had similar reservations about cottage living.

Another artist was Sam Hunter (1858–1939), the foremost political cartoonist of his day, whose work was published in four Toronto newspapers. He spent three months each summer at Stony exploring nature and sketching birds. His property on the McCracken's shore, 'Pepacton', became a gathering place for artists, writers and musicians who stayed in a large tent by the shore. Carol Winter recalls Stella Grier giving art lessons in the 1950s.[6]

Westel Willoughby's story included his memories of Fred Craig, noted especially for his watercolours and drawings of the steamers, the *Islinda* and *Stoney Lake*, published in *By the Sound of her Whistle* in 1966. For eight winters, a tiny cabin on the shore near Craig Island was both his living quarters and artist's studio. A small wood stove provided the only heat, its burned-out side showing a direct view of the flames only a few feet from Fred's head as he slept. "I have a genie that keeps me young—it isn't just the lake water here," he said.

The Art Festival, started in 1992, initiated by the vision of Andrew Ross and supported by the help of several enthusiastic volunteers, continues the artistic tradition. A success right from the beginning, the festival began with 20 artists and a viewing audience of over 600. By 1999, at the 8th annual festival, there were 38 exhibitors with a wide variety of paintings, drawings, sculptures and photographs. It is now held under the aegis of the Cottagers' Association, which receives a percentage of the sales. The show is juried and hung on Saturday morning, the second weekend in August, then opens with an early evening reception with cash bar and hors d'oeuvres provided by community cooks. The show is open all day Sunday for viewing and sales. The deep love for Stony Lake, shared by many, is reflected in the creativity of the artists and the enthusiasm of the volunteers.

In the early fifties, a new yacht club, evolving out of a more loosely organized group of ardent sailors, was formed. The 1952 "Stony Lake Programme of Events" provides this background: "The Stony Lake Yacht Club promotes and supervises recreational activities in the Stony Lake area, and the supervision and operation of the Yacht Club building on Juniper Island is the responsibility of the Yacht Club Organization.

"The furthering of the sport of sail boat racing and motor boat racing requires time and effort on the part of Yacht Club officials and, in addition to these activities, the Yacht Club has undertaken to organize and run the regattas at Juniper Island in August which include paddling and swimming events for contestants of all ages, particularly the younger residents and their visitors.

"All these heavy responsibilities have been carried on for many years by the former Aquatic Association and the present Yacht Club was formed in the year 1951 to succeed the Aquatic Association."

Over the past half century, the Yacht Club concentrated on sailing instruction and races with great success having turned the responsibility of the annual regatta over to the Cottagers' Association. Now in the 21st century, the junior sailing program involves more than 100 students and 12 certified instructors, with much hard work and organization provided by the executive. Two tennis courts are busy all day with play, clinics, round robins and tournaments. For these courts, appreciation goes to Peter Newton and Kenzie Dickson for their foresight and hard work in 1976–77 in organizing the construction of the courts. Could there be any other courts in the world where play is interrupted by gambolling red squirrels intent on mating? Players sometimes stop to decipher birdcalls. "Was that the osprey?" "No, that's a kingfisher's rattle." Ants, of course, are a problem for the court surface, and caterpillars can be slippery when squished; an errant ball may land in a tree branch or even in the lake, altogether creating an unique atmosphere for a game.

Other organized activities take place in different locations as part of the Cottagers' Association community. The Nature Walks, led by cottagers knowledgeable in geology, bird and plant life, and forestry are held at various properties around the lake. The Annual Ladies' Potluck Luncheon hosted by different cottagers is an opportunity for conversation and a fund-raiser for the Association.

In the 1950s and 60s, Alma Guillet taught crafts, first at 'Westaway' and later at different cottages. Known indelicately to some as "The Hookers," the women learned everything from bookbinding to drying and pressing flowers to glovemaking, (pronounced without the 'g' by some wags.) The Reeds remember that when it was their mother's turn to host the craft class, she would use her best china and iron the tea napkins with an iron heated on the wood stove.

A history of the craft class was written in 1980 by Elizabeth (Buell) Reed for David Anderson's archival research project: "During World War II the ladies of Stony Lake wanted to help the Peterborough Red Cross during the summers. The Red Cross asked us to make pyjamas for boys, size 12. These were turned out by the dozens!

"When the war was over, it seemed a shame to discontinue the meetings, which we had enjoyed, so Mrs. Cephas Guillet, who had long been teaching arts and crafts in the Riverside Church building in New York City, asked us to come to their house on Horseshoe Island on Wednesdays. We were to bring a sandwich for our lunch, during which Mrs. Guillet always served hot tea and her own cookies or the like.[7]

"We worked on the porch which ran along the south and east sides of the old house, and we learned one craft after another. How fortunate we were to learn, at no cost to us save the modest cost for materials that Mrs. G. had brought with her from New York—special paper, leather, powders for stencilling (trays and chairs), tools for bookbinding, materials for chair caning, etc. We carried home each object we'd made, if not proudly then thinking, "it's a poor thing, but mine own." Some actually went on and, with practice, turned out beautiful things. Mrs. Weatherstone likes to tell how she worked painstakingly to make a pair of long white gloves, only to discover later that they were both for the same hand."

Started in 1981 by Wil Tranter, the Stony Lake Triathlon is unusual in that paddling, not swimming, is the first section. The distances are 7 km. pairs paddling or solo kayaking, 30 km. cycling and 7 km. running. In 1999, some participants also swam in a quadrathlon. The present course is "out and back" centred at Crowe's Landing, and also includes a 200 metre portage. The Triathlon has been sponsored by six different firms over the years and is run by about 45 volunteers, some of whom have helped every year.

Fishing has been a mainstay of the Stony Lake area seemingly forever. Natives and early settlers fished for sustenance, but enjoyed the sport. An early settler, Colonel Strickland wrote: "I camped on an island in Stony Lake for a few days in 1849 when one morning between breakfast and dinner time my two eldest sons and myself caught with our trolling lines 35 salmon-trout, 8 maskinonge and several large lake bass, the total weight of which amounted to 473 pounds."[8]

With this sort of success, sport fishing soon became popular as Richard Choate's account in the *Peterborough Examiner* shows. "At the turn of the century in October a party was organized to fish for salmon trout up near the head of Stony Lake. These fish which vanished later were then plentiful and were caught in the fall. Average weight was about seventeen pounds. The use of seine nets was then permitted. The salmon came to the shores in two runs each night, at midnight and about 4 a.m. Making the nocturnal trips to the salmon beds, the tiny 18 ft. steam-powered *Lily* usually towed a skiff for use at the nets. At about 2 a.m. tea was made for the party, heating the water with the boat's steam jet. They returned to Peterborough with a good catch of these excellent fish and had a novel experience of running through a snowstorm on Clear Lake on the way home."

The 'Shanty' log for August 8, 1904

records: "Fishing at Burleigh the result of which was thirty bass and two lunge." In those days fishing was necessary for food as well as fun. Later in the log, Art Cole says, "I think canoe trips and fishing were very high on the 'I like to do' list." Velma Osborne recalls: "My sister and I often paddled Dad around the islands as he trolled. He told us it was impossible to catch any fish with us singing and laughing so loudly; however, after he snagged a beautiful muskie one evening he had to admit we were great guides and brought him good luck." Joyce Corner describes fishing with her grandfather, who used no fishing rod but a board with a heavy cord which he held in his mouth as he paddled. "We always came home with a muskie well over the size of a keeper. When I see the modern trolling motors and the fish finders I think how much these fishermen of today are missing." Sonny Cook remembers catching sunfish with a stick, string, safety pin and bacon. Tim Sherin's grandfather used to head out to fish when he spied the *Islinda* approaching with his guests. He knew he could catch dinner before the guests set foot on the dock. Blair Mackenzie adds this modern observation: "Today's fishermen will tell you of herons that have come to know they can find an easy dinner by squawking at a nearby fishing boat and waiting for something to be tossed their way."

Janet Smith tells an amusing fish story. George Greening, Fred Collins' brother-in-law, was salmon fishing in New Brunswick many years ago. He sent a large salmon, packed in dry ice, to his family at Stony Lake. Fred, who was there when it was delivered, borrowed it for a while. It was market day. "We all got in the boat with our 5 h.p. motor on the stern. The salmon was carefully attached to Dad's fishing line. As we passed 'Shota', into the water went the salmon, and as we got close to shore, he made a great play at landing it. When we got to McCracken's, he went to Jack Hunter, a fishing guide, to ask him to identify the fish. Sixty seconds later the boat was surrounded. Ten minutes later 'Shota' was surrounded. The story of the landlocked salmon made the international news in no time!"

Recently, an avid fisherman attempting to remove the lure from a large muskie was himself painfully snagged with three hooks imbedded in his hand. When his rescuer cut the hooks with steel cutters, the conservation-minded fisherman asked him to resuscitate the fish before putting it back in the water.

Excursion trips on the *Islinda* or *Stoney Lake* were very popular in the early days. Tom Cole writes: "One dressed very properly for the occasion, dresses for the ladies and white ducks or cream flannels and blazers with neck ties for the men. This somewhat inhibited helping at the capstans which closed and opened the lock gates."

A lengthy account in the *Norwood Register*[9] of September 6, 1894 describes a wonderful excursion from Boschink to Lakefield for a baseball game: "We began the day with the sun. By seven o'clock the camp was all activity, the ladies packing the lunch, the gentlemen arranging boats and sails. Three canoes started with a dozen persons aboard, and a favourable breeze wafted the white wings westward. At the Syndicate camp a boatload of merry young people pushed out and the steadily increasing fleet now prepared to form a line." The steam launch *Ojai*, captained by its owners Ernest Moore and Sammy Best, took them in tow, and "...the confused mass changed to a straight line as we headed for the Juniper Store. The last boat of the tow had secured a basket of apples, so the baseball team put in a little practice at fly catching, securing the fruit as it came forward on the fly from the rear. The grounders were left to be picked up by the last boat, so that of about fifty apples thrown, only three were left

behind." As they left the store, the party had increased by a skiff load and several canoe loads. On Clear Lake they met three steamers, the *Golden City*, the *Mary Ellen*, and the *Undine*. "Considerable excitement was created several times in this part of the voyage by the breaking of tow lines. The yacht, warned by the shouts of those left behind, slackened speed and all available paddles were pressed into service. Every turn the forward boat made had to be followed by those behind so that the line would wind like a serpent or zig-zag."

At twelve o'clock they reached Young's Point, locked through and headed for Lakefield, where they stopped for a picnic and prepared for the baseball match. Having handily defeated the Lakefield nine, they heard the yacht whistle for the return trip.

On the way home they had tea, as the *Norwood Register* continues: "As every third boat was supplied with a basket and there was lots of hot water available on the yacht, we had the wherewithal, but the difficulty was to transport it from one boat to another. It is almost impossible to raise a barrier between a camper and his supper, so the paddles were used as a means of transport. Before long a perfect system was organized and you could order a cup of tea from four to five boats ahead and have it delivered in less time than at a city hotel. It was delightful to watch a steaming cup arrive on the end of a paddle. You might shout back for a pickle, and in no time a cucumber would come whizzing into your hands, and so we feasted until Young's Point was reached about dark. News of our victory had preceded us and the crowd around the locks gave us a royal reception. We responded with 'Stony Lake, Stony Lake Rah! Rah! Rah!'

"And now as we wound into Clear Lake the moon rose in all her glory. The cruise was delightful and fast along the glittering water. At the store we left some of our fleet and paddled home. We all agreed that this was our best day on the lake and recognize that its success was due to the genial proprietors of the yacht, Messrs. Moore and Best."[10]

In the years between 1910 and 1927, the Gouinlock's steamer *Sunny Jim* could tow up to ten canoes on trips to Jack's Creek with its long log chute, or to Eel's Creek with its cave at High Falls which could only be entered by persons who were both agile and slim-waisted. Other possibilities were White Lake and Indian River with its smooth rock bottom, good for water-dancing. Dancing on the rocks at the top of High Falls was also considered great fun. Other trips were to Blue Mountain to pick blueberries or near McCracken's to pick raspberries. "Closer to home were walks into Fairy Lake, where one swam to the other side with lunch balanced on a floating cushion, or evening visits to Viamede," recalls Dottie Drake: "...with the juke box playing and a couple of dozen people at most dancing. One father said that Viamede was sinful but the worst sinner I recall was a visitor who put slugs in the jukebox." Jane Matthews and friends hitched rides, as she describes: "One perfect day we awaited the passing of the steamer *Wauketa* heading for Blue Mountain on her daily run. With pleading eyes, we raised our paddles and the captain responded by letting us put the canoes on the empty barge. What a thrill to travel in comfort!"

Swimming, for many, is the greatest summer joy. An early long distance swimmer from 'Inglestane' used to swim miles at night, greeting startled paddlers from the water. Sheer suicide today! Nancy Watson recalls waiting the required hour after breakfast and then spending the entire morning in and out of the water until being called in for lunch. Gerry Hill remembers Joyce Corner as a little girl: "All she ever did was swim!" Besides promoting and encouraging children's swimming classes at Stony Lake, Joyce became a certified judge of synchronized swimming. From 1967 to 1999, she has judged at the Olympics and Pan-Am Games and has been recognized with many awards. Today swimming is still fun and a challenge for her.

Do kids still learn to dive over a paddle balanced along the wharf so that they have to spring up? Do they still test their courage on the Sister Islands or High Rock on 'Plum Pudding'? Likely the answer is "Yes." Today, young people enjoy the outflow from Burleigh Falls just as swimmers used to cavort in Perry's Creek.

One of George Douglas' journals records a 7 a.m. departure for an expedition up the Trent Canal in 1924: "As we passed the various cottages we were impressed by the general addiction of the inhabitants to that vile and pernicious habit of early bathing. If it were really done for pleasure, excuse and pity might be found for such strange and uncomfortable tastes, but there is an overwhelming suspicion that the motive behind the act is mere conformity to a conventional idea that virtue resides in it and merit is acquired thereby."[10]

A different attitude to swimming is recorded by Jack Amys: "Away you go to the dock, wrapped in secret glee and a towel and carrying your trunks in your spare hand. On a nice day it is so pleasant to have dry trunks to wear after your swim. We shed our towel and step to the brink, and dive deep and far and peacefully. The cool, refreshing waters receive and embrace us. A swift glow of strange elation envelopes us."[11]

Recreation was a do-it-yourself pastime in early days. Art Cole writes: "We used to play "Kick the Can" on the island and also time ourselves going around the island by single canoe, tandem, single skiff and tandem." At 'Nakemi' the Allen family played "Run, Sheep, Run" and had paper chases. While "Peck the Crow" was a great favourite on the Leeming Island, there also were treasure hunts and scavenger hunts and "Capture the Flag." Phyllida Klück writes: "There were benches and a summer house and we children ran round a flag pole and up and down the paths, swung on the swing, did somersaults, handstands, cartwheels, climbed trees, played in the dollhouse made of logs especially built for us children, where we could actually enter and sit on tiny chairs just for us. Sometimes we would make jam there with wild strawberries, on a toy stove in a miniature pot."

The Griers and Mackenzies had a regular summer baseball series with added players from further up the lake. In 1916, Ottilie Ormsby at 'Kawana' was not allowed to play this unlady-like sport, so she hid her middy and bloomers in her canoe from her mother when she went to join her friends in the pasture behind the Cassidy's farm.

There were also quiet pursuits. "Morning chores and the bliss of unstructured afternoons, card games on wet days and making flotillas of shingle boats with my brother Angus," writes Kady Denton. Sonny Townsend remembers "...disappearing into the woods behind the cottage and down to the swamp where I sat enraptured by the sound of the frogs plopping in off the lily pads. The bass notes of the frogs, the singing of the "darning needles" and the delicate popping of the swamp bubbles as they reached the surface." And Velma Osborne relates: "Our children fondly remember the novels read to them at twilight as they sat swinging quietly on the daybed on the verandah." Back in 1904, the 'Shanty' log records: "With a little singing to the guitar and mandolin we retired." Judy Finch looks back upon "...the smell of those wood fires, the coal oil lamps, the warm low light they created and the cleaning of the glass in the morning. I remember the card games in the evening, the games of bridge, gin rummy and noisy snap and hearts, the wind-up victrola on the old verandah, the pots on the floor to catch the rain dripping through the

ceiling." The swamp at the back of 'Nakemi' was a favourite place to poke about in a canoe. Ken Allen and tomboy Jo Eddis took special delight in capturing little frogs and snakes to startle unwary pals.

Rob Guillet recollects: "Cephas [Guillet] used to lead us in singing rollicking French songs around the piano at the old cottage." Chris Greening remembers "...some pretty lively nights when the clan would gather for a heated game of rumoli. For some reason the games always got louder as the night progressed. Although I was too young at the time to be able to explain why that was, I am sure there are still some around that could."

Visiting was always important. In 1897, the 'Shanty' log mentions "...a most delightful visit to Mrs. Traill , a younger sister of Agnes Strickland, with her daughter and granddaughter are at 'Minnewawa.' Much later Don Cameron remembers: "A constant activity was of course visiting. We still visit today, but before the day of the telephone there was an element of compulsion to the visiting, quietly by canoe, or by walking through woods threaded with footpaths, the trails blazed on nearby trees with different daubs of paint so as not to pick up the wrong path."

Blair Mackenzie recalls that "...my grandparents would expect much more socializing back and forth amongst island residents than they would find today. A regular afternoon bridge game, complete with (depending on the participants) lemonade, or gin and cigarettes, was a fixture in front of the Fairbairn cottage, with the participants wearing the most improbable combination of formal clothing and wide-brimmed Vietnamese-style coolie hats."

Phyllida Klück, now in New Zealand, in her recollections places her grandmother, Isabel Fairbairn Smith, in the rather grand setting of 'Boscobel,' a well-equipped cottage of a bygone era. Picture what Phyllida recalls of her summer birthday party: "On the long,

Left: Posing for the camera in 1926. *Courtesy Heather Elliot Collection.* Right: Bathing suits of yesteryear. *Courtesy Nancy Watson Collection.*

screened-in verandah of the main house, my grandmother sat in an enormous red upright rocking chair and viewed the proceedings. Behind her was the sitting room with an immense fireplace in which a huge iron cauldron hung, stuffed animal heads and birds bedecked the walls and, tethered to the cathedral ceiling, the most beautiful hand-made canoe which had never known the sound of lapping water or a trip to Eel's Creek. The sitting room was surrounded by the screened-in porch and, on either side, were two large connecting double bedrooms. As my grandmother quietly rocked, she sewed handmade tea bags put together with tiny stitches, then filled with her choice of imported China or India tea, indeed sometimes a mixture of both, and then finally closed in such a manner that, when the bags had been used, they could be opened with ease, their contents disposed of, washed and returned to my grandmother for careful re-filling."

When the young guests arrived, they knew there was a protocol to follow: "Although greeted by my mother, my sister and myself, the children innately knew that, on arrival at the large grassy opening in front of the house,

they must first go up onto the verandah and say how-do-you-do to my grandmother, such a lovely woman but perhaps formidable to other children with her long, straight back and alert and watchful gaze. The formalities finished, the presents produced and opened with excitement by me, meant that finally the longed-for treasure hunt could begin."

Finally, at the end, "...my grandmother remained on the verandah overseeing the tidying up of the lawn by Millie and later Violet when she came back from her steamer dock duties. Not long after Sam and the *Redbird* would return and it was time for the flag to be lowered, perhaps a paddle with Violet round the island in a canoe or rowing in one of the carpeted rowboats with a tiller at the stern which Violet and I would take turns at steering. And, finally, to bed exhausted and happy, a story read to me by my mother, excited chatter about the party itself, what we would do tomorrow, and the awareness that I was drifting off to sleep. Phyllida's birthday had ended."

What would Stony Lake be like without the flair for gardening? Jill Farrow, one of the lake's most passionate gardners, writes: "While gardening is for many the passion of the 90s, cultivation has a long history at Stony Lake. Wild rice beds flourished in quiet bays, and produced a coveted harvest for the local Natives. 'Minnewawa,' now Patsy and Jamie Anderson's cottage, was once owned by Catharine Parr Traill who was captivated by the amazing diversity of wildflowers in the surrounding area. Her 1894 collection of Stony Lake grasses is preserved at the Plant Research Institute in Ottawa. They were collected according to a slip in the album, 'from the island of Minnewawa and Otter Island in Stony Lake.' The paper used for mounting the labelled specimens is from a discarded Eaton's catalogue.

"Small wonder then that subsequent cottagers have found solace and inspiration in our rich landscape. Don Walter's grandfather left a legacy of perennials from his early 1900s' garden. While we children were off sailing and picnicking, many mothers were identifying and exchanging plants. Berenice Knapman was our local source, and her lily-of-the valley, day lilies, sneezeweed and, yes, loosestrife now flourish on many islands.

"Valiant efforts have been made to grow fruits and vegetables. Winnie Weatherstone tried to grow strawberries on the weeping tile bed, then had to rescue the determined bird who penetrated her umbrella netting and devoured half the crop. Art Cole and his father Cooper before him spent years perfecting their version of the Potager, mixing vegetables with flowers. Several islands now have flourishing beds of chives, collected during a picnic stop at Chive Island. The McKerrachers produce vegetables in raised beds and grow grapes on their tennis court fencing. The most unusual vegetables are grown in the Benthams' boats (retired red Flippers), in soil dredged during the clearing of 'Muskrat Marsh.' The Oxley gardens

west of Mt. Julian on the mainland were begun early in the 20th century.

"At 'Roxie' on Eagle Mount Island, Hugh Jones built stone and concrete flowerboxes. On 'Tarbox Island' an exquisite "Friendship Garden" is filled with exchanges of perennials from grateful guests. On 'Fairhaven' natural rockeries were constructed by Jim Binnie and at the "Glass House" near Viamede large rock faces and massive perennial planting provide an expansive interpretation of a Canadian garden. Ann Binnie's woodland walk to Fairy Lake is Japanese-inspired, while Del Walton plants a rocky slope with an eclectic mixture of suitable plants. Jill and Grant Farrow have transformed Bare Island with deep soil pockets, filled with both shade and sun-loving perennials, grasses and ferns, set amid paths meandering along the steep slopes.

"Local Lakefield mentors are Thelma Madill with her unique daisy and Ralph Millage, everyone's plumbing expert, who grows and shares everything. Local growers and nurseries are springing up, and artisans such as Pete Hillman are creating appropriate garden art and furniture.

"Challenges that face the Stony Lake gardener are lack of soil, constant wind, wildlife in the compost and having to wait till the ice goes out for access. But the reward comes after escaping the Friday traffic—the walkabout to see 'what's up.' What a fulfilling vacation hobby!"

Having fun at the lake for children and adults helps strengthen that important sense of community. Through enjoyment with others or in quiet contemplation of the surroundings while in solitude, the spirit is enriched and something is given back to this land so loved by all of us.

Ten

"WE WILL SERVE THE LORD"

"A s FOR ME and my house, we will serve the Lord." Joshua 24:15

This quotation surely reflects the conviction of many of the early settlers around Stony Lake who worshipped God in their own homes or with neighbours. Soon these small groups formed congregations of various denominations and began to build churches on land donated by parishioners. Eden Methodist Church on Northey's Bay Road, Holy Trinity Anglican at the top of the Mt. Julian Road, and St. Aidan's Anglican and St. Mary's Roman Catholic, both at Young's Point, were all built late in the nineteenth century. Zion United at Hall's Glen and Carmel United served residents south of the lake. Services were organized at Mount Julian Hotel, Roman Catholic, and at Viamede, non-denominational, to serve travellers on the Burleigh Road.

Because early cottagers came to the lake by train, steamboat and canoe, access to mainland churches was difficult for them, so some cottagers conducted services on their islands. One of these was Thomas S. Cole who attended the American Canoe Association Regatta in 1883 and later bought Otter Island. A visitor to the lake in the '90s described the services: "Almost everyone came in canoes, and as there was little space on the island we stayed in them, holding each adjoining canoe. A wide fan-shaped group listened to the service and sang hymns, supported by a portable organ. Most memorable, after the benediction, as the canoes started to move away, the hymn 'God be with you 'til we meet again.' Voices echoed back from old Eagle Mount and surrounding islands."[1]

Any visiting clergyman, or Mr. Cole himself, led the service since he was a travelling evangelical lay preacher. His grandson, Tom Cole, comments wryly, "I'm not sure that many families had Bible readings and morning prayers right after breakfast daily, which my grandparents did—wasting good fishing time."

A further example of verandah or lakeside worship is found in the recollection of Mrs. Mary Acton Yardley, a lifelong resident of Stony Lake. Her grandfather purchased Acton Island in 1903 after renting 'Yonanda' and then 'Chateau du Lac.' Mr. Acton conducted services for a "throng of canoeists" from a pagoda on the point of Acton Island, now called 'Endiang'.

Ken Brown, married to the great-great-granddaughter of William Brownscombe, has researched the family's history on Stony Lake, which began in 1886. He writes: "On a nearby island, Dutchy Stone would deliver a

Top: St. Aidan's Anglican Church, built at Young's Point in 1909, was sold in 1998 as the congregation had dwindled considerably. *George Douglas Collection, courtesy Katharine Hooke.*
Bottom: St. Mary's Roman Catholic Church, also built in 1909 at Young's Point, is shown before the porch was built. *George Douglas Collection, courtesy Katharine Hooke.*

message from the bare rock to an assembled Sunday morning crowd in their boats. There is a story that one day he announced that if your faith was strong enough you could walk on water. He apparently then proceeded to try, and nearly drowned."

When the pavilion at Juniper was built in 1896, services were held there and the minis-

ter and family lived in what is now the Yacht Club. At the 'Shanty,' where the Buell-Wahl cottage was built in 1887, the logbook for July 18, 1904 records: "Another perfect day and just the day to heed the cry of the denizens of the lake 'Give us a rest.' It was strictly observed as a day of rest except by the captain of the ship and others who attended service at the pavilion and listened to a sermon on the fish story of Jonah and his whale."

A 1909 Cottagers' Association *Yearbook* announced that: "Sabbath Services will be held at the pavilion at 11 o'clock a.m. It is strictly non-denominational and speakers are asked not to introduce controversial questions." This last request may have been in response to an incident, nay, a fracas, involving an earnest internationalist, who whisked the Union Jack off the altar-table to demonstrate the evils of nationalism. Rising swiftly to defend the honour of the Empire, several stalwart members of the congregation had to be restrained from attacking the demonstrator.

The *Yearbook* also admonished readers not to loiter near the pavilion or to interfere with the decorum of the service. That decorum was disturbed one Sunday in the late 1890s by the arrival of a group of young men from Echo Bay Camp on Emerald Isle. "We had been reproached for our non-appearance at the Sunday morning services in the Pavilion, which were then attended by all the respectable elements of Stony Lake. Navy blue jackets, spotless white ducks and yachting caps were de rigueur on the occasion of any public appearance. Sadly enough, spotless white ducks were not always to come by in the hurly-burly of life many miles from a laundry." So they asked a kindly matron on the Dummer shore to help them. "She worked faithfully with a hand-power washer, the scientific marvel of the age, far into Saturday night. The ducks arrived, spotless, starched and ironed, by rowboat early

Holy Trinity Haultrain, located on County Road 29 between Burleigh and Haultrain, the interior shown decorated for "Harvest Home". *George Douglas Collection, courtesy Katharine Hooke.*

Sunday morning. Alas, our laundress had pressed the white trousers to a board-like flatness and rigidity – the creases not fore and after, but sidewise. What was to be done? Nothing, to be sure, except for Echo Bay to march in a body up to the front row of the assembled worshippers. What if the customary austerity and decorum of religious exercises went by the boards one Sabbath morning? Perhaps a good many long and solemn services would be the better for a few ripples of merriment." The steamers did not run on Sunday, partly out of deference to the worshippers. For a time, the YWCA campers from nearby 'Inglestane' swelled the congregation, but the services at the pavilion ended after World War II.

The Kawartha Park Chapel was founded by the Rev. John Edmison in 1920. Services were held in a circus tent on land donated by R.B. Rogers until the chapel was built in 1925. A loyal and devoted group still attend non-denominational services worship at this Chapel.

Meanwhile, church services conducted regularly by Michael Mackenzie at 'Lochend' in Mackenzie Bay moved to a cottage with a larger verandah at 'Kiluna' on the Burleigh Channel in 1913. Even earlier, services had been held at 'Headlands' as noted by George Douglas in his 1903 diary. This group of cottagers spearheaded the building of St. Peter's on-the-Rock, where the first service was held on June 28, 1914.

St. Peter's story is well told in the book entitled *St. Peter's-on-the-Rock—Seventy-Five Years of Service*, commissioned for the 75th anniversary of the church in 1989, and written by Kathy Hooke. The celebration included a successful potluck dinner at the Juniper Pavilion on Saturday night, followed the next day by a communion service of worship and thanksgiving attended by over 600 people including eight past rectors. The church could not accommodate this number, so 350 people were seated on the newly refurbished tug the *Trent* and its adjoining barge. The tug overflowed with communicants who clambered over the side and onto the barge to partake of the sacrament at the altar there. Latecomers sat on the rocks or in boats anchored nearby.

Life at St. Peter's abounds with stories: of clergy lost on the lake at night or accidentally helping themselves to a cottager's boat from the landing; of volunteer organists valiantly struggling to pump the old organ and keep their music from blowing away; of lost communion wine; of church-going canoeists dumping at the dock; a wedding where the tour boat failed to return to take the guests on to the reception; of an irreverent organist who played "Satin Doll" as an interlude; of a funeral in a storm when the coffin slid across the wet wharf almost into the lake; and of the epic tale of the rebuilding of the church in time for services in July after the collapse of the roof under the snow in the winter.

During the 1950s, there were frequent "vestry meetings," festive cocktail parties related to church only because they followed services at St. Peter's. An announcement from

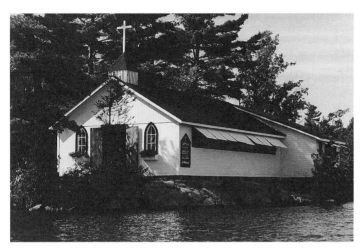

Above: St. Peter's-on-the-Rock. *Courtesy Alan Wotherspoon Collection.*
Right: Members of the congregation at the front door of St. Peter's-the-Rock in 1914. *George Douglas Collection, courtesy Katharine Hooke.*

the pulpit gave the location of each Sunday's "meeting."

Changing times have greatly affected life on Stony Lake. Some people felt that attendance at St. Peter's would dwindle because telephones rendered churchgoing unnecessary for arranging the week's social calendar. However, at St. Peter's, participation and singing are hearty, baptisms and weddings are increasing, and family reunions often centre around the church. The church and the lake have come a long way from a verandah phenomenon. Succeeding generations of worthy people of every faith will continue the prayer, "God of power, the glory of your works fills us with wonder and awe. Help us to live in harmony with all your creation."

Eleven

TELLING TALES

Legends old and new are told about Stony Lake. Like many stories, these can often be credited more to the imagination of the teller than to his or her memory.

The "Legend of the Lost Channel" relates the tale of two unfortunate Jesuits caught by the Iroquois. "Entering the Channel at the end where the church is now, they paddled frantically, with the Iroquois in hot pursuit. As fate would have it, they took the false dead end exit near the north end of the Channel and had no retreat. The Indians caught them and sent them to their Maker, kicking the severed heads about like footballs and leaving the bones to be scattered by the animals. To this day a venture up this dead end with its strange quietness will be short as the fearfulness of the past still lingers." This account as presented by Wes Willoughby is "guaranteed" by both himself and Angus MacDonald!

A tale published in the *Star Weekly* concerns Huron lovers whose trysting place was a large lichen-covered rock in Fairy Lake. "Arriving one evening to meet his maiden, the young brave was horrified to find her dead, the arrow of a jealous rival buried in her breast. Long sat the young brave with his beloved in his arms and, when day was near, he arose and, with the maiden in his arms, plunged to his death in the deep waters. It is said that when the moon is full the shadowy figures of the lovers may still be seen upon the rock, wrapped in eternal embrace, and the voice of the young brave may be heard lamenting the death of his beloved."[1]

A third story is told by the ghost herself, Emma Jane Davis, with the assistance of Bernie Morin. She describes her death on August 18, 1943: "I observed my body drowning in perspiration and graceless age as I floated above myself near the ceiling. How I managed to be in two places is of some confusion to me still. I have spent my life since at Davis Island Manor, vexed by the progression of strangers who, uninvited, have taken up residence in my house. To remind these interlopers of their 'place', I have brushed past them in the hallway in the night, or appeared in mirrors, though I am careful to choose my victims carefully. A rational and intelligent being with a good respectful dose of fear is best."

Stony Lake has other ghost stories. According to Janet Smith, two young girls were sleeping in a bedroom at 'Cordach' on Juniper Island, with the door bolted from the inside. In the night they found themselves very wide awake, conscious of the sound of someone with a cane slowly walking towards the room and opening the door. The next day Derry Smith met the ghost as he was walking on the

An early view of Fairy Lake (not dated). *Courtesy David Card Collection.*

path from 'Kincardine' to 'Cordach.' The little old lady in flowing robes said that she was lost. Derry, aged 12, spoke to her politely but kept his hand on the little hatchet at his waist. She wandered away, but later two of Derry's relatives, paddling into a bay behind the cottage to investigate, encountered the spectre. She beckoned them to the shore and then evaporated.

Humourous stories are told in Stony Lake families. Doreen Foote describes a trip to Spencley's Landing near Burleigh: "In his square-nosed red punt, Fred Hawkins was transporting a family of five, dressed in their Sunday clothes, from the landing to his island for a visit. With six people, the boat was full, and by the time they were out in the open channel Fred knew he had a problem. He pulled in beside the red buoy marking Black Rock and ordered his friend Fred Stinson out of the boat. Thinking that Hawkins was simply going to rearrange the seating, Stinson

'Davis Island Manor', the residence of Emma Jane Davis. *Courtesy Bernie Morin Collection.*

126

complied. To his amazement, the boat pulled away. There was no use calling out, as Fred Hawkins was stone deaf. Observers later remarked that it was strange to see a man in a navy blue suit standing in the middle of the channel. Much to Fred Stinson's relief, his friend returned to pick him up, after he had deposited the rest of the family on the island."

Eric and Aileen Grier's honeymoon got off to a rocky start—for that very reason. As they were leaving 'Kawana' after their wedding reception at Jessie Grahame's, Eric's launch *Waunita* hit a rock. Aileen was taken back to her family cottage, 'Lochend,' while Eric and his best man, Geoffrey Grier, repaired the propeller. While the wedding guests and family waited for the two men, the bride's grandfather proposed a toast "to the roving blades."

On a stormy day years ago a capsized taxi boat dumped a family of five plus dog into the lake. Fortunately, they were spotted by an elderly farmer who set out alone in an old rowboat in the midst of a squall. When one oar broke, he paddled the rest of the way, rescuing six people and a dog. He brought a bottle with him to ward off the chill, for which the dog was grateful because he received the first drink. This story was told to Diane Ferguson by Berenice Knapman.

Hugh Jones remembers from his boyhood an encounter between his grandfather and a small terrier named Peter: "Grandfather decided to sleep on the verandah so that he might view the sunrise. Peter slept under the verandah. My grandfather had a full set of dentures which each night he placed in a tumbler of water beside his bed. One morning the entire family was wakened by Grandfather screaming, 'My teeth, my teeth.' Of course, everyone rushed to the verandah and immediately saw that the tumbler was on its side and the water running between the floorboards. A search of the ground and flowerbeds gave us no clue, until Peter, the terrier, crawled out

from under the verandah with Grandfather's teeth intact. For the remainder of his stay at 'Roxie,' my grandfather placed his dentures on the kitchen shelf at nighttime."

Doreen Jones tells a more recent story of landing on a small rock at midnight and of 'camping out' until dawn broke. The Bankes also hit a rock just off their island, Little Otter. Jack said to Betty Jean, "Oh, you're always imagining boat accidents. Don't worry, we can't sink that fast." But the boat went down in a few seconds and needed a crane to pull it up.

Agnes Upper, on her way home in a fog after visiting the Matthews at 'Anchorage' spent two and a half hours circling in vain. Finally, the Hookes at 'Singkettle' heard her shouting. They went out to help and loaned her a compass. But this wasn't the end of the weather's pranks that day. A thunderstorm accompanied her as she headed for home in Upper Stoney. Thinking her husband Bruce might be worried, she rushed to the cottage, only to find him sound asleep and unconcerned.

Being lost because of adverse weather is one thing, but there's little excuse if you're captaining a Canadian Navy Fairmile on inland waters on a clear day. These ships were built at Penetanguishene during World War II and taken through the Trent-Severn system on their way to the sea. Imagine the surprise of residents on the Mt. Julian shore when they saw one of these ships obviously off course and steaming dangerously close to the wrong side of the black buoys marking the Viamede reef. After waving mightily from shore and getting no response, some cottagers headed out and managed to catch the wheelman's attention. Without so much as a rueful word of thanks, he changed course and headed toward Clear Lake to catch up to the rest of the fleet.

As for the Hookes, over the last few years 'Singkettle' has experienced a marked increase in boats landing unintentionally in, on and around the island, as cottagers and cruise boats circle close by in an effort to better view the "Glass House" or visit the boathouse bar at Viamede. The proximity of the visiting Stanley Cup to Dallas Stars' current general manager Bob Gainey's home will surely bring more unexpected arrivals to 'Singkettle'.

Araby Lockart relates how in the '30s her father, Jim Lockhart, accepted a ride to Toronto in Keith Russell's float plane. "Dad had lost a leg in the war, and that morning was wearing his wooden leg rather than a peg, as he was heading to work. On Monday morning the engine wouldn't start, so Jim suggested they pour gasoline in the exhaust ports, a method he had found useful in World War I aircraft. This they did; Dad cranked the propeller, the engine caught and the plane began to move from the dock, pushing Dad inexorably into the water. He was dressed in a suit to go to work. When he came up spluttering, he had to remove the leg, pour out several quarts of water, and get into the aircraft soaking wet, for Keith would brook no complaints." Another plane story involves a World War II pilot who somehow managed to commandeer an empty bomber in which he buzzed the lake with the bomb bay doors open. Undoubtedly humans were startled, but so were the cattle that were grazing north of Mount Julian. They stampeded across the fields in great agitation causing several farmers to phone Don Fowler of Mt. Julian wanting an explanation.

Many of us can remember stories of Rusty Dodworth, who owned a fleet of hovercraft, one to use and several for spare parts after crashes. His spectacles with diminutive windshield wipers, his player piano device and his donut-making machine are the stuff of legends, but true.

Bill Hamilton once asked a local workman, Dick Crowe, about his long underwear, and received the reply, "I wear those longjohns in winter to keep in the heat and in summer to keep it out." Another apt answer was given by an elderly Amea Brewin to a youthful and somewhat cheeky Robbie Willoughby, who suggested that the solemn old lady "buck up." "Robbie," she replied with great dignity, " I was not aware that I needed 'bucking up.' " Jeannie Guillet recalls that story about Robbie, while Earl Shewen remembers transporting a drunk cottager and his wife. "He slipped and fell under the seat. He was stuck. His wife said angrily, 'Now you are loaded in more ways than one.' "

Of course, there have always been tricks and pranks at Stony. A quick sleight of hand allowed a young Jack Gouinlock to dump sand into the punch at a wedding in 1920. Another incident is recalled for the 1930s. In the old cottage at 'Spree Island', the floor sloped so steeply that the older boys made sure that they sat on the high side of the dinner table. Any spills inevitably went towards the younger cousins on the low side. Many have undoubtedly noticed the "inscription" on Elephant Rock that has been there since the late 1960s, but may not know the story of its arrival. Two Upper Stoney cottagers, Ed and Bob, painted their names quite clearly in white paint on the west side of the "elephant," and Angus Matthews, Hal Corbett and Shelagh Morris thought it would be a very clever idea to paint the word "loves" in between. However, being without paint, they decided to visit Pam Hooke at 'Singkettle' to see what she might have. Pam was babysitting her younger siblings at the time, but decided that a painting expedition would be much more fun, so, leaving her younger brother David in charge, she departed for the rock with the others and her father's can of bright red paint. The four might have gotten away with it; however, the tell-tale red painting drippings left behind in the Matthews' wooden boat were a clue. As well, David decided not to keep the secret and, when Pam's father Hal insisted that she go back to remove their "artwork," she argued that the environmental damage to the lake through the use of the paint remover would be greater than the aesthetic damage. For years "Ed loves Bob" has greeted boaters travelling east up to Upper Stoney.

Some pranks involve skill, timing and coordination, as this one recounted by Blair Mackenzie: "In the summer of 1979, Doug Smith, Beverley Hicks-Lyne and their friends decided that Gordon Collins had carried out a few too many practical jokes at their expense. It was time to even the score. This they proceeded to do, by moving Gordon's beloved Volkswagen Beetle to a most unusual location. Late one Saturday night, with her grandfather Mackenzie's full support, Beverley unhooked the front dock of 'Kincardine,' the Mackenzie family cottage opposite 'Shota'. The conspirators towed the dock over to Carveth's Marina. Having stolen a key, they opened up Gordon's car and, under cover of darkness, rolled it down to the waiting dock. By 1:00 a.m., the car was securely on the dock. It then began a very slow trip to Collins Island. In absolute silence, they secured this dock, with Gordon's car on it, to the Collins front dock. Next, they thoughtfully placed a no parking sign beside the car and a parking ticket under the windshield wiper. I well recall paddling to church the next morning , and passing by the Collins cottage just as Gordon emerged, no doubt having been told by his family that there was a sight that might interest him out front. For once, Gordon was speechless. He saw that a variety of eyes were trained on him from the Leeming Island and made a mental note of this. To his credit, he enjoyed the joke as much as anyone and, in due course, he moved the Volkswagen back to the mainland, and the dock back to 'Kincardine,' with no outward sign of protest.

"It did not take Gordon long to conclude who was responsible. In due course, he made off late one Saturday night with Doug Smith's aluminum runabout, with the intention of suspending it in the air between two trees on the Church island, for the amusement of the worshippers arriving the next morning. With engineering assistance from Peter Dickson, the boat was duly hoisted in the air. Unsuccessful efforts were made to induce Kevin Dickson to go to sleep in it. Revenge was thwarted by the arrival of an alert Bob Trennum, who insisted that everything be taken down at once. To this day Gordon speaks of his car as having been stolen, despite the fact that it was only moved, with the greatest of care, right to his doorstep."

Of course, the YWCA camp was a temptation to youthful pranksters. Tom Cole describes one raid: "The camp emblem, a blue triangle with the letters on a bar across the centre, stood on a garden wall back of the steamer dock. Paddling with great stealth we lifted the emblem into the canoe and off to Juniper, where we silently raised the blue triangle to the top of the tall flagpole. There it met the eyes of early passersby, and the storekeeper left it up all morning as an attraction." There were other raids on that camp, one as late as 1944, which remains in the memories of the some of the participants.

Christie Bentham remembers V-J night in 1945: "I had carefully planned my party, but we did not know of the war's end until the first guests arrived, because a violent storm had knocked out the electricity, making the radio useless, along with the refrigerator, lights, record-player and stove. My chief emotion was not elation but disappointment that the party arrangements were disrupted and all the older boys got drunk."

Chris Greening remembers cottage life during the era before phones: "The nice part about that time was that if you wanted to be

The YWCA Camp on Eagle Mount, at an earlier time (not dated). *Courtesy David Card Collection.*

left alone it could actually be done. On the other hand, there was a downside to having no phone. When guests were arriving for a stay at the cottage, you would set a predetermined time to meet them at the landing. Now this usually worked out, give or take a half-hour of waiting one way or the other. However, if your friends took a wrong turn because they could not follow your crystal clear instructions, problems arose. They could not phone you to explain their delay or ask for further instructions. So there you sat waiting at the dock for hours. Not bad as long as it was not raining."

Phones and fast boats have altered Stony Lake life immeasurably. Again, Chris gives an example of how much cottage life has changed in his lifetime: "In the summer of 1998, some friends and I were having refreshments on the deck of Viamede's boathouse. At some point in the evening, one of my companions decided he was hungry but, to his dismay, was told that the kitchen was closed for the night. Being a true outdoorsman, this did not prevent him from putting food on the table. Out came his trusty cell phone and in no time flat

he was ordering up a veritable feast from one of Lakefield's finer pizzerias to be delivered to Young's Point. The group of us piled into one boat to head for our host's cottage. At the same time one brave fellow set out in a flying wedge he calls a boat in an attempt to set a new round trip speed record from Viamede to Young's Point and back. Although not documented I believe he did. It was only a short 15 minutes later that we were all enjoying take-out pizza and wings on the dock under the light of a beautiful full moon."

Blair Mackenzie also comments about change: "I think my grandparents would be fascinated by the laptop, cellphone and fax machine that occasionally are there, not to mention the concept of Internet e-mail."

Yet some things don't change. Judy Finch "...cannot imagine another place where all the generations and cousins can have such a good time together. In this world of ours in which no one ever stays in one place very long, at Stony Lake this is just not so. We not only have our friends, but we know their children and their parents. The continuity of people, year after year, is a rare gift."

Twelve

STONY LAKE LOVE STORIES

"Moonlight glistens like silver, on a Stony Lake summer's night.
The wind whispers through the pine trees and a loon calls out in flight
And the silence seems so endless when the forest it is still
As the jewelled lake called Stony casts its endless magic spell.
Oh may you live forever! Oh Stony Lake so clear!
You seem to give us inner peace whenever we are near."[1]

So sings Bob Trennum in a beautiful musical tribute to Stony Lake. While most of us cannot provide a melody for our feelings about Stony, we do express them in words as shown here:

"My heaven on earth"
> Annette Collins Greening

"My private Eden"
> Emma Jane Davis

"My true surroundings"
> Cecily Morrow

"That wonderful feeling I get every time I am at the cottage"
> Chris Greening

"Granddad claimed that never in his travels had he seen a more beautiful spot than Stony Lake"
> Mary Jane Dickson

"There's healing in the pines"
> Aileen Grier

"A veritable Venice without any Bridge of Sighs"
> a guest at 'Cordach'

"Alec and Alice Collins agreed that it would be hard to imagine a Heaven that could be better than Stony Lake, a little piece of terrestrial paradise"
> Carol Winter

"I've had a good life here on Stony. I don't think I would do it much differently"
> Earl Shewen

For some, cottage living has small appeal. "Courting discomfort!" one city dweller remarked. Another found the loons too noisy and never visited the lake again. But for most, Stony Lake is the central stillness around which the rest of the year revolves. When Peggy and Andrew Brewin visited Tanzania, "...they were taken out to a tented camp in Mikumi National

Park," writes their son John. "As the sun set beneath the African plain with a herd of giraffes walking in stately fashion through the acacia trees, Peggy looked at the scene and sighed, 'It's almost as beautiful as Stony Lake.' "

Some people have drawn on enormous reserves of strength from their times at the lake. Jack Gouinlock was one of those during World War II. While stationed in Quebec City with the RCAF, he was given an extra day on a 48-hours pass, and decided to come to Stony. "Train from Quebec, sitting up from Montreal to Port Hope, and hitchhiking via trucks, occasional car, and funeral director's van, I ended up on the north shore. I borrowed a canoe and paddled across the lake to 'Sandhaven.' It was a perfect weekend. Going back, I was able to hitch a ride to Port Hope, train to Quebec, buttons polished for Parade."[2] That visit to Stony sustained Jack through ten bombing missions and several months in Belgium after his plane was shot down.

Elizabeth Dann suggests: "For all its quiet, natural beauty, Stony offers fond memories of people too. We felt as if we were the only residents from the United States and that we were blessed to have Stony Lake Canadian friends, adding a unique asset to our lives."

Hugh Porter makes a list of his childhood memories:

Oil and gas lamps
Handpump in the kitchen
Gardening on rock
Wood stove with the hot water well
The outhouse
Roaring fires in the fireplace
The ice house
Disappearing propellor boats
The market at McCracken's
Steamer excursions
Juniper and Viamede dances
The *Islinda*, the *Empress* and the *Stoney Lake*
The ice-cream parlour at McCracken's
Annual canoe trip to Eel's Creek
Dick Crowe, handyman extraordinary
Lorne and Mary Morrison at Choate's Supply Store
Slot machines at Wantasa
The sail and leeboards we used in our canoe and skiff
St. Peter's on-the-Rock.

The first arrival at the lake always remains as a vivid memory. "It is impossible to describe the welling up of emotion I felt when we approached the island for the first time each season. The cat would feel it too, for even though I held her tight, she always leapt out of my arms toward the dock, as I would have liked to do. After we arrived, the former pet melted into the island scenery like the wildlife creatures we all became." So writes Cecily Morrow.

Another cottager, Gerry Hill has vivid memories. "In the '40s we got to the cottage after dark and, as it was before hydro, the meal was cooked on the wood stove with the use of flashlights. I still remember what we ate—corned beef hash."

Such were the beginnings for our memories, for most of us lifelong. Where else in the world would you recall, as Michael Allen does, this warning as you set out for your evening paddle. "Come home when you hear the whippoorwill."[3]

Harold Knapman carried photos of Stony all through World War I, and saved the letters, which his sisters wrote to him, on birchbark. Perhaps he was remembering the joys his daughter, Dottie Drake, now recalls, "...the back bay full of croaking bull frogs, all-night music. The morning swim followed by the welcome heat of a pine cone fire in the big kitchen stove. The smell of baking powder biscuits and fresh caught bass. The silky soft water, the glow of coal oil lamps and the tinkle of an untuned piano."

Harold died at Stony Lake, as did Helen Russell and Ralph Hendren, whose daughter Velma Osborne writes: "We all agreed it was exactly what he would choose, as most of us would when we're 83 years old and at our favourite place in the world."

The following delightful story evokes the sustaining love of Stony Lake. Shelagh Morris writes: "Nothing stirs the soul like the haunting sounds of the bagpipes floating over still water on a moonlit night. Better yet if the water is Stony Lake. Favourite visitors to our island cottage 'Wee Croft' on Cassidy Bay have been our friends from Paris, Ontario, Gordon Black and his wife Barb. In addition to his construction abilities (generally the reason for an invitation), Gordon is also an accomplished piper of world class calibre. Despite this lofty distinction, however, Gordon is typically reluctant to perform at social gatherings. As a result, whenever he visited the cottage we needed some type of inducement to get him to play. Shamelessly, we used my father!

"Like Gordon, my father hailed from Bonnie Scotland. If anyone could cajole Gordon into breaking out the pipes, it was Alex. News of an impending cottage visit by Gordon and Barb would delight my father to no end, as he knew it would undoubtedly involve some type of construction project, in which he would be anxious to participate, not to mention a Saturday evening bagpipe concert.

"On one particular occasion, the weekend project (well, actually it was a week project that ran into the weekend) involved the construction of a sleeping cabin. At the conclusion of this arduous endeavour, it was finally time for the long awaited 'concert.' Despite the fact that Gordon was exhausted from all the work, he good-naturedly agreed after dinner to entertain my family (my mother and father, my husband John and me) and of course Barb, with an impromptu bagpipe concert around the fire pit down by the lake. Plas-

"Moonlight Glistens like Silver." *Courtesy David Card Collection.*

tic chairs were hastily gathered and assembled as the sun sank slowly in the western sky. A supply of beverages was proffered to all as we settled in for the show.

"As dusk approached, the soft breeze and the lapping waves on the shore created the perfect setting as all eagerly awaited the entertainment. After a brief tune-up of the drones, which quickly sent our three cats and other wildlife off to the other side of the island, the skirl began. A medley of tunes poured forth as Gordon played on and on to his appreciative toe-tapping, knee-slapping audience, which now included friends and neighbours across the bay and down the shore to as far as Kawartha Park Marina. Unfortunately, as the night wore on and wind died down, the infamous Stony Lake humidity level rose, aggravated by the heat of the fire, and soon poor Gordon looked as if he had just emerged from a Turkish steam bath. A brief respite was in order.

"No sooner had Gordon collapsed into a chair and grabbed the nearest spirituous libation, than my father leapt to his feet, scurried down to the boat and quickly set off for my parents' cottage just down the shore, muttering something about a list. In short order, he returned to the gathering and proudly announced that in anticipation of Gordon's visit, he had put together a few 'requests.' The next thing we knew he brought out what looked to be a replica of the Dead Sea scrolls and proceeded to rattle of his selections, each one preceded with 'Doo ye kno' this one, Gordon?' Gordon could only smile weakly and nod 'aye' as the rosy flush from the heat quickly drained from his face.

"After much persuasion, the bagpipes were again assembled and the concert resumed. Gordon continued his feverish pitch going from one selection to the next, as the sweat poured down his face. He looked like a sausage about to burst. However, from the look on my father's face, he was obviously in the proverbial seventh heaven as Gordon tirelessly made his way through the 'wish list,' much to our delight as well.

"Now as anyone who has ever tried to build something on a Stony Lake island knows, there is no level ground anywhere. Trying to set four legs of a chair on even ground just won't work, and invariably the chair rests on only three legs. Such was the case with the plastic chairs we were using that night. It was no wonder then, that during a particularly rousing rendition of some reel or other that Gordon was playing, my father suddenly managed to toe-tap his way ass over teakettle backwards in the chair and

onto the ground. Unfortunately, we were all so caught up with the music, and whistling, clapping and toe-tapping ourselves that no one noticed my father's upending until we heard Barb exclaim, 'Alex, are you all right?' We immediately turned to see two feet up in the air, wildly flailing in time to the music, apparently oblivious to the circumstances of the situation. He hadn't missed a beat!

"Sadly, we lost my father to a brain aneurysm in 1998, but it always brings a smile to my face whenever we sit around the fire on a Saturday night at the cottage and remember the famous concerts of Gordon the Piper."

Most of us have felt our own special love of the lake. And many have experienced abiding human loves at Stony, such as the long-lasting marriages of Effie and Earl Shewen and Grace and Orval Bolton, who celebrated their sixtieth wedding anniversaries in 1999, and Marg and Doug Dunford, nearing their fiftieth in 2000. Cottagers with marriages of over fifty years are Anne and Art Cole, Lorraine and Bob Cochran, Marg and Jack Gouinlock and Marianne and Tom Cole.

Many a cottager found romance here, as did three of the six Gibson sisters who wed Stony Lakers. A photo of Gibson descendants taken at a reunion in 1994 gives an idea of the many interlocking families resulting from Stony Lake marriages.

But other Stony Lakers have found their loves off the lake, only to find that these lake adoptees are also avid Stony Lakers. Why, if a husband stays around Stony long enough he may even get to be called by his own surname, instead of "Jane Doe's husband." For many of us the lake is important enough that a prospective fiancé(e) comes on a trial basis to test his or her adaptability and enthusiasm.

Some Stony Lake second marriages occur after a first non-Stony one, when teenaged sweethearts re-unite in the place that gives them the happiest memories. Tim Sherin tells a touching story of his mother, Gretchen, returning as a widow after 30 years, to find her beau Harry still waiting for her. After their marriage, "Harry became a wonderful Dad to me," says Tim.

Stony Lake marriages have stood not only the test of time, but also remarkable stresses. The ideal honeymoon for husbands in the Dodworth, Guillet and Douglas families was a six-week camping trip, a rocky start in more ways than one. A more recent groom spent his entire two-week honeymoon building a set of outside stairs, a project that involved spending the days at a nearby island to benefit from the expertise, tools and rye of his neighbour.

Early wives, with husbands absent during the week, managed with half-built cottages, wood stoves, local help and children, often without a motorboat or any means of communication. One wife after the Second World War could have readily dispensed with communication of a more unconventional mode. This bizarre communication involving vigorous "pulling" on the generator housed in a shed next to the privy, then returning to the house to talk to her husband in Toronto via ham radio on an enormous war surplus transmitter from a destroyer.

Stony Lake's mystique was beautifully expressed in Phred Collins' tribute at his father Jim's funeral. "Being with my dad during his

Flory Gibson MacDonald (centre, behind baby) with the next three generations, all descendents (with spouses) of the six Gibson sisters who first came to Stony in the 1920s. Most still summer on Stony Lake. *Courtesy Kady Denton Collection.*

Sun breaks through over the waters of Stony Lake.
Courtesy Katharine Hooke Collection.

time of transcendence convinced me that the human spirit does not die, but rather it moves into the loving essence of the Greater Spirit that moves within all things, like the warm August wind spreading the summer smells of a pine forest, or the morning mist hanging low over Stony Lake.

"Dad told me his experience of paddling one morning when the fog was so thick that he couldn't really see where he was going. He decided to stand up in the canoe to see if that would help. As his head still wasn't clear of the mist, he stood up on the gunwales and found that his head and chin just barely broke through the upper surface of the low-lying mist. He could now see into the clear light of day and find his way home."

Phred also described his appreciation of "the absolute value of community" where Stony Lake friends and others joined the family to share their memories of Jim. That is the community we have extolled in this book.

As Jill Trennum writes: "Memories of Stony Lake sweep over many of us year after year, with waves of nostalgia and fondness. Life-long friendships, special times, special people, special memories - how lucky we were, and still are today."

NOTES

The area represented in this book is rich in history that has been recorded in many forms and served in many institutions. Staff are knowledgeable about their own collections and generally can accurately direct a researcher to another source as necessary. Readers who wish to preserve, duplicate or donate historic material will find expert help in the Peterborough area.

INTRODUCTION

1   The Association of Stony Lake Cottagers' records include this undated short, typed account of the spelling controversy. Helen Guillet estimates it was written in the 1970s.

2   This account of the never-to-be settled question of the spelling of our lake refers to a heated discussion at an annual Cottagers' Association meeting, probably in the early 1970s. For further information about local names see E.C. Guillet, *The Valley of the Trent* p. xxxvi–xxxviii. See also *The Peterborough Review, under water.* Summer/Fall 95 p. 38–46 and "Water Circle" for the Anishnabe names and meanings for various local bodies of water. Unfortunately, this fine quarterly journal of essays, poetry and interviews ceased publication with this 1995 issue. See also Andrea Ryder, "Metamorphize Kiluna," *Peterborough Review, under water.* Summer/Fall 95, 51.

3   Samuel de Champlain, *The Works of Samuel de Champlain*. (Trans. W.L. Grant, 6 volumes), (Toronto: The Champlain Society, 1922–36) 56–62.

4   As associate professor in the Department of Anthropology at Brandon University, Trevor Denton has extensively researched Champlain's journeys. He has developed a particular interest because of summers spent at Stony Lake. This excerpt is the precursor to a book based on history, linguistics and Huron studies.

5   Susanna Moodie, Chapter xvi "A Trip to Stony Lake, " in *Roughing it in the Bush*. (Toronto: Bell and Cockburn, 1913) **367–372**. In her writings about her earliest days in the area, she often refers fondly to Mr. Y -, Francis Young, the founder of that family dynasty.

6   Catharine Parr Traill, "The Mill of the Rapids," *Chamber's Edinburgh Journal*, Nov. 3, 1938, 322–323. In her writings, the Young family are the "Yorricks", whose mill and rapids she describes in some detail.

7   James Logan, *Notes of a Journey through Canada, the United States and the West Indies*. (Edinburgh: 1836) 44–46, cited in a letter excerpt from E.C. Guillet to G.M. Douglas. Logan travelled up from Cobourg to Lakefield to visit Thomas Traill "whose lady has published an account of Canada." Logan may have been a fellow-officer of Traill's. He writes as if he is a young man, for in his brief account of viewing Clear Lake, he notes that he and two English companions stopped at a deserted shanty, "resembling in shape a pig-style" where they baked their bread and roasted potatoes.

8   John Huston (surveyor), *Field Notes of Some of the Land in the Township of Burleigh, 1834*. Ontario Archives Survey Diaries, shelf 73, box 7.

9   Carl Baldstadt et al. *Susanna Moodie Letters of a Lifetime*. Letter #114 to an old Belleville friend, Maggie Rous (Toronto: University of Toronto Press 1985) 305–6. Susanna was living with her sister Catharine Parr Traill, at the time but by 1877 had moved to Toronto, where she died in 1885. See also Charlotte Gray, *Sisters in the Wilderness*. Chapter

18 "A Trip to Stony Lake" (Toronto: Penguin Books, 1999) 302–321 for a broader picture of Susanna and Catharine in their final years together.

ONE. THE LAND AND THE LAKE

1 C.D. Howe & J.H. White, *Trent Watershed Survey*. (Ottawa: Commission for Conservation Canada 1913) 5.

2 This species information is cited in E.C. Guillet *The Valley of the Trent* "II Preparations for Settlement," (Toronto, The Champlain Society 1957) especially from 28. These excerpts taken from surveyors' reports and letters provide an excellent picture of the impenetrable forest and rocky landscape of the north shore of Stony Lake. See also land registry records for maps of specific townships, these include some notes. Other survey records are in the Ontario Archives. Check Ministry of Natural Resources (MNR) for surveyors' maps.

3 C.D. Howe et al, 61.

4 Stony Lake Project Lifeline began as a joint three-year environmental project with the Trent-Severn Waterway in the late spring 1966 because of concern about the increasing degradation of water quality, fish habitat and shoreline flora and fauna. Now, a database is well-established and Sir Sandford Fleming College environmental studies students use the project as part of their course work.

5 See reports in Association of Stoney Lake Cottagers' (ASLC) newsletter *Islander* for annual updates of this on-going project. See also website *http://www.stonylake.on.ca/*

6 Catharine Parr Traill, *Studies of Plant Life in Canada*. (Ottawa: A.S. Woodburn 1885) 113–114. Of further interest to readers are her references of "vegetable treasures to be found in the peat marsh near Hurricane Point." Mrs. Traill noted several plants "scattered round this lovely lakelet"—that is, Fairy Lake, within Hurricane Point. See also Molly Blyth, "History as storytelling: Mrs. Traill's Scrapbook of Stoney Lake Grasses" in the *Peterborough Review* vol. 1/number 1, 1994, 97–110. Blyth's article includes useful references to current interpretations of Traill's value as a botanist. Her scrapbook of pressed grasses is now housed at Peterborough Centennial Museum and Archives (PCMA).

7 A photocopy of this article is in the files of the ASLC 1984 files. It includes a comprehensive survey of fish species and their particular habitats in the lake.

8 Taken from the ASLC files.

9 Peter Adams and Colin Taylor (eds.) *Peterborough and the Kawarthas*. (Peterborough: Heritage Publications 1992) 67, tables 6.2 and 6.3, 95 and 96.

10 Hahn/Hooke family letters pertaining to Stony Lake, property of the Hooke family.

TWO. FIRST NATIONS—FIRST HERE

1 Jean Cole, *Origins of The History of Dummer Township*. (Peterborough: Township of Dummer 1993) 9, as cited in Phil Mayer & Poulton and Associates, "An Archealogical Overview of the Quackenbush Provincial Park," Unpublished report to the Ontario Ministry of Natural Resources, 1986.

2 Lorenzo Whetung, "Ke-No-Mah-Gay-Wah-Kon The Teaching Rock" in the *Kawartha Native*. (Compiled by the Peterborough Field Naturalists, 1992) 26–27.

3 Marc K. Stengel, "The Diffusionists have Landed," *The Atlantic Monthly*, January 2000, 35–48. This article examines possible early Stone Age settlers in North America. Academics are divided in their beliefs, based primarily on their own fields such as linguistics, anthropology or archaeology. See references to the Stony Lake Petroglyphs (called the Peterborough Stone in the article). See also a flurry of articles in August, 1999 in the *Toronto Star* and *Peterborough Examiner*.

4 Harvey N. McCue, "The Kawartha Lakes Indians: A Brief History 1800–1852" in *Kawartha Heritage*. Proceedings of the Kawartha Conference, 1981, 3–12.

5 Charles Richardson Weld, "A Vacation Tour in the United States and Canada." (London: n.p. 1955) 93–118, as cited in E.C. Guillet, *The Valley of the Trent*, Chapter XI, "Selections from Writings Descriptive of the Region #12 (Toronto: Champlain Society 1957) 409–416. When Weld was visiting Peterborough, he was taken to Lakefield by two friends (unnamed) and introduced to Sam Strickland who organized a hunting and paddling expedition to clear and Stony Lake for his English visitor.

6 Robert Hatton, "400 Years of Indians in the Kawartha," in (*Peterborough: Land of Shining Waters*. Centennial Committee 1967) 18–19.

7 Tony Hall, "The Kawartha Indian Missions The Larger Picture" in *Kawartha Heritage*, 13–21. See also Douglas Williams with Harvey and A. McCue "A Legal History of Curve Lake and the Kawartha Indians." *Kawartha Heritage*. Proceedings of the Kawartha Conference, 1981, 23–26.

8 Aileen Young, *Yesteryear at Young's Point*. (Privately published, 1997) 7. The author provides two

accounts of the story of Polly Cow Island, the burial site of the beloved daughter of Jack Cow whose territory, alongside that of his brother Eel, included much of the land and streams on the north shore of Stony Lake.

9 From a telephone interview with Rick Beaver. A well-known Native artist, Rick is one of four Natives on the exhibit design committee of the Canadian Canoe Museum in Peterborough.

10 James Redpath (1872–1953) Lakefield's newspaper publisher and printer was father of two well-known canoeists, Clayton and Jack. They competed locally and at the Canadian National Exhibition. Their uncle, Bruce Redpath (1885–1925) began his canoeing career in Lakefield and later joined the Toronto Balmy Beach Club. All three men were superb athletes who would paddle from lake to lake to compete in regattas.

11 This quotation occurs near the end of a sketch entitled "A Visit to the Camp of the Chippewa Indians" which appeared in *Sharp's London Journal* No. 7 (1848). It expands on the stories of the Ojibwa families, the Nogans of Curve Lake, in Letters VIII and XVI found in Catharine Parr Traill's *The Backwoods of Canada*. (Later edition: Toronto: McClelland and Stewart 1989).

12 Fay Tilden and Kathy Woodcock, *History of the Burleigh Falls Métis Settlement*. (Peterborough: Ontario Métis and Non-Status Indian Association [Kawartha Branch] 1978) 31. This area has seen year round Native families living and working at Burleigh in lumbering, trapping, guiding, hunting, road construction and building.

13 Ibid, 32

14 *The Rural and Native Heritage Cookbook*, Lovesick Lake Native Women's Association Collective, 1985. Back cover information.

15 *Globe and Mail*, May 24, 1958. See also the Lakefield *Katchawanooka Herald*, March 24, 2000, for a reference to Moses Marsden and his wife Nellie. Their daughter, Mrs. Ruby Hicks, has dedicated a bench to be placed along the Lakefield Millenium Trail. The Marsdens were the first Native family to live and build a home in the village of Lakefield.

THREE.   THE EVOLVING COTTAGERS' ASSN.

1 Ralph Ingelton, speaking at the Annual General Meeting of the Association of Stony Lake Cottagers, July 10, 1999.

2 The *Peterborough Examiner, Daily Evening Review* and the *Morning Times* all covered activi-

ties on and around Stony Lake and are a wealth of information about who was camping, building or taking a trip. Boats, islands and cottages are named, along with anecdotes about lost fish, and minor and major accidents. The many advertisements provide a useful picture of supplies and services of the times.

3 Excerpts from an updated (probably 1950s) photocopy of a letter to the editor of the *Toronto Telegram* recalling evening services on the south end of Otter Island. To end the service, a semi-circle of canoes would be towed back to various cottages, while canoeists continued singing a final hymn.

4 The records of the Ladies' Pavilion Committee are intact, although included within the Association records of each year. The plan is to collect and file all material of this group as a separate entity.

5 *Islander* Vol. 7 Issue 2. November, 1999.

FOUR.   LIVING HERE

1 Eleanor Douglas, letters to her son George M. Douglas, 1889–1892. These letters will be transcribed and donated to Trent University Archives to provide an earlier picture as background to the Guillet/Douglas correspondence.

2 This group of young Peterborough businessmen also met throughout the winter in one another's homes. They appear to have been lively, talented fellows who could entertain athletically, socially and musically. Their names are carved in a dark cupboard under the main stairs of the Emerald Isle cottage. The Echo Camp began in 1897; the Banjo Club was an off-shoot of the Camp.

3 The 'Shanty' log is typical of many of the Stony Lake cottage journals that were kept by family and guests, and enhanced by occasional sketches and snapshots.

4 *Eaton's Camp and Cottage Book*, available in the Baldwin Room of the Toronto Metro Library; 658–871 E 13. 6AR.

5 "The old red Boathouse" is a delightful account of the life and antics of family members of the Collins' clan. Copies were distributed to the Collin's family in the 1950s.

6 Russell Dodsworth, a quotation for a display in an exhibition "Canoeing, Camping and Cottaging: Fifty Years in the Kawartha's 1883–1993," curated by Kathy Hooke, August 4–September 8, 1991, Peterborough Centennial Museum and Archives.

7 Florence (Tedford) Stone, personal interview, April 1, 1991 for the exhibit at the Peterborough Centennial Museum and Archives.

8 George Douglas (1875–1963) son of Dr. Campbell M. Douglas VC, was an engineer by training and a skilled canoeist following his early years on Lake Katchawanooka. He is known primarily for his expedition to the Coppermine River (1911–12) which he later described in *Lands Forlorn*. He made four more short trips to the Arctic in the late 1920s and '30s. Most of those written records and photographs are housed in the National Archives.

At that time, 1913, George Douglas was working for his Douglas mining relatives in Arizona and Mexico, and only back in Canada briefly. He was delighted to go to Northcote Farm but, with no families nearby, he enjoyed the friendship of the Griers, Mackenzies and Stuarts at Stony and Clear lakes. There he could do much more paddling, canoe sailing and exploring from his little island.

9 From the George Douglas Collection, courtesy Katharine Hooke.

10 Diary of George Douglas at 'Wee Island', November 17, 1915–November 25, 1943. Various visitors would be invited to record their activities. This diary contains intermittent entries, covering all seasons and includes recipes for Raspberry Acid, Ginger Beer and the dressing for treating the canvas of a folding boat. Courtesy Katharine Hooke.

11 Diary of Kay Douglas at 'Wee Island,' March 25, 1921. Courtesy Katharine Hooke.

12 Ibid, March 26, 1921.

FIVE. GOING UP THE LAKES

1 John Marsh, "Early Tourism in the Kawarthas, " *Kawartha Heritage Conference, 1981*, 43.

2 Aileen Young, *Yesteryear at Young's Point*, 5. See also Robert Bowley, *Plaqued Historic Sites in Peterborough and Area*, for names and recognition of people who appear in the annals of Stony Lake.

3 E.C. Guillet, *Valley of the Trent*. Chapter 5 "Transportation: The Trent Canal" (Champlain Society 1957) Initial survey for the Trent Canal, Rice Lake and Lake Simcoe, 1835, pp 161–191. See p. 164 for description of early efficient dam work by pioneer, Francis Young. See also James Angus, *A Respectable Ditch: History of the Trent Severn Waterways 1833–1920* and numerous pamphlets about the Trent-Severn Waterway published and distributed by Parks Canada.

4 Richard Tatley, *Steamboating in the Kawarthas*. (Belleville: Mika Publishing Co. 1978) 85. This is still the most comprehensive account, but others well worth reading as noted in the bibliography include

works by John Craig, Daniel Francis and Howard Pammett. Occasional references to steamers appear in works by Doris Huffman, Greg Knox, as well as in *Nelson's Falls to Lakefield*. See also Aileen Young *I hear a Boat a' Whistling* in which she recollects a trip up the lake in her beloved *Islanda*. Many references to local cottagers and special sites exist in the Pammett papers and memorabilia in the PCMA, TUA and PPL in the Peterborough Collection.

5 George Greening, "The old Red Boathouse," 1958.

6 *Peterborough Review*, Feb. 10, 1914. The newspapers regularly reported on waterway traffic.

7 R.B. Rogers' typed proposal for the Lotus Club, (not dated but probably circa 1908), from the files of Doris Hoffman, author of *Kawartha Park by Path and Paddle*.

8 Dunford, Hugh and Glenn Baechler, *Cars of Canada*. (Toronto: McClelland and Stewart, 1973) 248–9.

9 Thomas F. McIlwraith, *Looking for Old Ontario*. (Toronto: University of Toronto Press, 1997) 61–62.

SIX. ENTERPRISES AND ENTREPRENEURS

1 These soldiers had been treated at the Chelsea Hospital in London. Their pensions were allocated based on disabling wounds. The British government encouraged this emigration scheme in order to relieve the costs to the British treasury for nearly 85,000 pensions.

2 Jean Cole, *Origins The History of Dummer Township*, 16.

3 Copy of a letter from the Boyd Papers housed in the Trent University Archives.

4 Reported in *Peterborough Examiner*, August 3, 1889.

5 Jean Cole, *Origins of the History of Dummer Township*, 80.

6 Nepheline syenite is a mineral derived from rocks formed 1.3 billion years ago. These rocks are quite rare world-wide as they lack silica. The mineral is used in making glass and ceramics.

7 Charles Hallock, *The Sportsman Gazetteer and Guide of 1877*, Toronto, 189.

8 Kawartha Heritage Conservancy. This relatively new group is a member of the Ontario Nature Trust Alliance. Part of its mandate is "...to acquire, maintain and preserve lands or interests in lands of ecological, recreational, scientific, scenic, heritage or open space value." Phred Collins is an active member of the local volunteer committee.

9   As noted by Nick Nickels in the *Peterborough Examiner* of May 14, 1949. Gledden Charles Burnham "Nick" Nickels (1906–1988) was a freelance reporter for the Toronto *Globe and Mail* and a nature/local history journalist for the *Peterborough Examiner*. As a relative of both the Burnham and Choate families, he was very familiar with Stony Lake, especially McCracken's Landing. His books include *The Lunge Hunter, Indian River Mills* and *Master Canoe Builder Walter Walker*. His daughters are currently collating his extensive newspaper articles.

10 Nancy Watson was told of Gary Braund's exploits by Wes Willoughby, a contemporary of Gary's.

11 As stated in the purchase agreement between the Cottagers' Association to the Peterborough Canoe Company.

12 Garth Duff, *Hazy Days in Dummer*, p. 64. See Duff also for detailed accounts of ice cutting and storing.

13 Aileen Young, *Yesteryear at Young's Point*. 26.

SEVEN.   BUILDING AND REBUILDING

1   Interview with Earl Shewen by Ralph Ingleton, August 1999.

2   Interview with Orval Bolton by Hugh Drake, summer 1999.

3   Interview with Earl Shewen by Ralph Ingelton.

4   Taken from the deed for August Island, 1889.

EIGHT.   WATER, WIND AND WAVES

1   Written by Wes Willoughby and used with permission.

2   Dot Easson, now nearly one hundred years of age, gave permission for this publication of her poem.

3   See Georgia Elston (ed.) *Nelson's Falls to Lakefield A History of the Village*. Chapt. X "Trails, Rails and Water" (Lakefield Historical Society, 1999) for relationship of trains, steamers and canoes and wooden boat building.

4   Ibid, 108.

5   For more detailed history of the various canoe builders and companies see *The Canadian Canoe Co. (Limited)*. reprint Roger MacGregor, 1999; *Peterborough Canoes*, reprint Roger MacGregor, 1995; Bob Spelt, *A Real Runabout Review of Canoes*, 1991; Kenneth Solway, *The Story of the Chestnut Canoe*, 1997.

6   "Young Men's Stony Lake Club of 1897 Recalls Holiday Life in the Gay Nineties," by Richard F. Choate, *Peterborough Examiner*, Sept. 9, 1954.

7   Maynard Bray, *The Guide to Wooden Power Boats*. (New York: Wm. Norton, 1998) 9. This small volume of excellent photographs includes launches,

runabouts, raceboats, power cruisers, motor yachts, motorsailers and working boats from North America and Europe. All are restored classic boats.

8   The *Canadian Canoe Co. (Limited) Catalogue*. Peterborough 1894. Reprint by Roger MacGregor, 1999) 23.

9   Many boat companies turned to war work during World War II. The Lakefield Canoe Company made flexible wooden mats for warships.

10 The Chris Craft archives are housed at the Mariners' Museum, Newport News, Virginia. Chris Craft out produced other boat builders for years. For example, in 1941, it offered 110 models to the public.

11 Georgia Elston, *Nelson's Falls to Lakefield: A History of the Village*, 110.

12 This opinion of "dispros" was quoted by Jack Amys, *Ishpeming Stony Lake 1900* Privately published, 1950s. Taken from Harry Symons, *Ojibway Melodies*, 1946. (Privately published, 1946) 248.

NINE.   HAVING FUN

1   Bill Lech, a long-time member of the Peterborough YMCA and a superb swimmer, was concerned about children's ability to stay afloat should they be in a boat upset on Stony Lake. He reckoned that if one could swim about a mile, one could reach land- either the mainland or an island from anywhere on the lake. This annual event, the Mile Swim, is an ideal testing method to develop confidence in deep water, regardless of the length of time it takes a swimmer to finish the course.

2   *Peterborough Examiner*, September 9, 1954. Reprint of Article "Young Men's Stony Lake Club of 1897 Recalls Holiday Life in Gay Nineties" by Richard F. Choate.

3   Ibid.

4   From J.H. Amys, *The Story of Ishpeming Stony Lake 1900*. See also A.O.C. Cole and Jean M. Cole, *Illustrated Historical Atlas of Peterborough County 1825–1875*.

5   Letter was found by the present owners of the cottage, Angie and Warren Venner.

6   Stella's father, E. Wyly Grier, noted Canadian portrait painter, built his cottage 'Woodonga' in 1908 in Mackenzie Bay. It was here that he formed a friendship with George Douglas, painting his portrait *Master of Northcote* which is now in the Ottawa National Gallery. Stella Grier was known for her pastel paintings, primarily of children.

7   As noted in the Toronto *Globe and Mail* August 18, 1962, Alma Guillet published her first book, *Make*

Friends of Trees and Shrubs, (New York: Double-day, 1962) at the age of 83. Based on a life long study of trees and shrubs in New York City's Central Park, Mrs. Guillet completed her manuscript at her family cottage 'Westaway.' During the winters, she was deeply involved in handwork as director of Arts and Crafts in the Baptist Educational Centre in Harlem. She also taught an art appreciation class at the Metropolitan Museum of Art.

8   Sam Strickland, *Twenty-Seven Years in Canada West or the Experiences of an Early Settler*. (Edmonton: M.G. Hurtig 1970) 238. Volume one of this book covers Strickland's experiences with the Canada Company in the Huron Tract and his life in Goderich. In the shorter second volume, he returns to the Lakefield area and makes several forays into the lake and bush country.

9   The *Norwood Register* is a weekly paper which began on December 22, 1870 in the village of Norwood, Asphodel township. Most Norwood and area residents who became Stony Lake cottagers tended to travel due north of Norwood on the 9th line of Dummer, leading into Crowe's Landing on Upper Stoney Lake. They then bought shoreline property near the township road which was the only land access to the east end of Stony Lake until the early 20th century.

10   As an inveterate record keeper and observer, George Douglas produced written and pictorial logs of summer trips up the Trent Canal for the years 1921, '24, '26, '27 and 1930.

11   Amys, *The Story of Ishpeming Stony Lake 1900*. 30.

TEN. "WE WILL SERVE THE LORD"

1   From a letter to the Editor, *Toronto Telegram*, by Mrs. C.A. Johnson in the 1950s.

ELEVEN. TELLING TALES

1   Taken from "The Legend of Smithtown Point" written by Gordon Hill Grahame for the *Toronto Star Weekly*, (date not available).

TWELVE. STONY LAKE LOVE STORIES

1   Poem used with permission of Bob Trennum, Stony Lake cottager, teacher, musician, composer and paddler.

2   From Jack Gouinock as told to Christie Bentham.

3   Telephone interview with Michael Allen by Christie Bentham, November, 1999.

ACKNOWLEDGEMENTS

1   Simon Schama *Landscape and Memory*, (New York: Alfred A. Knopf 1995) 19. This comprehensive, historical account covers Europe and the United States through the ages, exploring nature through rock water and wood in attempt to connect our memories to real and imagined landscapes. Superb coloured and black and white visuals enhance the text. See also Amy Willard Cross, *The Summer House A Tradition of Leisure* for a focus on Canadian summer experiences, also encompassed in an historic background. References to extended families and summer recreation are evocative.

ACKNOWLEDGEMENTS

This book would not have been possible without the considerable contribution of many people on and about Stony Lake. The project began in 1999 with a question from Ralph Ingleton, president of the Association of Stoney Lake Cottagers. How are we going to celebrate the new century? How can we best commemorate our community? The steering committee gathered together by Ralph in January 1999 agreed wholeheartedly with his proposal of a 100-year book. The directors of the Association of Stoney Lake Cottagers (ASLC) endorsed the project at their February 1999 meeting. Christie Bentham then sent out a letter to all Association members asking for written recollections, especially of collective memories of all one's family. Sixty some accounts arrived in due course, ranging from a single sheet of pad paper to a 25 page typed essay, all of which are now saved in the Association's archives. Next Christie organized 15 researchers who gathered specific details and background over the summer. This information became the framework of the book: living on the lake; getting here; building; working; boating and a myriad of recreational activities. The recollections are priceless accounts that now will not be lost. Photographs, drawings and other ephemera amplify the written word as only pictures can.

We have not changed the spelling or punctuation of writings from publications or from the submitted accounts. Any minor changes were made for clarity and are noted by square brackets [ ].

This book is only a beginning. We hope that readers take what is here and fill in the gaps, expand on what is only touched upon and, of course, correct any errors. We have documented and authenticated the facts to the best of our knowledge but memories can be fragile and fragmented. We have also tried "not to wallow in nostalgia" as one oral historian sternly warned us.

This book represents the memories, the myths and the recognition of something enduring that land and water give us. To many, Stony Lake means coming home from wherever we spend other parts of the year. To the settlers, it became home. The recollections and observations forming this book of memories are, in the words of a nature historian, "…a journey through spaces and places, with eyes wide open, that may help us keep faith with a future on this tough, lovely old planet."[1]

A number of people reponded to the call for written accounts of memories associated with Stony Lake, much of which has been incorporated into the text. We thank them for their stories:

Christie Bentham
Robin Brooks-Hill
Ken Brown
John Brewin
Jack Brownscombe
Don Cameron
Lorraine Cochran
Art Cole
Tom Cole
Jim Collins
John Collins

Phred Collins
Sonny Cook
Joyce Corner
Delight (Elizabeth) Dann
Kathy Dembroski
Kady Denton
MaryJane Dickson
Art Dobson
Dottie Drake
Marg Dunford
Don Elliott

Jill & Grant Farrow
Diane Ferguson
Judy Finch
Doreen Foote
Joyce & Michael Fowler
Marg & Jack Gouinlock
Jean Gillespie Graham
Chris Greening
George Greening
Helen Guillet
Jeannie & Rob Guillet

Terry Hall
Norma & Art Hamilton
Rick Hauth
Gerry Hill
Kathy Hooke
Nancy Hunt
Doreen & Hugh Jones
Berenice Knapman
Jean Koller
Beth Lech
Araby Lockhart

ACKNOWLEDGEMENTS

Susan Lumsden	Bernie Morin	Janet Smith	Marg Walter
Blair Mackenzie	Shelagh Morris	Phyllida Smith	Nancy Watson
John "Bubs" Macrae	Cecily Morrow	Marj Sonley	Wes Willoughby
Jane Matthews	Velma Osborne	Marian Teamerson	Carol Winter
Robin McGraw	Marilyn Ott	Ted Thomson	Jean & Bev Wood
Helen McKerracher	Hugh Porter	Mike Townsend	Mary Yardley
Margaret McKibbon	Robin Prince	Wil Tranter	
Jane McMyn	Doug Reed	Jill Trennum	
Lois Miller	Tim Sherin	Connie Wahl	

Also used in the preparation of this book were several accounts collected in 1980 by David Anderson. These were written by the following individuals and incorporated into the text:

Jim Binnie	Jack Collins	Flory MacDonald	Kathleen Moore
Larry Bonnycastle	Tommy Eisdell	Isobel Mackenzie	Anne Nichols
Pam Bonnycastle	James Guillet	Margaret McDonald	Elizabeth Reed
Margaret Buck	Sheena Hunter	Betsey and Robin Merry	Puss Sherin

A number of people gave generously of their time to compile the written account into categories, as represented by the chapter titles. This book would not have been possible without their work:

Christie Bentham	Helen Guillet	Marilyn Ott	Jean and Bev Wood
Dottie Drake	Kathy Hooke	Janet Smith	
Don Elliott	Beth Lech	Ted Thomson	
Jack and Marg Gouinlock	Jack Matthews	Nancy Watson	

To those listed below who helped in countless ways, from granting or conducting interviews, providing photographs, identifying names and generally providing support and encouragement, we give you untold thanks.

Michael Allen	Frank Crouse	Katharine Hooke	Barb Rimmer
Sheila Amys	Betty Currelly	Suzanne Hooke	Ginny Ross
George Baird	MaryJane Dickson	Pam Hough	Rob Roy
Rick Beaver	Dottie & Hugh Drake	Martha Hunt	Flo Ryder
Ann Binnie	Kathy Dembrowski	Carol & Ralph Ingleton	Dottie Scullin
Orval Bolton	Kady Denton	Phyllida Klück	Earl & Effie Shewen
Fred Brooks-Hill	Doug Dunford	Penny Little	Dave Smith
Lee Brumet	Heather Elliott	John Lyon	Derry Smith
Kay Bruce-Robertson	Dot Easson	Paul Martin	Art Teamerson
David Card	Jill Farrow	Babe McClelland	Florence Tedford
Peter Chittick	Michael Fowler	Maureen McDougall	Connie Wahl
Art Cole	John Greening	Jane McMyn	Marg Walter
Jean Cole	Jack Gouinlock	Bernie Murin	Nancy Watson
Tom Cole	Bill Hamilton	Bea Morris	Alan Wotherspoon
Marion & Robin Collins	Barb Harris	Tibs Partridge	Marnie Young

ACKNOWLEDGEMENTS

Particular thanks go to Heather Elliott who performed the duties of copy editor with an unerring eye from the beginning. To Blair Mackenzie we give our thanks for visualizing and organizing a cohesive whole emerging out of our joint efforts. To Suzanne Hooke who somehow kept all the drafts and revisions in order on her computer and produced a clean, correct manuscript for the publishers, we express out gratitude. To publisher Barry Penhale and editor Jane Gibson who believed in this book from the beginning, we express appreciation for their guidance and patience. Their professional skills were immensely helpful to us in organizing the material and tidying up loose ends.

We are especially grateful to our husbands, Will and Hal, who offered kind and valuable criticism and were our firmest supporters, we couldn't have made it without your love.

Thank you all. This books is for all of you.

Christie Bentham
Kathy Hooke

With the help of so many people, much effort has gone towards ensuring accuracy of information. The authors and the publisher however, would be pleased to receive information regarding any errors. All such will be corrected in subsequent editions.

SELECTED BIBLIOGRAPHY

Adams, Peter and Colin Taylor (eds.), *Peterborough and The Kawarthas*. 2nd ed. Peterborough:Heritage Publications, 1992.

Adams, Wm. Richard, "The Rice Lake Serpent Mound Group." *Bulletin of the Division of Art and Archeology*. The Royal Ontario Museum, 24 (1956) 14–19.

Amys, J.H., *The Story of Ishpeming Stony Lake 1900*. Privately published, c. 1950.

Angus, James, *A Respectable Ditch History of the Trent-Severn Waterway 1833-1920*. Montreal: McGill Queens University Press, 1988.

Angus, James, *Severn River An Illustrated History*. Orillia: Severn Publications Ltd., 1995.

Aron, Cindy S., *Working at Play A History of Vacations in the United States*. New York: Oxford University Press, 1999.

Ballstadt, Carl, Elizabeth Hopkins and Michael Peterman (eds.), *Letters of a Lifetime*. Toronto: University of Toronto Press, 1985.

Barker, Grace, *Timber Empire The Exploits of the Entrepreneurial Boyds*. Fenelon Falls: Dawn Publishing, 1997.

Benidickson, Jamie, *Idleness, Water and a Canoe*. Toronto: University of Toronto Press, 1997. Bond, Hallie, *Boats and Boating in the Adirondacks*. Syracuse: Adirondack Museum/Syracuse University Press, 1995.

Bowley, Robert, *Plaqued Historic Sites in Peterborough and Area*. Peterborough: Rebel Publishing, 1998.

Bray, Maynard, *The Guide to Wooden Power Boats*. New York: Wm. Norton, 1998.

Brunger, Alan G. (ed.), *Harvey Township An Illustrated History*. Peterborough: The Greater Harvey Historical Society, 1992.

Cameron, Dr. G. Donald, "Canoe Trip to New York 1914." Unpublished manuscript. Peterborough: November, 1968.

Cameron, Dr. G. Donald, "The Development of the Canoe in the Kawarthas." Monthly Meeting, Peterborough Historical Society, PCMA, March, 1975.

_____,*The Canadian Canoe Co. (Limited)*. Peterborough: 1894. Reprint Roger   MacGregor, 1999.

_____, *Peterborough Land of Shining Waters*. Peterborough: Centennial Committee for the City and County of Peterborough, 1967.

_____, *Through the Years in Douro*. Peterborough: Centennial Committee of the Township of Douro, 1967.

Clarke, Ruth, *Before the Silence Fifty Years in the History of Alderville First Nation 1825-1875*. Victoria, BC: Alderville First Nations, 1999.

Cole, A.O.C. and Jean Murray Cole (gen eds.), *Illustrated Historical Atlas of Peterborough County 1825-1875*. Peterborough: The Peterborough Historical Society Foundation Inc., 1975.

Cole, A.O.C. and Jean Cole (gen. eds.), *Kawartha Heritage Proceedings of the Kawartha Conference, 1981*. Peterborough: Peterborough Historical Atlas Foundation, 1981.

Cole, Jean Murray, *The Loon Calls A History of the Township of Chandos*. Peterborough: publ. Municipality of the Township of Chandos, 1989.

Cole, Jean Murray (ed.), *Origins The History of Dummer Township*. Peterborough:Township of Dummer, 1993.

Cole, Jean Murray, "Sandford Fleming No Better Inheritance." Occasional paper 11. Peterborough: Peterborough Historical Society, 1990.

Craig, John, *The Clearing*. Markham: Longman Pocket Book Edition, 1976.

Craig, John, *By the Sound of her Whistle*. Toronto: Peter Martin Associates, 1966.

Craig, John, and Nick Nickels. *The Lunge Hunter The Life and Times of Alex Sharpe*. Woodview, Ont.: Frances Craig and Nickels, 1983.

Cross, Amy Willard, *The Summer House A Tradition of Leisure*. Harper Perennial, 1992.

Denton, Trevor, "Samuel de Champlain's Trip from Lake Simcoe to Lake Ontario September 1615 AD: Route, Readings, Recognition." Brandon University, unpublished ms., 1996.

Dibb, Gordon, "A Review of Archeological Investigations and Site Potential along the west side of Lake Katchawanooka in Smith township, Peterborough, Ont.: Lakefield to Young's Point." Document prepared by York North Archeological Services regarding proposed aggregate development. Peterborough: January, 1998.

Duff, Garth, *Hazy Days in Dummer*. Peterborough: Self-published, 1991.

Durant, Kenneth, *The Naphtha Launch*. Utica: Adirondack Museum of the Adirondack Historical Assoc., 1976.

Durnford, Hugh and Glenn Baechler, *Cars of Canada*. Toronto: McClelland and Stewart, 1973.

Elston, Georgia (ed.), *Nelson's Falls to Lakefield A History of the Village*. Lakefield Historical Society, 1999.

Ferguson, D., "It's Summertime....and the dippys are coming! (back)." *Katchewanooka Herald* [Lakefield, Ont.] 10 Dec. 1999.

Francis, Daniel, *"I Remember..." An Oral History of the Trent-Severn Waterway*. Peterborough: Friends of the Trent-Severn Waterway, 1984.

_____,*The Gathering The Rural and Native Heritage Cookbook Vol. 1*. Lovesick Lake Native Women's Association, 1985.

Grant, Shelagh, *The Hope Mill*. Occasional publication by the Otonabee Region Conservation Authority. Peterborough: 1979.

Gray, Charlotte, *Sisters in the Wilderness The Lives of Susanna Moodie and Catharine Parr Traill*. Toronto: Penguin Books, 1999.

Guillet, Edwin C., *The Valley of the Trent*. Toronto: The Champlain Society, 1957.

Guillet, G. Robert, "Mining at Nephton". Occasional Paper 19. Peterborough: Peterborough Historical Society, 1998.

Hodgins, Bruce W. and Margaret Hobbs, *Nastawgan: The Canadian North by Canoe and Snowshoe*. Toronto: Betelgeuse Books, 1985.

Hooke, Katharine N., "From Campsite to Cottage: Early Stony Lake." Occasional Paper 13. Peterborough: Peterborough Historical Society, 1992.

Hooke, Katharine N., *St. Peter's-on-the Rock Seventy-Five Years of Service*. Peterborough: Anniversary Committee St. Peter's-on-the-Rock, 1989.

Howe, C.D. and J.H. White, *Trent Watershed Survey A Reconnaissance*. Ottawa: Commission for Conservation Canada, 1913.

Huffman, Doris, *Kawartha Park by Path and Paddle*. Peterborough: Archival and History Committee of Smith Township, 1987.

Jennings, John, Bruce Hodgins and Doreen Small (eds.), *The Canoe in Canadian Cultures*. Toronto: National Heritage/Natural History Inc., 1999.

Kirkpatrick, George and Julie Rouse (eds.), *The Peterborough Review*. Vol. one, Number one, "In the Garden," 1994.

Kirkpatrick, George and Julie Rouse (eds.),*The Peterborough Review. under water*. Vol. one, Number four, 1995.

Knox, Gregory H, *Bellvidere Fond Reflections of a Stony Lake Hotel at Crowe's Landing*. Woodview: Gregory and Elizabeth Knox, 1987.

Mallory, Enid, *Countryside Kawartha*. Peterborough: Peterborough Publishing, 1994.

Mallory, Enid, *Kawartha Living on These Lakes*. Peterborough: Peterborough Publishing, 1991.

Martin, Norma, Catherine Milne and Donna McGillis, *Gore's Landing and the Rice Lake Plains*. Bewdley Ont.: Clay Publ. Ltd., 1986.

Moodie, Susanna, *Roughing it in the Bush*. Toronto: Bell and Cockburn, 1913.

Nickels, Nick, *Indian River Mills*. Lakefield: Paddle Press, 1975.

Pammett, Howard, "The Steamboat Era on the Trent-Otonabee Waterway: 1830-1950." *Ontario History* LVI (1964) 2: 67-103.

Peterborough Canoe Co. Ltd. Letter to G.M. Douglas specif. for Lake Erie Pound Net Boat and engine, Oct. 23, 1922.

_____,*Peterborough Canoes*. Peterborough: Peterborough Canoe Co. Ltd., 1929. Reprint Roger MacGregor, 1995.

_____, *Peterborough County Natural History Summary of 1998*. Annual report. Peterborough: Peterborough Field Naturalist et al, 1999.

_____, *Kawartha's Nature*. Compiled by the Peterborough Field Naturalists. Toronto: Stoddart, 1992.

Peterman, Michael and Carl Ballstadt (eds.), *Forest and other Gleanings The Fugitive Writings of Catharine Parr Traill*. Ottawa: University of Ottawa, 1994.

Schama, Simon, *Landscape and Memory*. New York: Alfred A. Knoff, 1995.

Solway, Kenneth, *The Story of the Chestnut Canoe*. Halifax: Nimbus Publ. Ltd., 1997.

Spectre, Peter, *Different Waterfronts A Wooden Boat Reader*. Gardiner, Maine: Tilbury House, 1989.

Speltz, Robert, "A Real Runabout Review of Canoes." Unpublished manuscript, 1991.

Stengil, Marc K.. "The Diffusionists Have Landed." *Atlantic Monthly*. Jan 2000: 35-48.

Stephenson, Gerald F., "John Stephenson and the Famous "Peterborough Canoes." Occasional Paper 8. Peterborough: Peterborough Historical Society, 1987.

Tatley, Richard, *Steamboating on the Trent-Severn*. Belleville: Mika Publ. Co., 1978.

Theberge, Clifford and Elaine, *At the Edge of the Shield*. Peterborough: Smith Township Historical Committee, 1982.

Tilden, Fay and Kathy Woodcock, *History of the Burleigh Falls Metis Settlement*. Peterborough: Ontario Métis and Non-Status Indian Association (Kawartha branch), 1978.

Tozer, Ron and Dan Strickland, *Pictorial History of Algonquin Park*. Toronto: Friends of Algonquin Park, 1986.

Traill, Catharine Parr, *The Backwoods of Canada*. Toronto: McClelland and Stewart, 1989.

Traill, Catharine Parr, *Studies of Plant Life in Canada*. Ottawa: A.S. Woodburn, 1885.

Turner, Larry (annot.) *A Boy's Cottage Diary, 1904*. Ottawa: Petherwin Heritage, 1996.

Verhurst, Dirk and Walter Greenway, *Peterborough Folklore and Folklife*. Vol. 1. Peterborough: Peterborough County Board of Education, n.d.

Vidakovich, Steve. Column, " 'Where to Go' Stony Lake," *Ontario Out- of- Doors*. April, 1984, 27-35.

Weaver, Emily P., *The Counties in Ontario*. Toronto: Bell & Cockburn, MCMXIII.

Willcox, Helen Rutherford, *Chemong Park Story*. Peterborough: Archival and History Committee Smith Township, 1986.

Young, Aileen, "I Hear a Boat a' Whistlin' " *My Stoney Lake Memories*. Privately publ., 1992.

Young, Aileen, *Yesteryear at Young's Point*. 3rd ed. Peterborough: privately publ., 1997.

INDEX

ABOUT THE AUTHORS

Christie Bentham's love affair with Stony Lake is lifelong and inherited from three generations of her family. She hopes that this book will inspire future generations to love and preserve the lake.

Katharine Hooke's roots at Stony Lake go back to 1907 when her Grier and Mackenzie forebearers spent the summer camping before building their cottages. She has written about local history and is undertaking family research having retired from Sir Sandford Fleming College in Peterborough. Her husband, two daughters and five grandchildren share her abiding love of Stony Lake.

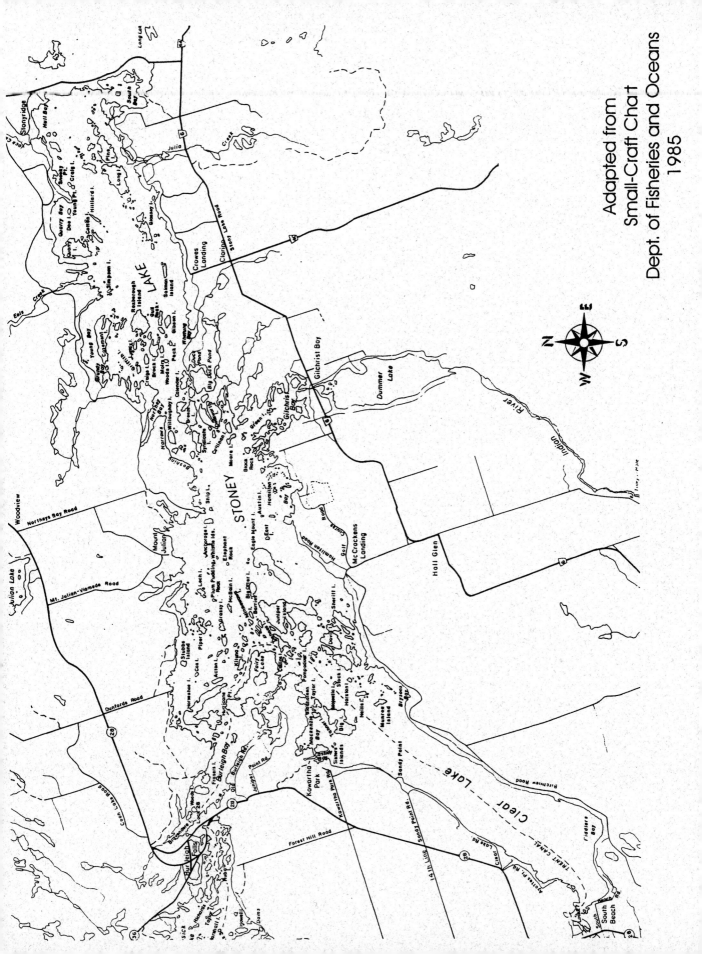

Adapted from
Small-Craft Chart
Dept. of Fisheries and Oceans
1985